HISTORICAL HERITAGE OF THE TAMILS

HISTORICAL HERITAGE OF THE TAMILS

K K Pillay, M.A., D. Litt., D. Phil (Oxon.)
Director, Institute of Traditional Cultures of South and South-East Asia
Former Professor of Indian History, University of Madras

MJP PUBLISHERS
Chennai 600 005

First Published : 1979
MJP re-series first reprint : 2008

ISBN 81-8094-047-0 **MJP PUBLISHERS**
© Publishers, 2008   47, Nallathambi Street
All rights reserved Triplicane
Printed and bound in India   Chennai 600 005

MJP 040

To

Dr. B R Ambedkar

PUBLISHER'S NOTE

India has a rich heritage of tradition and culture which dates back to the beginning of human existence. But unfortunately, most information of the past has not been properly documented. The few books published in the past are not within the reach of the needy, and in the present e-age with its modern communication techniques, many may not find time to preserve our heritage. But a few academicians and historians who may come forward in the future for research studies may lack the needed resources.

Keeping this in mind, MJP Publishers has endeavoured to revive the oldest rare books to serve the academic community and the society at large. In this effort, a series of rare books would be republished under the banner, "MJP's re-series". These rare books have been carefully selected based on the significance and authenticity of their contents as we perceive.

The books in the "re-series" have been recomposed in an elegant style and format to suit the interest of the present-day readers. Only slight modifications have been made for better presentation, and care has been taken to keep this to a minimum and to not affect the contents of the original edition.

This book is an extract from the original edition *Studies in the History of India with Special Reference to Tamil Nadu* written and published by K.K. Pillay in 1979.

We hope that the "re-series" books would prove to be of immense help to researchers and general readers to have a better understanding of many important facts and happenings of the past, thus exposing the richness of our culture, tradition and knowledge.

MJP Publishers

In remembrance . . .

A casteless society and human brotherhood is my ideal.

Dr. K K Pillay
(1905–1981)

Dr. K. Kanagasabapathy Pillay, as Dr. K.K. Pillay was known, was born as the eldest son of Kolappa Pillay and Parvathy, 3rd April, 1905 in an agricultural family in the small hamlet of Aloor of the Kalkulam Taluk of Kanyakumari district—the then Travancore State. His father Kolappa Pillay was a village school master proficient in both Tamil and Malayalam, and Dr. Pillay used to fondly recollect his father as "Thinnai Pallikooda Vathiyar." His sister Mrs. Ammu was married and settled in Kanyakumari district.

K.K. Pillay had his primary education in the village school and later joined the English High School at Kottar, Kanyakumari district. After schooling, he joined the Scott Christian College, Nagercoil, when Raw Eastaff and G.H. Marsdan were the Principals, as a student of History for his intermediate course with his optional subjects as Ancient History, Indian History and History of Great Britain.

He completed his Honours degree in history with distinction from Maharaja's Arts College at Trivandrum, when Prof.K.V. Rengaswamy Iyengar and Prof. C.V. Chandrasekaran were the Principals. He started his career as a lecturer at Government Arts College, Kumbakonam, in 1927 and subsequently became the

Professor of History at the Presidency College, Madras. In 1946, he received the D. Litt. degree for his historical research publication titled *The Suchindrum Temple,* for the complilation of which he was motivated and inspired by Kavimani Desikavinayagam Pillay to whom he dedicated the volume. Undoubtedly, the book is a distinct contribution to our knowledge of south Indian history. In 1948, he obtained his D. Phil. degree from the School of Oriental and African Studies of the Oxford University for his work "History of self governance in the Madras Presidency (AD 1882–1918)," under the guidance of Prof. C.H. Philips. Appointed in 1954 as Professor of Indian History in the University of Madras, he became in 1961 Professor of Area Studies in the same University. After retiring from the University, he took up the directorship of the Institute of Traditional Cultures of South and South-East Asia, succeeding Prof. K.A. Nilakanta Sastri. Thus he has had the association with the handling of problems of history and culture for well over half a century.

Dr. K.K. Pillay was one of the pioneers to encourage research in historical studies. His historical research works have paved the way to unearth many historical facts. He reiterated that historians should possess the basic qualities of honesty, sincerity, judiciousness and impartiality, and that a narrow-minded, one-sided and emotional approach towards issues relating to caste, language and regional issues should be strictly avoided. He also had the strong notion that historians should not rely totally on data from stone inscriptions alone to put forth their research findings but should be well-informed about the fields of literature, anthropology, psychology, sociology, philosophy and politics, to present their research findings in an effective and unbiased manner.

Dr. Pillay has delivered presidential addresses at the Indian History Congress at Jubbalpore, 1970, and at the History Associations at the Madurai Kamaraj, Annamalai and Calicut Universities, the Presidency College, Pachaiyappa's College and the Christian College, Madras.

Besides several books in Tamil on the history and culture of Tamil Nadu, Dr. Pillay has several other publications which include

- *The Suchindrum Temple*
- *A Social History of the Tamils,* Vol. I
- *South India and Ceylon*
- *History of Local Self Government in the Madras Presidency 1850–1919.*
- *Studies on the History of India with Special Reference to Tamil Nadu.*

Dr. Pillai was married to V. Saraswati Ammal from Theroor, Kanyakumari District. They had three daughters and one son, Mani.

The eldest daughter, Rajam, pursued her research on the Kanyakumari Temple. She was married to Yogeswaran, a Tamil Professor Sabapathy, their son, is a lecturer at Venkateswara Engineering College, who married Ambika, and has a son named Aswin. Their daughter Rajeswari is married to Mariappan, an Engineer in AUDCO, and they have a son named Manikandan.

Dr. Pillay's second daughter Thangam was married to Perumal of Veerani, Kanyakumari District. They have a son Srinivas married to Kohila, and they have a daughter and a son.

His third daughter, Vimala, was married to Kanniperumal, an Engineer. They have two daughters—Ambujam who is a lecturer at Anna University and is married to Madhusoothana also a professor at Anna University, and Vanitha Vedam who is a sociologist, and married to Madhavan, working at Neyveli Lignite Corporation. The former have two daughters Manu Vaasanthi and Vimala Madhangi. The latter have two sons, Dinesh Damodar and Vimalesh Kannan.

CONTENTS

1. Introduction   1
   Lemurian Theory   10
2. Tamil Literature as a Source Material of History   17
   The Sangam   18
     Chronological Basis   19
     Historical Value of the Literature   22
     The Pandyas   23
     The Cholas   24
     The Cheras   26
     Minor Chieftains   27
     Social Life   29
   Quasi-Historical Literature   36
   Classical Literary Works—Their Direct and Indirect Value for the Historian   43
   Chronological Background   51
   The Religious Works   54
   The Modern Epoch   58
3. Narrinai in its Historical Setting   67
   Political History   71
   Porayan   78
   Cholas   78
   Tittan   79
   Chola Chiefs   80

Alisi	80
Anni	81
The Pandyas	82
Independent Chieftains	83
Ay Andiran	83
Kari	84
Anji	85
Aruman	86
Vanan	86
Periyan	87
Talumpan	87
Pulli	87
Social Life	92
Velan Veriyadal	99
Madalerutal	102
Marriage	103
Parattayar	105
Standards of Moral Conduct	108
Diet	111
Dress and Decoration	113
Games and Amusements	115
Festivals	116
Occupations	117
Customs	121
Religion	122
Superstitions	124
Conclusion	124
4. Inscriptions of Tamil Nadu and their Historical Value	135
The Inscriptions of the Pandyas	140

The Dalavaipuram Plates of Viranarayana	143
The Sivakasi Plates of Vira Pandya	148
The Kudumiyamalai Inscription	149
Chola Inscriptions	150

5. The Brahmi Inscriptions of
   South India and the Sangam Age 159

6. Aryan Influence in Tamilaham During
   the Sangam Epoch 173

7. Origin of Muruga Worship 189

8. The Temple as a Culture Centre 205

   Decline of the Position and Service of the Temple 217

9. The Bhakti Movements in Tamil Nadu 223

   Saivism 225
   The "New Bhakti Cult" of South India 227
   The Bhakti Cult in North India 227
   Sufism 231

10. Date of Manikkavachagar 233

1

INTRODUCTION

"Most history is guessing, and the rest is prejudice" said Will and Ariel Durant in their well-known "The Story of Civilization".[1] Developing the same idea further, these writers added that "the historian always oversimplifies and hastily selects a manageable minority of facts and faces out of a crowd of souls and events whose multitudinous complexity he can never quite embrace or comprehend."[2]

Great as these writers were, their sweeping generalization is unacceptable. Even in respect of the major part of medieval and modern history of countries like India much data have been collected and conclusions formulated. No doubt, there is still much that is unknown or indefinitely and incompletely known. But this, too, has to be explored by assiduous effort; we must remember that many facts unknown some decades ago have since been brought to light. It is important to remember that the progress of archaeology, sociology, linguistics and other studies has disclosed several new facts and ideas.

In respect of known facts deliberate perversion of truth actuated by chauvinism, prejudice and such other reprehensible factors must be cast aside. It is unwarranted to assume that at no time can we reconstruct the true history of many countries of the medieval and modern periods. But it calls for a sustained effort and a balanced outlook.

Equally important is the need for delving deep into the relatively unknown periods of the early history of the various countries. Regarding India, for instance, did we know any thing about the marvellous Indus Valley civilization before 1922? We had known only about the Egyptian, Assyrian, Sumerian, Babylonian, Syrian and Chinese civilization, to mention some. But the discovery of the Indus Valley or Harappan, as it is briefly known, culture has revolutionised the history of India and of the world. Thanks to the C-14 Test it has been taken to have flourished between 2500 and 1900 BC. It is important to notice in this connection that very recent excavations in certain sites now in Pakistan throw new light on the extent, and more important, on the date of the Indus Valley civilization. Excavations at Rehman Dheri, 14 miles north of Dera Ismail Khan city, have revealed the amazingly wide extent of the so-called Indus Valley civilization. There appears to have existed a cultural closeness between the northern part of Pakistan, Mundi Gak in Afghanistan, Hissar in Iran and even so far as Namaz Gah and other sites in Soviet Turkemania. Moreover, this discovery establishes the beginning of Rehman Dheri a few hundred years earlier than Mohenjodaro and Harappa. The first major steps towards urbanization on the Indus plain, as well as the initiation of a proto-literate society, are evident from the recovered material. The date of the rise of Rehman Dheri as a town associated with the Indus civilization is reckoned by experts as about 3200 BC.

Even more arresting is the fact that a factory site believed to have existed at Lewan in North Pakistan about 4000 BC connected with the Indus civilization. The excavators have said that the Lewan factory was used for the manufacture of stone tools of different types, including querns, grinding stones, axes, hammers and ring stones. It may be noted that the relics discovered at Rehman Dheri produced striking jewellery and pottery. Artisans there made beads of gold, lapis lazuli, carnelian, agate, jasper, turquoise, ivory and bone, terracotta and bone ivory bangles. Cultivation of wheat and barley, chillies, mustard and wild oat seeds also seems to have been adopted. It is likely that the area was irrigated by the Comal Tank-Zam River and by the Indus River, which apparently flowed nearer the site then. Thus Rehman Dheri, Lawan and the adjoining places were at once agricultural and industrial; they witnessed a stage of transition from the rural to the urban setting.

Now there arises the question of the identification of the Harappan script; it continues to this day a baffling problem. Fr. Heras thought the language of the Harappan inscriptions was proto-Indian, Proto-Indo-Mediterranean or more specifically Proto-Dravidian, supposed to have been the parent of all the modern Dravidian languages of India.[3] This has been supported more recently by the Russian and Finnish experts, who, working independently, concluded that the language was Dravidian. Moreover, Iravadam Mahadevan has made an intensive study of the script and the words occurring in the Harappan inscriptions and thinks that they represent old Tamil. They are recorded in his "Corpus of Tamil-Brahmi Inscriptions", the product of an intensive study.

But as against these, Dr. S.R. Rao of the Archaeological Survey of India claims that the old Indus Valley script can be deciphered on the basis of its later development. He conducted excavations at Lothal, Rangpur, Rojdi and Prabhas and concluded that in those places the old Indus script has survived and undergone certain modifications between 1900 BC and 1500 BC. The script had become simplified as found from the writing on the pottery in the post-Harappan period similar to that in Lothal, Rojdi and Rangpur which had become simplified and disciplined into an alphabetic system of 21 letters, with only two vowels, of which one was rarely used. According to Dr. S. R. Rao, this late Harappan script is identical with the north Semetic writings of the 18th to 12th centuries BC. It is significant that vestiges of the late Harappan culture have been discovered recently in Andhra Pradesh in painted pottery.

Another interesting fact stated by him is that he read nearly 85 inscriptions in Lothal, Rangpur and other places and from them he found the names of Rishis, Deities, Asuras and Demigods and also the names of ordinary individuals, of commodities, of planets and constellations. He added that the names of deities, which later came to be identified with Shiva, Vishnu and other deities were also found. Dr. Rao added that of the nearly 70 words read so far, at least 60 are traceable to the Indo-European group of languages. They showed the transition from the old Indo-Iranian to the Indo-Aryan (Vedic) branches of the Indo-European group.

But he added that a small section of the Harappan population spoke a language not of the Indo-Aryan group but, at the same time, not Dravidian. His contention was that "the phonology and structure of the Harappan script so far deciphered did not suggest any appreciable connection with the Dravidic or so-called Proto-Dravidic group of languages." However, he thinks that the Indus population must have been cosmopolitan in character.[4]

While these are the two main lines of thought regarding the Indus people, several writers have yielded to wishful thinking and chauvinism one way or the other. Many are the Tamil chauvinists who assert that the Harappans were the ancestors of the Tamils. They associate Tamil to have been derived from a language spoken by a group of early people like the Elamites and Hurrians who came from the West and settled in and near the Indus Valley. Several European archaeologists like Bork and G.W. Brown suggest the Elamite and the Hurrian connection with the Indus inscriptions. It is hoped by some that the survival in Tamil of place and personal names which can be traced to Hurrians and Elamites leads us to suspect that some of them may turn up on the Indus Valley seals. The affinities between Elamite and the Dravidian languages have led Dyakonov, the Soviet historian, to assume that tribes related by language to the Elamites and the Dravidians were scattered throughout Iran in the 4th and 3rd millennia BC and perhaps later as well. T.B. Nayar shows how certain words in Tamil and Malayalam correspond to Hurrian words. He thinks that the name Porunan occurring in the Sangam age has its parallel in the Hurrian Pur-hu-un-ni. Elini in Tamil corresponds to E-ez-ni-ia in the Hurrian language. But all these conjectures seem to be far-fetched. They do not indubitably prove the connection of the Tamils with those who had come and settled in the Indus Valley. More striking is the fact that I. Mahadevan has read several names from the earliest stratum of Tamil literature in the Indus seals. Particularly notable is that he reads the original name of Agastya (Akattiya) in one of the Indus Valley seals. It is well known that Agastya is the legendary originator name of Agastya (Akattiya) in one of the Indus Valley seals. It is well known that Agastya is the legendary originator of Tamil language. It is interesting that in Hurrian Akku-teia is a common personal name. It is made of two elements 'ak' meaning bring, guide and teia representing a Hurrian deity. A Hurrian personal name Ari-Harpa is said to be connected with Ayyappa in Kannada and Malayalam.

Now the question is whether these examples indicate a connection between Hurrian and Dravidian as represented by Tamils.[5] These require further study. Among the pieces of evidence which suggest the Dravidian connection with the Indus culture the following may be mentioned. Firstly, the pottery of the Harappan culture and that of the Tamil country in the megalithic period, particularly in Uraiyur, Tirukkam-puliyur and Korkai are similar. Secondly, ring wells were used in both regions; particularly in Kanchipuram there are many ring wells buried in the river beds and on the bank of the Vegavati river. Thirdly, it has been recently announced by Dr. Sankalia, the well-known archaeologist, that one of the terracotta dancing figures (3"h) from Harappa bears resemblance to the South Indian Nataraja of the Chola period. But can this be taken to be anything more than a matter of chance? Fourthly, among objects of worship there were among the Indus people lingas and yonis. The yonis were pierced with a cylindrical hole in the centre, and were either round or had a wavy outline. It is well known that the Rig Vedic Aryans condemned the worshippers of the Linga. Again the Siva Pasupati cult, believed to have existed among the Indus Valley people, was non-Aryan and probably Dravidian.

Moreover, unlike the Rig Vedic Aryans the Indus people lived a highly organized urban life. Besides, among the skeletal remains recovered from Harappa and Mohenjodaro, the Austroloid is one pattern that shows affinity with skulls unearthed from the ancient cemetry of Adichchanallur in Tamil Nadu and with the Veddas of Sri Lanka.[6]

In this connection an oft-repeated argument must be reiterated. The cow as held in veneration by the Rig Vedic Aryans and the horse was also esteemed by them. On the other hand, neither the cow nor the horse appear in the Indus Valley sites, where the place of the cow is taken by the bull, while the horse finds no place whatever.

Perhaps one of the most important pieces of evidence of the Dravidian and particularly Tamil association with the Indus Valley culture is the presence of the people speaking the Brahui language is Baluchistan. It is well known that the Brahui is basically connected with Tamil. To imagine that Tamils from South India had proceeded to Baluchistan and beyond is to think of an improbable hypothesis. Again, as noticed earlier, the Lycians of Asia Minor described themselves in their inscriptions as Trimmlai, a name which seems to have affinity with Dramila or Tamil. Moreover, it is notable that several ancient place names in Afghanistan, Iran and particularly in Mesopotamia like Ur, Yertur and Nippur have a Tamilian similarity.[7] Again, the discovery of twenty Dravidian words in the Rig Veda by Prof. Burrow shows that prior to the Aryans portions of North India too must have been occupied by Dravidians.

In this connection attention may be called to the inferences drawn by R. Raghava Iyengar and M. Raghava Iyengar to tribes like the Velir and the Kocar having migrated from the north to the region of Tamil Nadu. It is shown from Puram 201 that the Velir chief Irunkovel is described as having been descended through fortynine generations from the Velir who emerged from the pitcher of a northern sage. This pitcher myth is associated with the history of the Chalukyas as well as with certain North Indian legends. It is significant that the jar is an important symbol in the Indus script. Can these facts help us formulate a connection of the Indus people with the Dravidians? Another popular legend is that Agastya, the accredited father of Tamil, led a migration of 18 kings descended from Lord Krishna to Potiyil in the extreme South, Dr. Nikita Gurove refers to the vibrant legends in ancient Tamil literature as well as in Telugu folklore about a distant motherland and suggests that they indicate a wave-like emigration of cultural groups of ancient Indus civilization to the South.

The Kocar are also believed to have come down from the north. The fact that they are known as Ilam Kocar suggests, as I. Mahadevan points out, that Ilam may refer to Elam, the hilly region near Baluchistan. These facts gathered from the Sangam literature reinforce the hypothesis of the connection of the Indus people with Elam on the one hand and the Tamils on the other. Though this strengthens the hypotheses suggested earlier, a more convincing piece of evidence is needed to settle the question once and for all.

While on the one hand some of the suggestions made on the bases of verbal similarities, connecting the Indus civilization with Tamil have yet to be proved, some writers have sought to indicate certain pieces of additional evidence in support of the Vedic connection. T.N. Ramachandran claims to have discovered a similarity between the Indus Valley seals and the Rig Vedic patterns of sacrifices.[8] He states: "It would seem possible now to discover a remarkable correspondence that the scenes on the seals depict many events and scenes described in the various Rig Vedic hymns themselves". But he does not substantiate his hypothesis by specific evidence. He says again that the episodes narrated in the Rig Vedic hymns are reflected in the Indus seals. He adds that the "description of Agni as surrounded by the seven Hotarah or other sacrificial members in a ritual as given in the hymns is virtually depicted to a detail on these seals". This is nothing but a figment of the imagination. Again, he adds that the Great Bath in Mohenjodaro was constructed for the final purification of the performer of a sacrifice like the Asvameda. This is fantastic. If anything, the Great Bath resembles the large tanks near South Indian temples. There is thus no convincing base for his association of the Rig Vedic Aryans with the age-old Indus civilization.

In fact the real identification of the Indus script and its relation with a known language can be determined only if we get a bilingual inscription in the Indus script and another script which has been already identified. The situation is not so desperate even though the efforts have so far failed to discover such a bilingual inscription. There was a time when the hieroglyphic writing in Ancient Egypt was not made out. But the problem was solved after the discovery of bilingual inscriptions engraved in hieroglyphic writing in which the figure of an object represented a word or syllable. It must be remembered that the Brahmi script itself was deciphered only in 1837 by Prinsep. He was able to achieve this from bilingual coins of the Greek rulers of north western India, in which their names and titles were given both in Greek letters and in Prakrit in Brahmi letters. Thus it is hazardous to make venturesome assertions about the relationship of the Indus Valley civilization with either the Aryan or Dravidian civilizations though the probability alone may be indicated on the basis of the extant evidence. It cannot be too often repeated that neither wishful thinking nor chauvinism should handicap authentic history.

One form of chauvinism has led to the view that both the Aryans and Dravidians were natives of India and were not outsiders. This seems unacceptable for the simple reason that the

Iranian and Sumerian elements noticeable respectively in the Aryan and Dravidian civilizations of old could not have appeared but for their having come from or through these respective regions.

LEMURIAN THEORY

In this context a reference to the so-called Lemurian theory is essential because it has relevance to the origin and antiquity of the Tamils. But a detailed consideration of the theory need not be undertaken here, since it has been examined at some length in my book on the Social History. It is well known that several Tamil scholars of old believed that there existed in the bygone ages an extensive mass of land connecting South India with Sri Lanka, Malaysia, Indonesia and other countries of South East Asia and Australia on the one hand and Madagascar and South Africa on the other. This view was vaguely stated by Tamil scholars and was described as the Lemurian continent by certain Western writers. Tamil scholars developed this theory on the basis of Nakkirar's commentary to the Iraiyanar Ahapporul, which commentary appeared only about the 9th century AD. Recently some Tamil writers speak of it as Kumarikandam. Nakkirar referred to it in connection with his description of the Tamil Sangams. Certain references in Kalittohai and Silappadikaram advert to the submergence of land to the south of Kumari. The commentators of the Tamil classics, like Adiyarkkunallar and Nachchinarkiniyar who lived between the 12th and 14th centuries AD developed these views at considerable length.

According to the theory expounded by them, in that vast expanse of land there was Madurai, later known as Ten Madurai, which was the capital of the Pandyan king and the seat of the first Tamil Sangam. Many details furnished about the Sangam are probably incredible, though it might have been true that several Tamil works ascribed to the first Sangam are lost. Old Madurai was engulfed by the sea after which the second Sangam flourished in Kapadapuram. Several of the works produced by this Sangam also are lost, except a fragment of Tolkappiyam.

Another deluge devoured Kapadapuram and ultimately the Pandyan capital and the third Sangam appeared in Madurai of the present day. There are many who believe that this was the real and only Sangam or Tamil academy under the auspices of which all the extent Sangam works were produced.

It may be held that the theory of three Tamil Sangams is not a pure myth. In this connection it may be mentioned that there is a small island called Madurai very near the northern part of Java. There is also another island called Madurai near the coast of Borneo. The common people call them Marudai. But this is how the modern Madurai of South India is also called by the illiterate folk. One or the other of these might have been the seat of the first Tamil Sangam. It is probable that the island near Java was the Madurai associated with the Sangam because, early mankind might have first appeared in Java, a fact suggested by the discovery of a skeleton of a creature resembling early man. Kapadapuram could well have been the seat of the second Sangam. Its existence in the past is indicated by the references to it in the Epics, the Ramayana and Mahabharata.

European scholars supported the Lemurian theory on geological and geographical grounds. The genesis of the name Lemuria was found in the monkey-like animals, Lemur, as they were called, which lived in that region. The name 'Lemuria' was first employed by an Englishman, Sclater, to this wide expanse of land.

There arises the question of the presence of the Negrito element among the aboriginals of South India. Several ethnologists and anthropologists support this view and suggest association of South India with South Africa or South East Asia. The totems found among certain tribes of South India as well as the practice of using the boomerang by the Kallans of South India are found to exist among certain original inhabitants of Indonesia and Polynesia. Moreover, the languages spoken by the Maories in New Zealand and by people in the neighbouring islands are pronounced by experts to have affinity with Tamil.

On the other hand, affinities of certain backward classes with the Negros of South Africa have been stressed by certain recent researchers. Of course in respect of the black colour and flat nose there is some resemblance. But when it comes to a matter of the 'straight hair', 'wavy hair' or 'curly hair' the resemblance is by no means clear, though some European experts like Snowden Junior think there is not much difference.[10]

Some writers have felt that African negros had come and mixed with South Indians and that they constituted the ancestors of some of the Harijans in Kerala and Tamil Nadu. Geologists have advanced a hypothesis that a great land bridge once connected India and Africa. Whether the Negroid element in South India is traceable to Africa or to Australia, is another difficult question. Probably they all formed inhabitants of one vast land mass. The Negroids of Africa in the West and Oceania in the East came to be separated by the expanses of the Indian Ocean. But his, too, is a piece of guess. It is not possible to be more specific about this difficult question, although some assert that the contact between South India and East Africa rather than South Africa is more probable. But the assertion made by L.S. Senghor that there was kinship between East Africans and Dravidians[11] seems to be wide of the mark. Lilian Hamburger held that there is a kingship between Kannada and the Bantu languages.[12] Alfredo Trombetti went to the extent of suggesting that Dravidian and Negro-African languages represented a common language, akin to Sumerian.[13] This too seems to be a sweeping generalisation.

The only reasonable conclusion is that there are some probabilities in respect of the Lemurian theory and Negroid element in South Indian population. It is not possible to assert as to how far they are true. Further advances in archaeology, ethnography, anthropology and other sciences alone can settle these riddles.

In the present state of our knowledge the possible conclusions are that the Dravidians came from Sumeria through Elam, settled in North India and established the Indus Valley civilization. Their language was in all probability akin to the language, later developed as Tamil. As a consequence of repeated deluges the people of the Indus Valley moved south and east and some of them ultimately reached South India and settled in modern Canarese, Telugu, Tamil and Malayalam regions.

In this distant past there must have existed a few places in South East Asia, where some of the ancestors of the Tamils lived. These people might have developed the Tamil language and established in due course the Tamil Sangams. These hypotheses alone can explain the early history of Tamil in Ten Madurai, Kapadapuram and Vada Madurai. Perhaps some of the early Tamils had travelled westwards by the ocean and settled in Baluchistan, Elam and the Indus Valley. These postulates provide a plausible relationship between Tamil words and those found in the Elamite and the Hurrian languages. At a later stage people from Sumeria and other regions of Western Asia might have immigrated into the Indus Valley and mixed with the earlier immigrants.

Still earlier, certain people of the Negroid stock either from South East Asia or from Africa might have come and settled in South India. It is not unlikely that some of them are the ancestors of the Negroids in Tamil Nadu and other regions of South India. Up to a certain measure we have to agree with the castigations of History of Will and Ariel Durant indicated in the opening para of this paper. There are palpable guesses and over-simplifications.

But it is important to urge that these pessimistic writers themselves admit in another part of their work the historicity of the Indus civilization. They state moreover that "between the heyday of Mohenjodaro and the advent of the Aryans a great gap stands in our knowledge or rather that our knowledge of the past is occasional gap in our ignorance".[14] Refreshingly they add a more positive conclusion. "The Dravidians were already a civilized people when the Aryans broke down upon them; their adventurous merchants *sailed the sea even to Sumeria and Babylon*; and their cities knew many refinements and luxuries. It was from them apparently that the Aryans took their village community and their system of land tenure and taxation. To this day the Deccan is still essentially Dravidian in stock and customs, in language, literature and arts".[15] But unfortunately one is constrained to add that there are still uncertainties and contradictions in the conclusions advanced by these learned critics. The gaps have to be filled and the ultimate truths have to be arrived at only after further investigation. As mentioned earlier, the situation is not desperate. Geologists, geographers, sociologists, anthropologists, linguists and historians most all work in collaboration in order to arrive at the truth.

ENDNOTES

1. The Story of Civilization, Chapter I, p. 12.
2. *Ibid.*, p. 979.
3. Certain writers have ascribed to Fr. Heras the conclusion that the ancient inhabitants of the Indus spoke the Tamil language. He protests indignantly against this erroneous interpretation. However, he shows that the original name of the Proto-Indo-Mediterranean was 'Tramilar' which was later transformed into 'Tamilar' in India.
4. These details are gathered from the address delivered by Dr. S. R. Rao in the Museum Society of Bombay on June 14, 1971. Dr. Rao is at present working on the Indus script as a Nehru scholar.
5. We leave out the consideration of Lahovary's fantastic theory that the civilization which flourished once in the region beginning from Iberia in Spain down to India were all connected with each other in respect of religious rites and customs. His theory was based on the study of linguistic affinities but other similarities like ethnological and anthropological features do not support his theory.
6. Bulletin of the Institute of Traditional Cultures, Year 1976, July–December, pp. 155–6.

7. See the author's A Social History of the Tamils, Vol. I, p. 51/F.N.

8. Transactions of the Archaeological Society of South India, 1957–8, pp. 457–54.

9. Slightly different in area is the Gondwanaland which comprised South America and Antartica also.

10. Snowden, Jr.: Blacks in Antiquity, Harward University Press, 1970. Some photographs show that certain primitive inhabitants in Kerala had almost a similar kind of hair like the Negros of Africa.

11. K.P. Aravanan: Dravidians and Africans, Ed. 1977. p.4.

12. *Ibid*, p.12

13. *Ibid*, p.10.

14. Will and Ariel Durant: The Story of Civilisation, Vol. I, p. 396.

15. *Ibid*.

2

TAMIL LITERATURE AS A SOURCE MATERIAL OF HISTORY

It is indisputable that professedly historical works are conspicuous by their absence in early India. Several writers, commencing with Alberuni, the discerning scholar who visited the country in the 11th century AD, have observed that Indians of the past, despite their high intellectual attainments, lacked the historic spirit. This feature is as much true of the Tamils as of the rest of the Indians.

However, the Sangam classics, comprising the extant literary works of the early Tamils, contain extraordinarily abundant data of historical value. They throw some light on the political, and still more on the social and religious conditions of the early Tamils. But the determination of the chronology of the Sangam age on the one hand, and the sifting of the historical data from the vast mass of miscellaneous material on the other, is by no means easy. The origin of the Sangam, the celebrated literary Academy, is itself enshrouded in mystery.

THE SANGAM

The earliest account of the Sangam appears in the Commentary on the *Iraiyanar Ahapporul* (Grammar of Tamil Poetry)[1] which is not assignable to a date earlier than 8th century AD. Moreover, it is coloured by the belief in the supernatural agency. It speaks of three successive Sangams which lasted altogether for 9,990 years and had in the aggregate 8,598 poets, who included certain Gods as well! On the face of it this account is incredible.

Nevertheless, the entire tradition concerning the Academy does not seem to have been a fiction, for in the first place, traditions do not arise normally without any basis. Secondly, certain kings and poets figure in more than one classic of the Sangam age. Apparently, fact and fiction seem to have become mixed up in the account recorded in the Commentary on the *Iraiyanar Ahapporul*. While it is quite probable that an academy of poets flourished under the patronage of the Pandyan kings, as mentioned in the *Velvikkudi grant*,[2] many of the details concerning the Sangam are clearly figments of the mythmakers' imagination.

It is not possible to determine whether there existed three Sangams or only one. The legend that the Pandyan kings changed their capitals twice before they settled in the present Madurai, is supported partly by the reference in the Mahabharata and by the evidence of Pliny.[3] The fact of the three capitals was perhaps responsible for the legend of the three Sangams. Tradition is, however, persistent that the two earlier Sangams had produced numerous literary works, most of which have perished and that the extant classics are mainly the products of the third Sangam. It must be admitted that it is impossible to arrive at a finality in respect of this question.

Chronological Basis

Nor do the extant Sangam works provide a firm chronological foothold for the history of the early Tamils. The determination of the age of the Sangam has proved a vexed problem, for speculation on it has ranged from 500 BC to AD 500 not to speak of the extreme views on its upper and lower limits.[4] Doubtless, the Academy flourished prior to the 7th century AD because of the Saiva hymnists, Sambandar and Appar, who were the contemporaries of Pallava Narasimhavarman I of 7th century AD refer to the Sangam.[5] Besides it is obvious that several centuries must have intervened before the rather archaic style of the Sangam works attained the simple pattern of the devotional hymns of the 7th century AD. Then again, it is unlikely that between the 4th and 6th centuries AD, when Tamilaham was under the chaos caused by the Kalabhra eruption, the Sangam would have flourished under the patronage of the Pandyan kings.

In fact, the generally accepted view which assigns the Sangam to the early centuries of the Christian era seems to be based on valid grounds.[6] Besides the *Gajabahu Senguttuvan* synchronism, the so-called sheet-anchor of South Indian chronology, which ascribes the events embodied in the *Silappadikaram* to the 2nd century AD, the remarkable coincidence of the Tamil literary references with the data furnished by the Greek geographers of the 1st and 2nd centuries AD, reinforced by the discovery of the Roman coins of that period in South India lends support to this view. However, this conclusion has recently been challenged on the ground that the Sound Indian Brahmi inscriptions of the 3rd and 2nd centuries BC, reveal Tamil of a crude form and that the well-developed language of the Sangam classics could not have appeared prior to AD, 500.[7] But this challenge is based on a doubtful hypothesis. The language of these inscriptions represents a hybrid of Prakrit and Tamil and not the real Tamil of the age.[8]

The extant Sangam literature comprises the eight anthologies called *Ettuttogai* of short lyrics and the Ten Idylls known as *Pattuppattu*.[9] These poems are broadly classifiable into two groups, viz., those called '*Puram*' works which deal with external matters like war and patronage of king and '*Aham*' works which concern themselves with love.[10] The anthologies and Idylls were no doubt compiled several centuries after the Sangam age. Further, all the works in each of these categories were not composed at the same time either. Even verses in the *Purananuru* belong to different periods of time within the Sangam age. *Kalittogai* and *Paripadal* seem to be later than *Ahananuru*, while *Tirumurugarruppadai* among the Ten Idylls was unquestionably a late composition, posterior to the 3rd century AD.

According to tradition the *Eighteen Minor works* called *Patinenkilkanakku*, was well as the two great epics, *Manimekalai* and *Silappadikaram*, are classed among the Sangam classics. But the language as well as the ideas contained in most of them indicate a later date for them. However, all the '18 didactic poems,' as they are described, do not belong to the same time, though they were grouped together because of the 'venba' metre in which all these poems were composed. Tradition which assigns the celebrated *Kural* to the Sangam age might well be true to fact.[11] That *Kural* speaks of love marriages typical of the Sangam age as contrasted with those of the *Silappadikaram* epoch is a pointer in this direction. *Kural* (verse 475) mentions the example of the cart loaded with the feathers of peacocks; it is suggestive of the cart loads of feathers sent abroad during the 1st and 2nd centuries AD. Again, *Kalavali*, another of the 18 minor works, was not far removed from the date of one verse in *Purananuru* (v. 74). But *Tirukadugam* and *Sirupancamulam* are the latest in the series and were composed in the 9th century AD. The references to *Peru Muttaraiyar* in *Naladiyar* indicate the contemporaniety of the work with these chieftains of the 9th century.

The twin epics are anterior to many of the 18 didactic works, although the tradition which assigns, them to the Sangam age seems unacceptable. The themes of the epics belong in all probability to the 2nd century AD. The political background of the stories, and in particular the *Gajabahu Senguttuvan* synchronism, indicate this. The supernatural element in the epics apart, the principal events mentioned in *Silappadikaram*, could well have occurred in the 2nd century AD. The omission of the Pallavas in the political picture confirms it. Some time after, popular imagination had spun stories out of the events, talented poets would have shaped them into epic form. Besides the larger proportion of Sanskrit words than in the early Tamil literature, the improved forms of the language, the appearance of the northern pattern of marriage ceremonies and the prominent role assigned to the festival of Indra in *Silappadikaram*, all indicate a later date for the epics than for the Sangam works.[12] It is interesting to find that a recent writer proceeding on astoronomical data furnished by *Silappadikaram* and its famous commentator, *Adiyarkunallar*, suggests AD 465 as the date for the composition of the epic.[13]

Manimekalai is totally Buddhist in its setting and though it is not indisputably established that Dinnaga's *Nyayapravesa* had influenced the epic, the Buddhistic philosophy of 3rd and 4th centuries AD. is clearly discernible in it.[14] *Manimekalai* reveals that Kanchi had become a centre of Buddhist learning. It may be recalled that Buddhist and Jain devotees had found their way into South India as early as the 3rd and 2nd centuries BC. On the whole there is little justification for assigning the epics to a period later than the 5th century AD; in all probability they belong to the 4th or 5th century AD.[15]

HISTORICAL VALUE OF THE LITERATURE

Against the chronological background outlined above, the historical value of the different classes of early Tamil literature may be assessed. Among the Sangam classics, *Purananuru*, *Pattuppattu* and *Padirruppattu* are the most important works of the reconstruction of the people's history. Though the *Aham* poems which deal with love, occasionally advert to historical events and social customs, they are not as full and vivid in these aspects as the *Puram* works in general.

The short lyrics of *Ettuttogai* furnish a clue to the date, authorship of the poems and the occasion for their composition by means of a colophon appended to each poem. The Idylls also provide similar epilogues, padigams, as they are called, but generally they are far too brief and little more than the authors' names are available from them. Among the *Ettuttogai* collections themselves the historical value of the colophons is not uniformly of the same character. The padigams of the *Padirruppattu* appear to have been appended long after the poems were composed, for they mention important facts which are not found in the poems. For instance, Senguttuvan's northern expedition, the most important achievement ascribed to him by *Silappadikaram*, is found mentioned in the padigam of the 5th Decad and not in the poem itself.

Far different is the case of the colophons in *Purananuru*, since they seem to have appeared contemporaneously with the poems themselves.[16] Besides, there is no valid reason for disputing the claim registered in the colophons of *Purananuru* that the poems were contemporary compositions dealing with particular situations to which the poet themselves were eye witnesses. If this claim is true, the historical value of the work is great.

A remarkable feature about the *Puram* poems is that they deal with the situations in an objective and realistic manner. There is little of the conventional pattern either in their themes or in their treatment of the subject as we find in later poems. It is important to observe that the Sangam poets were not petty minded supplicants who praised their patrons indiscriminately. There are a number of courageous outbursts of poets expressing their contempt of those rulers who failed to treat them in the befitting manner.[17] Thus the poets maintained their self-respect, despite their poverty. Their poems were generally true to their convictions, though extravagant praises of generous patrons have occasionally found their way into the poems.

A principal drawback of the data provided by the Sangam works is that a continuous political history of the dynasties of the age cannot be reconstructed, for it is difficult to determine the genealogy or chronological relationship of the kings who figure in the classics. The Pandya, Chola and Chera dynasties dominate Tamilaham in their respective divisions, while in between their territories, there ruled several minor chieftains. But the achievements of prominent rulers and incidentally the character of monarchy are about the only data of political history which can be gathered from the poems.

The Pandyas

References to several Pandyan kings are found in the Sangam poems. *Maduraikkanci*, for instance, speaks of two kings,

Nediyon[18] and *Palyagasalai Mudukudumi*,[19] but unquestionably the hero of the poem is *Nedunjeliyan* who won the famous victory at *Talayalanganam* against a combination of the contemporary *Chera* and *Chola* kings and five minor chiefs. Unfortunately it is not possible to determine the distance of time which intervened between this *Nedunjeliyan* and the king of the same name. *Aryappadaikadanda Nedunjeliyan*, figuring in *Silappadikaram*.

The victor of *Talayalanganam* is praised also in numerous poems in *Purananuru*,[20] *Ahananuru*,[21] *Kuruntogai*[22] and *Narrinai*.[23] An ambitious warrior, a generous patron of poets, and a staunch Hindu who performed a Vedic sacrifice, *Nedunjeliyan* was one of the outstanding Pandyan kings, celebrated in the Sangam classics.

Among the successors of *Nedunjeliyan* known to Tamil literature there appears *Ugraperuvaluti*, a valiant warrior who subdued his opponent, the chief of *Kanapper*.[24] A poet of eminence, he himself, is believed to have caused the anthology of *Ahananuru* to be made. Another Pandyan king, famous in the Sangam literature is the poet king *Bhutappandiyan* who captured Ollaiyur.[25] An able warrior, a generous and affectionate friend as well as a loving husband, he was an enlightened ruler. The names of several other Pandyan monarchs occur in the classics; but few details about them are available.

The Cholas

The data regarding the Cholas do not differ radically in character from those on the Pandyas. A continuous history of the kings and their rule is not possible to be reconstructed. The schemes of genealogy attempted by V. Kanakasabhai and M. Raghava Aiyangar are not fully supported by the available sources.[26]

As among the Pandyas, certain Chola kings stand out prominently in the poems. *Karikala* is clearly the most outstanding personality among all the monarchs of the age. His brilliant victory at Venni against the Chera and Pandyas sovereigns[27] as well as his triumph over a confederacy of nine minor chieftains in a battle at Vakaipparandalai[28] and finally the havoc caused by his forces in the territories of his enemies[29] are all vividly described. *Karikala's* development of irrigation and his promotion of trade and industry in *Kaverippumpattinam* receive special treatment in *Pattinappalai*.[30] His exploits are mentioned also in *Purananuru, Porunararruppadai, Manimekalai* and *Silappadikaram*.[31] Many of his achievements specified in literature are echoed in later inscriptions like the *Malepadu Plates, Anbil Plates, Tiruvalangadu Plates, Larger Leyden grant* and the *Kanyakumari inscription*.

It may be observed that many legends have gathered around the personality of *Karikala* in the post-Sangam period. Later literature, as seen from *Kalingattupparani, Vikramacholan Ula* and *Rajarajacholan Ula*, all of the 12th century AD, present embellished accounts, which are clearly legendary in character. While *Karikala* of the Sangam works appears a realistic personality, he becomes enveloped in an admixture of legends and facts in later literature.[32]

A Chola king who ruled considerably later than *Karikala* was *Koccengannan*, the *Saiva* devotee, whose victory at the battle of *Kalumalam* against the Chera ruler *Kanaikkal Irumporai* is found described in a rather conventional manner in *Kalavali*. The author of *Kalavali*, called Poygaiyar, a benefactor of the Chera king, cannot be identified, as has been done, with the celebrated *Vaisnava* saint, Poygai Alvar, since the battle of *Kalumalam* is mentioned in *Purananuru*,[33] where it is stated that the vanquished Chera king himself composed that verse.[34]

The Cheras

The only dynasty about which a fairly consecutive genealogy can be constructed by the aid of the early Tamil literature is that of the Cheras. *Padirrupattu* (Ten Decads) concern themselves entirely with the achievements of the Chera kings. Of the original collection, unfortunately the first and last Decads have been lost. Each of the remaining Decads deals with the achievement of a particular Chera monarch. *Padirruppattu* furnishes a dynastic list of the Chera kings and the duration of each reign. K.G. Sesha Aiyar has made a commendable attempt at constructing a chronological framework. But he encounters certain difficulties, which he tries to overcome by means of certain hypotheses, some of which are clearly untenable.[35]

A serious obstacle to the framing of a succession list of the kings is that there were two lines of Cheras, one ruling at *Vanchi* and the other at *Tondi*, simultaneously for the most part. The exact relationship of the members of the collateral branch with those of the main line is not ascertainable in every case; nor is the capital of every ruler specifically mentioned. Moreover, the date of the Chera rule in terms of known chronology is not easily determinable, for *Padirruppattu* does not provide its account in terms of any era. Sesha Aiyar's basic date, viz., AD 125, the opening year of Senguttuvan's reign, is based on the Gajabahu Senguttuvan synchronism.

Of the eight Chera kings whose achievements are described in *Padirruppattu*, clearly Senguttuvan is the most outstanding personality. The famous poet, *Paranar* has devoted the 5th Decad to this sovereign, while many of his achievements are echoed *Silappadikaram*. Senguttuvan's northern conquests, his defeat of Nannan, the Velir chieftain, his overthrow of a confederacy of nine Cholas at Nerivayil and his triumph over the Kongar are all mentioned in the epic.[36] Senguttuvan was a devout Hindu who performed the Vedic sacrifices and worshipped both *Siva* and *Visnu*.[37] Senguttuvan was, in all probability, a kinsman of *Karikala*. From the references to these monarchs in *Padirruppattu* and *Silappadikaram*, it seems that Karikala was the maternal great-grand-father of Senguttuvan.

Purananuru speaks of nine more Chera kings besides those mentioned in *Padirruppattu*. The reason for the omission of these names remains a mystery. Perhaps the 1st and last Decads mention some or all of the rest; or more probably several of the Cheras mentioned in *Purananuru* were subordinate chiefs. However, it is significant that a few of the names found in *Purananuru* occur in *Ahananuru* as well.[38] Since the padigam of the 2nd Decad states that Udiyam Cheral was the father of Imayavaramban Neduncheralatan who is the hero of that Decad, it is likely that Udiyam Cheral was the hero of the first Decad. Thus while the historical data regarding the Cheras is more adequate than in respect of the other two dynasties there remain insoluble problems which make even the history of the Cheras far from complete or satisfactory.

Minor Chieftains

Several minor chieftains who ruled in various parts of the Tamil country are mentioned in the classics. The most prominent among them are Ay Andiran and Pari, both renowed for heroism and patronage of poets. Though we come across the names of five other chieftains who, along with Andiran and Pari, constituted the seven 'Vallas' (paragons of generosity), it is not possible to construct the genealogical line of these chieftains or determine their relationship with the rulers of the principal dynasties.

Thus, evaluating the literary source for the political history, it is found that though details are known about the achievements of several monarchs in each dynasty, the material is not adequate enough to help a systematic reconstruction of history. The knowledge of the Cheras is more full and continuous than that of the rest, but even here the lacunae are not inconsiderable. Nor can all the details furnished about the kings be considered historical. While the references to kings are realistic and sober in comparison with the data in later literature, it must be admitted that all poetic accounts have inherent limitations as a source of history. For one thing the focus of attention on the part of the poet would not have been the same as that of a chronicler or historian.[39]

Doubtless the inferences deducible from the literature about the general character of monarchy and the ideals and aspirations which guided the rulers are interesting. Kings were generally war-minded and wars were frequent. Heroism in war was held up as a great virtue. Death in the field of battle, valiantly fighting to the last, was considered a meritorious end for a ruler. The Chera king Atan II who was wounded on the back on the battlefield committed suicide on that account. Details concerning the army corps of the early Tamil kings, the different stages of an expedition, the pattern of military training and the ethics of warfare are all available from the early literature.[40]

There was a lofty conception of royal duties. The maintenance of impartial justice, protection of the poor and the helpless, the promotion of the economic well-being of the subjects[41] and the performance of religious rites for the sake of the people's welfare[42] were considered their legitimate duties. The *Kural* provides a systematic exposition of the responsibilities of an ideal king.[43]

It would seem that kings were remarkably enlightened. Invariably all kings were patrons of the learned. Even more interesting is the fact that many kings themselves were poets. Many of the early Pandyan monarchs and those of some other dynasties too, were gifted poets. The kings were intimately associated with poets, some of whom acted as advisers or messengers of the monarchs. The royal custom of according a warm reception to the wandering minstrels, Panar as they were called, contributed to the lively maintenance of the arts of poetry and dance.

The impression which the poems give us is that the monarch was an autocrat. But in reality, with the restraining influence of the poets and ministers and with a growing reverence for custom, the king was an ideal ruler suited to the times. Whether the groups of advisers called 'aimperungulu' and 'enperayam' denoted councils of representatives or merely attendants on the king, there is little doubt that the ruler was guided and influenced by several competent persons.

References to 'manram,' 'podiyil' and 'avai' in the classics suggest that there were frequent gatherings of the people. It is not possible to ascertain what role they played in the political life of the land. But it is presumable that they constituted a type of folk gathering where the people indicated their wishes. It cannot but be regretted that the light thrown on the political life of the common people is not adequate.

SOCIAL LIFE

It is concerning social life that an amazing wealth of material is provided by literature. True, the matter is available but indirectly. Incidental to the description of personalities or events there appear details of social habits, customs, religious institutions and practices and developments of arts and education. Normally, the more casual and indirect the data, the more true and faithful is the picture obtained. In comparison with professional history it suffers in one respect; it lacks a sense of proportion. Those details which are of great interest to the historian might or might not receive attention at the hands of the poets.

It is important to remember that for the most part, the Sangam poems were not produced by persons who pursued poetry for its own sake. Many of the poems came from the 'Panar,' the professional class of minstrels, who were the roving bards of the time. Some of them were poets of real merit, while others were musicians, who along with their womenfolk went about visiting kings and chieftains, delighting them with their songs and dances. They praised the liberal patrons while they condemned boldly those who were not warm or generous to them.

As a source of social history the early poems have their shortcomings. They do not touch upon all aspects of social life. Nor do they afford a connected picture of the past' throwing light on the changes which occurred from time to time. Historical averaging, which inevitably contains inaccuracies may be the result; it may provide an unreal appearance of flat uniformity and absence of change. In order to avoid this danger, it is necessary to limit our observations to the time indicated by the specific sources of information, except in such cases where there is definite evidence of the continuance of an institution or practice once established. For instance, meat and liquor were quite commonly used in the Sangam age; in the period of the epics they were condemned by moralists. Again, it is doubtful whether all the intricate patterns of dance described in *Silappadikaram* were known to the Sangam age.[44]

Here it is not possible to give a full picture of the social habits and customs gleaned from the early Tamil literature. The general character of the data available from the literary works, illustrated by a few examples, is all that can be indicated. Among the Sangam works unquestionably *Purananuru* and *Pattuppattu* afford the most abundant data for the social historian, though the other classics, too, are occasionally helpful.

The houses of the people in different strata of society, as well as the palaces of kings, are found described.[45] Food and clothing find numerous references.[46] Meat and liquor were commonly used in the Sangam age,[47] but by the time of the epics a tendency to prohibit their use is clearly in evidence.[48] Men and women dressed their hair with oil.[49] *Kurinjippattu* mentions the custom of women arranging their hair in five braids.[50] References to the habit of wearing *sandals* as foot-wear are found.[51] The habit of chewing betel leaves with lime and arecanut, prevalent in the Sangam age, continued in the period of the epics[52] and still later.

Descriptions of the agriculture and trade of the Tamils appear in numberless places in the classics.[53] While the life of the people belonging to the five natural divisions of the land is described in many of the Sangam works, the habits and customs of the *Paradavar*, the fisherman in Neydal, are vividly portrayed in *Maduraikkanci* and *Pattinappalai*.[54]

Occupation was the basis of division into castes among the early Tamils. But even as early as the age of *Purananuru* it is seen than the Aryan four-fold classification had found its way into the Tamil Country. The result was that from about the Sangam age onwards there commenced the fusion of the indigenous and imported systems.[55] Purananuru, while mentioning the pre-Aryan castes also refers to the brahmins and their high social position.[56]

By the time of the epics the amalgam of the two systems of caste had taken firm root, and what is more, the multiplication of subcastes had proceeded to an inordinate extent.[57]

Two forms of marriage, (marriage in secrecy and marriage in the open) were in vogue among the Tamils from early times. But beginning perhaps from the Sangam age these undergo a change and by the time of the epics the forms of Aryan marriage, together with fire rites seem to have become established in the Tamil country.[58] But it is important to observe that some of them were adopted by the brahmins as well. For example, the ancient usage of the bridge-groom tying *tali* (marriage symbol) around the neck of the bride,[59] as well as *Sati* and the tonsure of widows.[60] were continued side by side with the Aryan rituals and ceremonies.

There is little doubt that in the Sangam age woman was held in high esteem; she was considered the luminary of the home. *Pattuppattu* reveals that women enjoyed freedom and that they moved about in public without affecting prudery. '*Perumpanarruppadai*,' in particular throws much light on this question.[61] It describes, for instance, how girls in the *brahmin* villages sported in ponds, women mingled freely in the village festivals and how rich ladies participated in certain pastimes and amusements of their own. Of course, all through the ages, unstinting devotion to the husband was the high ideal of virtue held up for women. This is admirably emphasised in the celebrated *Kural*, though several earlier works also touch upon it.

Side by side with the high ideals for women who led the household life there existed harlots or public women, who enticed rich young men for the sake of their money. The Sangam works themselves speak of the harlots and the low social position they occupied. It is needless to add that by the time of the epics the institution had taken a firm root in the country.

The amusements and pastimes of the people reveal at once their rustic simplicity and robust outlook on life. While boys and girls had numerous kinds of interesting games,[62] adults enjoyed manly sports and physical contests, besides the training for warfare, which was provided in certain village organisations. Cockfights and ram-fights were common amusements which attracted vast crowds of enthusiastic spectators. Festivals were common. For example, during summer there appeared the *Kamavel* festival in honour of Kama, the God of Love. By the days of *Silappadikaram* the pastimes and festivals had increased in their number and variety.[63] Festivals in honour of Gods like *Muruga*, *Korravai* and *Visnu*, not to speak of the grand festival of *Indra*, all assume a great importance.

It was a common practice even in the Sangam age for monarhs and the rich to enjoy their leisure by listening to songs and poems of minstrels and poets, while sitting in pavilions in front of their mansions. Minstrels were provided with food and robes as well as presents of gold. Dancers also vied with each other in the display of their arts in these gatherings.[64]

The progress made by the early Tamils in the arts of dancing, music and poetry was remarkable. The ubiquitous *Panar* and *Viraliyar*, the roving bards, played a great part in the development of these arts. Many of the early classics furnish vivid descriptions of these arts as they flourished in the country. Tradition has it that several ancient Tamil classics on music have perished. However, there is little doubt that all these fine arts attained a high degree of perfection in the age of the Epics. Very graphic descriptions of the patterns of dance, the systematic training provided, the forms of music, vocal and instrumental, the wide variety of instruments are all described in *Silappadikaram*.[65] The *Panar* and *Viraliyar* do not appear in the Epic period as during the Sangam age. Apparently the artists had given up their roving missions and had settled down in towns.

It is also noticeable that by the epoch of *Silappadikaram*, the fine arts of music and dance[66] became associated with temples besides palaces and village parks. Temples existed no doubt in the Sangam period itself but they became more numerous and popular in the later epoch. The early religious beliefs and observances are found reflected in the classics including *Tolkappiyam*, the work on grammar, which tradition places among the earliest productions of the Sangam. There is no invocation in *Tolkappiyam* to any God as we find in later works. It is clear that the people of the age believed in a Supreme God and in a three-fold Trinity. But it is remarkable that their Trinity was not identical with that of the Aryans. The early Tamils had belief in several minor Gods, too. References to *Daivam*, *Devar*, and *Imaiyar*, all signifying 'God', indicate this and provide testimony to the Aryan influence. *Muruga* and *Korravai* appear to have been the most prominent deities of the early Tamils. Temples for *Muruga* were erected on top of hills as well as on the river side. The appearance of Aryan ideas, noticeable in *Tolkappiyam* and *Purananuru*, becomes increasingly prominent. In *Tirumurugarruppadai*, which was chronologically the last of the '*Pattuppattu*' and which was composed in honour of *Muruga*, the God is identified with *Kartigesa*, the Aryan God of six faces and twelve arms. *Korravai*, the war goddess of the Tamils, merges into the Aryan goddess *Durga*. A similar process is noticed in respect of several other deities. But it is still an open question whether the *Siva* of the Dravidians was adopted by the Aryans and given a new position in their pantheon. One thing is clear. A fusion, particularly marked in the sphere of religion, was taking place between the Tamilian and Aryan ideas and practices and this fusion became more and more marked as time passed. Even puja is stated to have been derived from the Tamil words Pu+sei i.e. the offer of flowers.

When we come to the period of the twin Epics, we notice the full-fledged fusion of Aryan and Dravidian religious practices. In addition to the Gods already worshipped by the people there now figured Balarama,[67] *Varuna* and *Indra*. *Devi* was worshipped not only in the form of *Korravai* but also as *Laksmi*, *Sarasvati* and *Parvati*.

Thus Tamil literature, which constitutes the only source of information, provides valuable data for the social history of the people. Care has to be taken, however, in utilizing them, particularly in relation to chronology. The basic conditions, as revealed by the Sangam classics, together with the changes reflected in the 18 minor works and the Epics, can be reconstructed with a fair measure of accuracy. It is important in this connection to remember that the literature of a particular period not only portrays contemporary life and events but may also embody in it earlier traditions. And a clear sifting of the one from the other is not always easy. Thus, subject to all these limitations, the social history of the early Tamils is possible to be reconstructed with the help of their literature.

Historical writing was conspicuous by its absence in Tamil, as in other Indian languages, including Sanskrit. Several writers have deplored the lack of historic sense on the part of the Hindus. R.C. Majumdar, the well-known historian of India says: "Historiography was practically unknown to the Hindus at the beginning of the nineteenth century." In spite of the large production of literary works, history as such received scant attention through the ages. One reason for this unfortunate circumstance was the domination of religion over all fields of thought and literary activity. In respect of Tamil literature this feature appeared more predominantly after the 7th century AD than earlier. Secondly, the didactic aim which motivated literary productions also vitiated an objective approach. Often, the didactic aim became commingled with the religious and philosophical treatment of ideas. Finally, certain literary conventions had taken shape which regulated the pattern of literary productions. This feature was particularly noticeable in the treatment of Love or Aham in the early Tamil classics. A truly historical or objective approach was vitiated by these literary conventions.

QUASI-HISTORICAL LITERATURE

However, in the whole range of Tamil literature, there have appeared certain quasi-historical compositions, which if carefully utilised, can be made to yield some historical data. Often they supplement or confirm the information gathered from certain other sources. Besides the Sangam works which provide indirect information on the political and social history, the most prominent among the types of semi-historical works are the Ula, Kovai, Parani, Kalambakam, Ammanai, Satakam and Pillaittamil. Several of the outstanding works under these categories were produced during the 12th and 13th centuries and are of value for the history of the Imperial Cholas.

These different patterns of semi-historical works vary in their historical value; and the particular compositions in each category, too, vary from one another in their utility for the historian. Thus the Ula is a poem sung in praise of a king or a deity. Where its subject matter is a king, some historical data may be gathered from it. But occasionally it is difficult to discern the subject of the poem; for instance, it is not known whether the Ekambaranathar Ula was composed in honour of the deity of Kanchi or a Sambuvaraya chieftain whose name was Ekambaranatha. Doubtless, the most celebrated of the Ulas are those of Ottakkuttan on the three successive Chola monarchs, namely, Vikrama Chola (1118–35 AD), Kulottunga II (1130–1150 AD) and Raja Raja II (1146–73 AD). He was the poet laureate of the Chola court during the reigns of all these three monarchs. From the standpoint of history, no doubt, the shortcomings of court poetry are there, and the truth has to be sifted from the laudatory verses.

The Ula assumes a conventional literary form, and it describes the supposed processing (parani) of its hero, the king, who is imagined as going around the city on a stroll along with his officers, apparently in order to ascertain the condition of his subjects living in the city. In the course of this description the poet provides a glorious and often an exaggerated account of the achievements of the king and his predecessors.

It is, however, notable that certain facts mentioned by the Ulas are confirmed by the epigraphic and other sources. For instance, the Vikrama Cholan Ula states that Rajamahendra, the son of Rajendra I, provided a serpent-couch set with precious stones for Lord Ranganatha of Srirangam. It is notable that, though the 'Koiolugu' of a later period does not mention this specific endowment, it refers to several improvements effected by Rajamahendra in the temple of Ranganatha. Again, the names of the feudatory chieftains and officers of Vikrama Chola, mentioned in the Vikrama Cholan Ula, are confirmed by the inscriptions of his time. It may be observed in passing that the information regarding generals like Naraloka Vira and Karunakara Tondaiman is gathered only from the Vikrama Cholan Ula and Kalingattupparani. Further the surname of 'Tyagasamudra' assumed by Vikrama Chola is mentioned both in the Vikrama Cholan Ula and in the inscriptions.

The Kulottunga Cholan Ula also describes the renovation of the Chidambaram temple, and describes how gopurams with seven tiers were erected, a shrine of the goddess was constructed and how several parts of the temple were thatched with golden sheets. It is significant that the improvements effected by this king, Kulottunga II, in the temple and city of Chidambaram are mentioned in the inscription of the 7th year Kulottunga's reign, found at Sripurambiyam.[68]

The 'Kovai' represents a collection of poems dealing with normal conditions in times of peace. The main theme of a Kovai centres round the conventional description of the course of love between lovers commencing from the moment of their accidental meeting. There are some works of this category which are purely religious, as for instance, the 'Tirukkovai'. Among the semi-historical Kovais, perhaps the earliest and the most notable one is the 'Pandikkovai'. But it is not available in full; some portions of it are cited in the later Commentaries and Anthologies. The historical value of this work labours under another defect, namely, that though it mentions several battles fought by the successors of Kadungon (590–620 AD), the central hero of the Kovai was not a single king of the time, but an imaginary hero to whom the achievements of the Pandya line are ascribed. Except, therefore, for securing confirmation of the references to battles found mentioned in the epigraphs, the 'Pandikkovai' is not of help to the student of history.

The 'Kulottungan Kovai', whose author remains unknown, deals with Kumara Kulottunga, presumably Kulottunga III; but its historical value is not considerable, though it throws some light on his participation in the Pandyan war of succession in the latter half of the 12th century.

The 'Tanjai Vanan Kovai', of Poyyamoli Pulavar, describes incidentally the exploits of Vanan, a general, presumably of the Pandyan king, Maravarman Kulasekhara (1268–1308 AD). The general's role in the Malai Nadu (Chera country) is an important theme which finds a place in the Kovai, and that enables us to identify the Pandyan king whom he served. Regarding the expedition of Maravarman Kulasekhara itself, the poem provides useful information.

'Parani' is pre-eminently a war poem; it describes the march of soldiers, the actual military operations and the result of the battle. The most well-known of the Paranis from the historical standpoint is the 'Kalingattupparani' of Jayankondar. It describes vividly the Kalinga expedition undertaken by Kulottunga, the Chola king (1070–1120 AD) and speaks of the ravages and depredations caused by the Chola army under its leader, Karunakara Tondaiman, during its progress in the Kalinga country. The Kalingattupparani provides incidentally other valuable pieces of information on the Chola history of Kulottunga's time and also on the genealogy of the Chola line of kings.[69]

In passing it may be observed that the Kalingattupparani provides the information that Kadiyalur Rudran Kannanar received from Karikala a munificent gift of over a million and a half gold pieces for his composition of the Pattinappalai.

There are several other Paranis in Tamil literature; but they are not of historical value. For instance, the Takkayagapparani of Ottakkuttar is composed on a mythological theme. Though it mentions Virarajendra's friendship with Vikramaditya VI (1076–1127 AD), the Western Chalukya ruler, and refers to Kulottunga II's new constructions in the temple at Chidambaram, on the whole, it cannot be considered to be of great historical value.

It may be mentioned here that Ottakkuttan is known to have composed another Parani on Vikrama Chola's Kalinga war, apparently in imitation of Jayankondar's work; but it is not now available.

The 'Kalambakam' is a quasi-historical poem which deals with a single theme. The best known composition of this category is the 'Nandikkalambakam' by an anonymous author. The poem is believed to contain several interpolations. As it stands at present, it consists of eighty stanzas, and it describes the victories of the reign of Pallavan Nandivarman III (844–66 AD). The poem mentions the principal towns of this Tellarrerinda Nandivarman's kingdom, particularly Mahabalipuram, Kanchi and Mylapore.

The 'Ammanai' is an historical ballad written in popular language because it is intended for the masses. An important poem of this class is the 'Ramappayyan Ammanai,' which dwells upon the military exploits of Ramappayyan, the general and minister of Tirumala Nayak (1623–59 AD) of Madurai. The historical data contained in this Ammanai are confirmed by other sources of information concerning the reign of Tirumala Nayak. Thus, the 'Ramappayyan Ammanai', though revelling in fanciful imagery at various places, is not devoid of historical value. It records not merely a conquest of the 'Malayalam' country by the ruler of Madurai, but it specifically states that the 'Nanchinad Raja', the foremost among the Nayak vassals, was appointed to guard the forts of the Pandyan capital. Further, it adds that the king of Nanchinad co-operated with Tirumala Nayak against the Setupati of Ramanathapuram.

Similar to the 'Ramappayyan Ammanai', both in style and subject matter, is the ballad known as the 'Iravikkuttippillai por', Por 'Iravikkuttippillaip Pattu', as it is alternatively known. This ballad describes how, in the battle of Kaniyakulam, Iravikkuttippillai, the courageous commander of the Venad forces, was killed while valiantly fighting against the Nayak invaders. The ballad does not at all state that the battle ended in a victory for the Venad ruler; in all probability, on the death of the commander, the Venad army dispersed without further fight, virtually conceding the victory for the enemy.[70]

Two other ballads of a similar nature are the 'Desingarajankadai' and the 'Khan Sahib Sandai'. The former deals with the war of Raja Jai Singh, the ruler of Jinji in the 17th century, while the latter describes the life and achievements of Muhammad Yusuf Khan of Madurai, who had joined the company of sepoys under Clive in 1752 and served the English during the siege of Tiruchirappalli. Appointed commandant of the sepoys in 1755, he defeated Haidar Ali in 1757, and at the time of Lally's siege of Madras, he played a valiant part in harassing the besiegers. Later, Yusuf Khan rebelled because he was made the servant of the Nawab of Arcot by the English. Eventually, in 1764, he was executed by the order of Nawab. His courage and ability have been praised by Lawerence and Hill. This ballad is of considerable value in throwing light on the personalities and events in South India during a critical period of the English struggle in the South.

The 'Satakam', another type of semi-historical composition of a local character, became popular in the 17th and 18th centuries. Padikkasu Pulavar was the author of the 'Tondaimandala Satakam' which dwells on Tondaimandalam and its early history. The author of the poem enjoyed the patronage of Raghunatha Setupati (1678–1710 AD) and of a rich Muslim merchant, Periyatambi Marakkayar. The 'Cholamandala Satakam' of Atmanatha Desikar was composed about 1720, and it dwells upon the glories of the Cholas. But both of these Satakams base their accounts on the then current traditions. There is little evidence of a critical approach to the sources. Nevertheless, they are of some use in providing certain details connected with the history of these regions.

The 'Pillaittamil' which describes the hero's childhood is historically the least useful among the semi-historical works, for it is pre-eminently of biographical interest. A notable example of 'Pillaittamil' is that composed by Ottakkuttan on Kulottunga II. No doubt Ottakkuttan was a gifted poet, but this poem is not of any considerable value as a piece of historical literature.

Then there are certain chronicles which profess to provide local history with the temple of the region as its nucleus. Thus we have the 'Maduraittalavaralaru' which deals with the history of the Sri Minakshi temple at Madurai. But, while it treats the later history of the institution fully, it is rather meagre in respect of the earlier period. Moreover, the dominance of the legendary lore obscures very often the historical utility of the account.

Belonging to the same category is the 'Koilolugu' which provides the history of the Sri Ranganatha Temple at Srirangam. From all points of view this is a more satisfactory treatment of the subject than the 'Maduraittalavaralaru', although here, too, legends vitiate the reliability of the account at various places.

Ananda Rangan Pillai's Diary is a unique record, which though not a high class piece of literature, is of considerable historical value in respect of a short period of South Indian history. Ananda Rangan Pillai was the 'Dubash' or interpreter and commercial agent of Dupleix. His Diary provides a full and vivid account of contemporary events from 1736 to 1760. The diary was continued for ten years more by Tiruvengadam Pillai, the nephew of Ananda Rangan Pillai. This is also of some use, though it is less vivid and incisive than that recorded by his uncle.

Ananda Rangan Pillai has provided a sound and a fairly impartial assessment of Dupleix and his activities. He shows how Dupleix had a remarkable skill in carrying out his plans. Though occasionally Ananda Rangan Pillai's personal predilections have influenced his account, on the whole, it contains the record of an acute observer of contemporary events. It throws abundant light on the Anglo French conflict in South India during a critical epoch of Indian history and on the social and economic conditions of the region. In addition, the Diary gives us some idea of the state of colloquial Tamil current in Pondicherry during that time.

CLASSICAL LITERARY WORKS—THEIR DIRECT AND INDIRECT VALUE FOR THE HISTORIAN

The early Tamil classics known as the Sangam works are remarkably helpful in the reconstruction of history. The penpictures provided by them are realistic for the most part, and therefore, though they do not constitute systematic history, they provide useful information on the political, social, economic and religious conditions of the age. No doubt, there are the shortcomings of court poetry in many cases, and these vitiate the data regarding the assessment of the political activities of kings. However, this limitation should not be exaggerated, for, generally the Sangam poets, unlike those of later ages, were conspicuous for their forthrightness and plain speaking. In respect of their indirect and casual references to social phenomena, their evidence is remarkably unimpeachable. Moreover, the Sangam literature was not so prominently dominated by religion, like the Tamil literature subsequent to the 7th century AD.

In respect of political history, the Puram works, namely those classics which deal with objective phenomena, particularly with war, are of considerable historical value. Of these, it is well known that the Purananuru and Padirruppattu throw abundant light on the kingdoms and feudatories of the Sangam age, their wars and other activities. It is clear that the political power was largely in the hands of these potentates, the Chera, Chola and Pandya monarchs who ruled over their traditional dominions, although on account of the varying fortunes of war, their boundaries were subjected to frequent changes. By the side of the three monarchs there were several chieftains who ruled over small principalities and others who were the feudatories of one or the other of the 'Muvendar', the three kings. The exact number of these chieftains and feudatories is not ascertainable. In connection with the famous battle of Talayalankanam, at which the Pandyan king, Neduncheliyan secured a brilliant triumph over his adversaries, only the two other monarchs and five chieftains are mentioned. But in other contexts we hear of seven chieftains who became renowned for their liberality.

Among the three monarchies, we have a remarkably elaborate account of the Chera kings from the extant poems of the Padirruppattu. Udiyancheral, the first Chera monarch,[71] is known to have been succeeded by his son, Neduncheral Adan, who was a valiant hero. Surnamed as Imayavaramban, he is stated to have conquered the whole of India and carved the Chera emblem on the Himalayas. The appellation, 'Imayavaramban' denoted that the northern boundary of his dominion extended up to the Himalayas. This is doubtless an instance of poetic exaggeration, but it may not be too much to infer that this Chera king was an intrepid fighter who had vanquished several of his neighbours.

The Padirruppattu poems narrate the exploits of five kings belonging to the Udiyan Cheral line. Three others of a collateral branch also are mentioned. It is not, however, easy to determine whether these three were successors or co-kings of the Udiyancheral line.[72] Nor has the controversy regarding the identity of the Chera capital been resolved. Evidence in support of Tiruvanchaikkalam as well as of Karuvur Vanchi is found in Tamil literature. Perhaps it is not a fantastic surmise to think that the Cheras had two capitals, Tiruvanchaikkalam near the Western coast as well as Karuvur Vanchi in the interior, identifiable with the modern Karuvur. Two early Chera inscriptions and Roman coins are found in Karuvur. As I. Mahadevan thinks the Irumporais, a branch of the Chera dynasty, ruled from Karuvur.

A significant fact concerning Chera history is that Paranar, the author of the Decad on the celebrated Cheran Senkuttuvan has also contributed a poem (No. 369) in the Purananuru anthology on the same monarch. This indicates the historicity of this king on the one hand and his contemporaneity with Paranar on the other. The Epilogue to the Vth Decad of the Padirruppattu provides the additional information that Cheran Senkuttuvan established a temple in honour of Kannagi, the paragon of chastity. It is stated that Cheran Senkuttuvan procured a stone for making the image of Kannagi after a fight with a chieftain of North India and that he had the stone bathed ceremoniously in the Ganges before it was brought to the Chera country. These events are described at greater length in a truly epic style in the Silappadikaram. Divergent views have been held as to which of these—the Epilogue to the Vth Decad of the Padirruppattu or the Epic, Silappadikaram—which forms the original source of the association of Cheran Senkuttuvan with Kannagi.

The Epilogues of the Padirruppattu are valuable for the reconstruction of Chera history. But there is little doubt that they were composed considerably later than the poems themselves, firstly because the simple style of their language is markedly different from that of the poems, and secondly, because there are discrepancies between the Vth Decad of the Padirruppattu and its Epilogue. The Epilogue speaks of the stone brought from the north for erecting a temple for Kannagi, while this is not mentioned in the text. To explain away the discrepancy as has been done by stating that the Padigam, unlike the poem, was composed after the king had returned from the north with the stone, is far-fetched. It is probable either that the Padigam incorporated certain ideas from the Silappadikaram or vice versa. However, though the late date of the Padigam and the consequent need for using it with caution are obvious, there is no justification for discarding the entire body of Padigams or Epilogues as valueless for the student of history.

As for the historical value of the Purananuru, it has to be noticed that at the end of most of the poems contained in it, we find colophons indicating the names of the poets, the Tinai, Turai and the occasions for the composition of the poems. The colophons were apparently provide a by the compiler of the anthology. But information as to who the compiler was, when the compilation was done and under whose patronage it was carried out, is lacking. Naturally, therefore, the reliability of the colophons is open to doubt. Perhaps they were based partly upon tradition and partly upon certain well-authenticated facts. Several scholars have attempted to provided connected account of the various dynasties of the Sangam age based on these colophons and have furnished different genealogies, one at variance with the other. Some have given up the attempt, despairing of their reliability.[73] But in this connection it is important to remember that the Kalittogai is stated to have been compiled by the poet, Nallanduvanar, who was himself the author of some poems in the same collection. In the case of Ainkurunuru, the compiler was one whose poems are found in certain Sangam classics themselves.[74] Therefore, all the colophons are not of a much later date and they cannot be dismissed as untrustworthy, though it must be admitted that they do not help us in weaving a continuous account of the political history of the Sangam age. It may be added that Nachchinarkiniyar, the celebrated commentator, does not challenge the authenticity of the colophons.

It is idle to contend that the kings and events mentioned in the Purananuru are figments of imagination. There are references to the Chola and Pandya kings mentioned in the Purananuru in the Copper Plates of later times. For instance, the Chola kings like Perunarkilli, Karikalan and Chenganan are referred to in the stone inscriptions and Copper Plates of 11th century AD. Again, the Pandyan king, Palyagasalai Mudukudumi Peruvaludi, about whom several poems are found in the Purananuru collection, is mentioned in the Velvikkudi Plates of the 8th century AD. The famous Talayalankanam battle, described in the Purananuru (Nos. 19 and 23) is mentioned in the Sinnamanur Plates of the 10th century AD. Unless it is fantastically imagined that these epigraphic references are all based on the literary works, the authenticity of the kings and the events associated with them is unquestionable.

More valuable, however, are the Sangam classics for the historian of the social, economic, religious and cultural conditions of the early times. It need hardly be added that it is now increasingly realised that history is not concerned only with kings and queens, wars and treaties but with the condition and progress of the people at large. In respect of social position, the Sangam works do not make a deliberate attempt at overrating the customs and manners, the institutions and the life of the people. They were the days when there was no conscious effort at glorifying one's own culture. Therefore, the penpictures and casual references provided by the poets of the Sangam age are refreshingly realistic.

The diet, dress, occupations, the institution of caste, marriage, pre-marital love the status of women in society, the state of education and learning as well as the manner of disposal of the dead are among the many features of social life learnt from the references in the Sangam literature. The Tolkappiyam, one of the earliest works, deals with many questions of social, organisation in the section on Poruladhikaram. The Ainkurunuru, Narrinai, Ahananuru and Kalittogai, and more particularly the Pattuppattu (Ten Idylls) provide a remarkable wealth of information.

The casual and indirect nature of the date furnished has the supreme merit that it was not dressed for the stage and that it was not deliberately exaggerated or underrated. However, it has a serious drawback, too. The details furnished are not always as full and comprehensive, as one may wish. For instance, it would be interesting to know the extent to which the caste system had taken root in the Tamil country during the age of Sangam. Again, it is not known whether Sati was then common among all classes of people, though we hear of a few cases of Sati from the literature of the time. In fact, one serious handicap in the use of literature for re-constructing social history is that, often, deductions have to be made from a few known examples. The limitations to the validity of such generalisations have to be remembered, though they should not be exaggerated.

At times conflicting deductions are possible from the inadequate and stray references, and great care has to be exercised in drawing conclusions from them. For instance, it is not easy to provide an answer to the question whether all Brahmins of the Sangam age were pure vegetarians or not. Kapilar, the author of Kurinchippattu and several poems in the Ahananuru, Purananuru, Kuruntogai and Narrinai, describes himself a brahmin, but speaks of the charm of meat and drink, as if from personal experience. On the other hand, we have a description of the typical brahmin diet which was purely vegetarian, found in the Perumbanarruppadai.[75] The attempt made by some modern writers to explain away Kapilar's reference as not applicable to himself, but to the inhabitants of the Parambu land of Pari, seems to be laboured and unconvincing.

Regarding the religious beliefs and practices we have several references in the Ettuttogai and Pattuppattu. The worship of Muruga and Korravai, Indra and Varuna is adverted to in several poems. The advent of Aryan ideas and rituals is particularly found in the Paripadal and Tirumurugarruppadai.

It is in respect of the fine arts, particularly of music and drama, that the data furnished by the classics, are strikingly abundant. References to the arts of music and dance practiced by the Panar, Viraliyar and Porunar are found in most of the Sangam works. Literary commentators of later times speak of several works on music having existed prior to the third Sangam. It is unreasonable to imagine that they are all inventions of the myth makers.

Music and dance attained a remarkably high standard of excellence in the days of Silappadikaram. The Arangerrukadai of this Epic is almost an encyclopaedia of these fine arts of the age. It reveals in particular how the professional dancers and courtesans were systematically trained in the fine arts. The custom was to provide the young girls of the class sound training for a period of seven years beginning from the 5th year. The training was provided by a dancing master, a music master, a composer of songs and those who played on the accompanying musical instruments like the flute, yal, drum and so forth. In fact, the references to musical instruments in the Silappadikaram, as well as in the earlier literary works are remarkably numerous. There were instruments made of leather, bamboo, wood and of strings derived from the veins of animals. The 'Yal' was a stringed instrument of great popularity among the early Tamils. We do not hear of the Yal subsequent to the 11th century AD.

The Arangerrukadai shows that the different kinds of body movement and limb movement, the poses, gestures, conformity to the time beats, the manipulation of the vocal chords and all other allied elements of the art were taught systematically. The pose of the hand, in particular, received very careful attention. The Silappadikaram speaks of thirty-three patterns of the hand pose. However, this development must have been the product of a gradual process, for the Kalittogai, one of the later Sangam classics also describes the attention devoted to the pose of the hand and to the facial expression during the dance.

CHRONOLOGICAL BACKGROUND

This raises the crucial question of the chronology of the early literary works in Tamil, which is by no means a settled affair even at the present day. But it may be observed that broadly the date of the Ettuttogai and Pattuppattu is determined to have ranged from the 1st to the 3rd century AD, the period which may be described as the Sangam age. Besides the Gajabahu-Senguttuvan synchronism, the so-called sheet anchor of early Tamilian chronology, which ascribes the events embodied in the Silappadikaram to the 2nd century AD, the remarkable coincidence of the Tamil literary references with the data furnished by the Greek geographers of the 1st and 2nd centuries AD, reinforced by the discovery of the Roman coins of that epoch in South India, particularly in Arikamedu, lends support to this view.

If it is taken that the Sangam age is assignable to the first three centuries of the Christian Era, what can be said regarding the dates of the different works of the Sangam? A study of the Ettuttogai poems indicates that the verses in the Purananuru belong to different periods of time in the Sangam age. Of the others, the Kalittogai and Paripadal seem to have been later than the Ahananuru and other Sangam works. The Pattuppattu are generally later than the Ettuttogai, while the Tirumurugarruppadai is the latest of them all. This conclusion is based upon the increased evidence of Aryan mythology and the occurrence of Sanskrit words, besides the differences noticeable in the social life depicted in them.

Then comes the question whether the Tolkappiyam, the earliest extant Tamil grammar, preceded or succeeded the Sangam classics. Some have assigned to it a date subsequent to the 4th century AD, but, every thing considered, it appears to have preceded the Sangam works. The deities mentioned in the Tolkappiyam are Varuna, Vendan, Mayon (Vishnu) and Seyon (Muruga). On the other hand, besides Muruga and Kannan (Vishnu) Siva and Baladeva also find a place in the Ettuttogai and Pattuppattu. Perhaps they are later introductions. Further, the Tolkappiyam states that the matter on Ahapporul should be composed in Paripadal and Kalippa. But, contrary to this prescription, the Sangam poets have composed most of the Aham verses of Ahapporul in Ahaval metre. Moreover, for certain rules enunciated in the Tolkappiyam, examples cannot be found in the extant Sangam poems. These indicate that the Ettuttogai and Pattuppattu appeared only subsequent to the Tolkappiyam. The traditional view, first stated by Iraiynar Ahapporulurai, that Tolkappiyam belonged to the Second Sangam may not be baseless.

That brings us to another controversial issue, namely, the number of Sangams. The Iraiynar Ahapporulurai and later commentaries have spoken of three Sangams, but most of the modern scholars have cast this aside as a piece of incredible legend. However, the references to the encroachment of land by sea in early Tamil literature and to the shiftings of the Pandyan capitals suggest that at first the Pandyans had Ten Madurai as the capital, then Kapadapuram and last Vada Madurai, the present Madurai. Poets might well have been associated with these respective capitals and the tradition regarding the works alleged to have been lost might have been based on reality. Numerous literary classics are said to have been lost, and although the fabulous legends connected with the Sangams are not true, certain fundamental facts like the existence of earlier Pandyan capital and the literary activities associated with them cannot be dismissed as baseless.

While Tolkappiyam seems to have belonged to the Second Sangam the common view held by Tamil scholars that the Padinenkilkanakku poems and the twin Epics, Manimekalai and Silappadikaram, also belong to the Sangam age are not acceptable. The Kural, no doubt, stands on a different footing. The parallelisms of ideas contained in the Narrinai, 32 and 355 Kuruntogai, 230, Ahananuru, 184, and Kurinchippattu 206–7 to certain corresponding couplets of the Tirukkural show that the latter had appeared earlier. Above all, verse 34 of the Purananuru anthology which states: 'Cheydi Konrorkku Uydi Illena Aram Padirre Ayilai Kanava' clinches the issue and indicates its earlier date.

But the other Padinenkilkanakku works mostly belong to the 5th or 6th century AD. The reference to Peru Muttaraiyar mentioned in inscriptions of the 9th century AD and the occurrence of their name in Naladi suggests a late date for the latter. Though inscriptional evidence need not be the only basis, the attempt to explain it away by stating that the argument of silence in epigraphy cannot be trumped up for suggesting a late date is not convincing. At any rate, the Muttaraiyar could not have lived in the Sangam age; probably they belonged to a century or two prior to the reference found in epigraphy. Further, the language of the Naladi, Inna Narpadu and Iniyavai Narpadu, for example, confirm the fact that they were later than the age of the Sangam.[76]

Regarding the date of the Epics, again, divergent views persist. Scholars who swear by the old tradition consider them as Sangam works, basing their position on the Padigams in the Epics and on the Cheran Senguttuvan synchronism. But while Cheran Senguttuvan is assignable to the 2nd century AD, the alleged authorship of the Silappadikaram to Ilango, the king's brother, seems to be an invention. The difference in style and more important, the different social conditions like the Aryan pattern of marriage and the higher stage of fine-arts reflected in the Silappadikaram suggest a date later than 3rd century AD but anterior to that of the Devaram hymnists of 7th century AD.[77] The view that they belong to the 5th or 6th century AD does not seem fantastic.

THE RELIGIOUS WORKS

Gradually the literary source became surcharged with the religious motivation. The themes dealt with are almost exclusively religious, and therefore, the mythical and legendary element predominates in them. To that extent the value of literature as a source of history diminishes. This is true of the age of the Bhakti movement in Tamilaham which was at its height during AD 7–9. Religious tolerance and goodwill prevailed among the Tamils only till about the 6th century AD. The Saiva Nayanmars and the Vaishnava Alvars traversed throughout the country visiting temples and pouring forth their devotional songs. This fervour was primarily provoked by the Hindu hostility towards the Jains and Buddhists. Though not directly valuable to the student of history these outpourings of the saints and devotees are of use in understanding the religious, and cultural conditions of the people.

The hymns of the Nayanmars and Alvars were collected and arranged in canonical form in the 10th and early 11th centuries. The works of the Saiva hymnist and of the religious writers were collected in the shape of twelve Tirumurais. Begun by Nambi Andar Nambi of the 10th century AD, the first seven books formed the Devaram, which contain the hymns of the great Nayanmars. Book VIII contains the Tiruvachakam of Manikkavachakar, while books IX and XI contain the hymns of several minor saints. Book X consists of 3,000 verses of Tirumular known as 'Tirumandiram' which is an obscure manual of Saivism. The Tiruttondar Puranam, commonly known as the Periya Puranam is the last and twelfth book of the Tirumurais and, used with care and discernment, they help the reconstruction of the history of early Saivism and the beliefs current in that age.

On the Vaisnava side, the Vaisnava canon, Nalayira Prabhandham including hymns of the Alvars, was arranged by Nathamuni.

The Periya Puranam narrates in an admirable manner the lives of the sixty-three Saiva Nayanmars. No doubt, many incredible legends find a place in it, but the author, a Chola administrator, who had access to official documents, has portrayed the social and religious conditions of his age as the background of his main theme. For example, Sekkilar's description of the brahmin village of Adanur and the slums of the pariahs living in the outskirts of Adanur may be taken as representative of the conditions of about the 12th century AD.

Some facts of political history are also recorded incidentally. It states that Pugal Chola Nayanar was a Chola ruler, presumably of the 7th century AD, who conquered Uraiyur. It reveals also that the Pandyan ruler during the time of Tirujnana Sambandar had married a Chola princess known as Mangayarkkarasi. It is learnt that when Sundaramurti and Cheramanperumal visited Madurai they found that a Chola prince had married a Pandyan princess. Thus the matrimonial relationship between the Chola and Pandyan royal lines seem to have been common in the 7th and 8th centuries.

The stories of persecution described by Sekkilar are partly based on legends and partly on the general tendencies of the times. Some have thought that the accounts of religious persecution described by Sekkilar were reflections of his age and not of the epoch of Devaram. But this seems to be the result of misreading the conditions during the epoch of the Bhakti movement. In reality the religious hostility must have commenced earlier. However, it may be added that from the 12th century onwards the Periya Puranam has influenced the life and thought of the Saivas in no small measure.

The Nalayira Prabandham, which describes the life and activities of the Vaisnava saints, assumed a proper form about the 11th century AD. Though the chronology adopted by it is fantastic, it traces the development of Vaisnavism in the Tamil country in the proper historical sequence. In passing, it may be observed that Tirumangai Alvar's works afford some historical data of value. The commentaries on the hymns of the Alvars were written later, probably in the 15th and 16th centuries, and they throw some light on the political and social conditions, though the material has to be sifted carefully from the accounts provided.

The Tiruvilaiyadal Puranam of Perumbarrapuliyur Mambi, probably of the 13th century, deals with the legends connected with the 64 sports of Siva. It mentions incidentally some details regarding the Pandyan rulers, but the whole account is so surcharged with mythology that it is impossible to sift historical facts from the legends. Subsequently Paranjoti dwelt on the same theme. His list of the Pandyan kings is different from that given in the Tiruvilaiyadal Puranam; but that, too, is unreliable.

The Saiva Siddhanta school of thought and literature connected with it commenced about the 12th century AD. Early in the 13th century there appeared the celebrated manual of Saivism of Meykandar in his Siva Jnana Bodham. On the basis of his brilliant work there grew up an extensive philosophical literature which has influenced the thought of the intellectuals among the Saivites through the succeeding centuries. The system stresses the importance of sincere devotion. It discards caste and ritual, and on the whole, the Saiva Siddhanta system is of importance in the social history of the Tamils.

The period extending roughly from the 12th century to 14th century AD is the epoch of the famous Commentaries on the literary works. Nakkirar's Commentary on Iraiyanar Ahapporul was perhaps the earliest of the series, but its exact date is not determinable. The commentators of Tolkappiyam, like Ilampuranar, Senavaraiyar and Nachchinarkkiniyar and the commentators of Silappadikaram like Arumpada Uraiyasiriyar and Adiyarkkunallar and above all, the celebrated Parimelalagar, the commentator of Tirukkural and Paripadal, are all learned writers. Though they adopted the traditional pattern of commenting on early works, they throw abundant light on the social, religious, literary and cultural institutions of the Tamils; however, they cannot be considered as systematic works on social history. Among these commentaties, those of Adiyarkkunallar and Nachchinarkiniyar seem to be of the greatest value for the student of the social and cultural institutions of the early Tamils.

From the 16th century onward there appeared numerous Sthalapuranas, many of which were translations from Sanskrit

Sthalamahatmyas. The 18th century was par excellence the age of Sthalapuranas. However, they are anything but history, though they are of use for local history of modern times.

THE MODERN EPOCH

Prose writing in Tamil assumed an importance during the age of the Commentaries, and it increased in popularity in the 18th century. In the 19th century and the recent times, fiction in the shape of the novels and short stories has appeared, and in some measure, it reflects the social conditions, habits and customs of people. Very recently some effort at writing history in Tamil has received encouragement, and it is likely to have a bright future, provided objectivity does not yield to sentimental chauvinism.

There is one source of importance which remains to be fully exploited. This is the vast body of manuscript material found in public bodies like Mathas and Churches as well as in the hands of private individuals. They pertain to a variety of subjects. Some are literary compositions, some are medical manuals, while a few throw light on political, social and economic conditions. Often the owners of these manuscripts are unwilling to make researchers use them. The Government must come to their rescue.

Col. Mackenzie, who was the Surveyor General of the East India Company in the early 19th century, took a great interest in the collection of manuscripts in the different languages of South India. It was at his instance that the 'Karnataka Savistara Charitam' and 'Kongu Desa Rajakkal' were written, but their historical value is not much, since many of the manuscripts on which the accounts were based are surcharged with legends. But doubtless, some historical facts can be gleaned from them.

There are, on the other hand, certain records like the 'Mudaliyar Manuscripts' gathered from the Periyavittu Mudaliyar's house at Alagiyapandipuram (Kanyakumari Dist.) which yield very useful data in respect of political, administrative, social and economic history of Nanchinad. More or less similar manuscripts available in various places of Tamil Nadu are of value, and have to be exploited with thoroughness and discrimination.

ENDNOTES

1. See Dr. S.K. Aiyangar: *Beginnings of South Indian History* (1918) pp. 249–56 for an account of the legend and P.T. Srinivasa Iyengar: *History of the Tamils* (1929), pp. 226–30 for a critical examination of the legend.

2. Madras Epigraphist's Report for 1908, pp. 50 ff. That there flourished a Sangam is evident from the statement alleged to have been made by Nedunjelian, the victor of the battle of Talayalanganam, that if he were to be defeated, the extent of his kingdom should not be sung by poets of world-wide renown, the chief of whom was Mangudi Marudan of great eminence (*Puram*, 72).

3. *Mahabharata*, Par IX. 36, See also E.H. Warmington: *The Commerce between the Roman Empire and India*, (1928) p. 167.

4. See V.R.R. Dikshitar: *Studies in Tamil Literature and History*, (1936) pp. 20–21 and K.G. Sesha Aiyar: *Cera kings of the Sangam period* (1937) pp. 97–122 for an enumeration of the different theories.

5. *Tiruttevar Tevaram*, II, 10 and *Tirupputtur Tiruttagam*, II, 1.2.

6. K.A. Nilakanta Sastri: *A History of South India*, (1955) pp. 112–13. While it is likely that the term Sangam was derived from the Jains or Buddhists, P.T.S. Iyengar's suggestion that the Tamil Sangam was established on the model of Vajra Nandi's Jain Sangha of AD 470 at Madurai, seems to be little more than a piece of guess work. (op. cit. p. 247).

7. Dr. N.P. Chakravarti: Presidential address to the 17th session of the Indian History Congress, December, 1954.

8. K.K. Pillay: 'The South Indian Brahmi Inscriptions and the Sangam Age,' *Tamil Culture*, April, 1956.

9. See V.R.R. Dikshitar: op. cit. pp. 24–45 for a brief account of the extant works of the Sangam literature.

10. Among the *Ettuttogai* anthologes, *Purananuru*, and *Padirruppattu* deal with Puram, and *Narrinai, Kuruntogai, Aingurunuru, Kalittogai* and *Ahananuru* with Aham: and while *Paripadal partakes* of the characteristics of both. Among the Ten Idylls, *Porunararruppadai, Sirupanarruppadai, Perumbanarruppadai, Tirumugarruppadai,* and *Malaipadukadam* are laudatory poems on patrons, and *Mullaippattu, Nedunalvadai, Kurinjippattu* and *Pattinappalai* are love poems, while *Maduraikkanchi* is a benedictory poem.

11. Contra. K.A. Nilakanta Sastri, op. cit. p. 350. The references to the author of *Kural* as the true poet (Poyyil pulavan) in *Manimekalai* (Canto 22. 11.60–1) suggests an established reputation and an early date for him. Besides, the extant *Tiruvalluvamalai*, an anthology of panegyrical verses sung by Sangam poets, proves the early appreciation of his splendid works.

12. *Indra Vila* (festival) is hardly mentioned in the Sangam classics. A faint reference to the temple of Indra occurs in

Puram (241). On the other hand, by the age of the Epics the Indra festival had become so important that Puhar is stated to have been destroyed by Heavenly wrath caused by the failure to celebrate it regulary.

13. M. Rajaro: 'The chronology of events in the *Silappadikaram*' *The Quarterly Journal of the Mythic Society*–Culture and Heritage Number, 1956.

14. See S. Kuppuswami Sastri: *Journal of Oriental Research* Madras, Vol. I, pp. 191 ff. Contra Dr. S. Krishnaswamy Aiyangar: *Manimekalai in its Historical Setting*, (1928). xxiv ff. Dr. Aiyangar thinks that the views of Dinnaga must have been independently anticipated by the author of *Manimekalai* which might have been composed a century earlier than Dinnaga, whose date, it may be added, is still matter of speculation.

15. Paranar, a Sangam poet has sung on Cheran Senguttuvan who figure also in *Silappadikaram*. Either Senguttuvan of Paranar was a different king, or more probably Paranar was a contemporary poet of Senguttuvan, while the author of the *Silappadikaram* was of a later period.

16. Madras Epigraphist's Report, 1907, p. 52 and K.A.N. Sastri: *Studies in Chola History and Administration,* pp. 14–18.

17. As example of poets who boldly remonstrated against ill-treatment may be mentioned *Perundalai Sattanar* (Puram 151, 165, 205); *Peruncittiranar* (Puram 207 and 206) and *Auvaiyar* (Puram 206).

18. *Maduraikkanci*, 1. 61. He has been identified with Vadimbalamba Ninravan by the annotator, Naccinarkiniyar.

19. *Ibid*. 1. 759.

20. Purananuru, briefly called *Puram*, verses 18, 19, 23–6, 76–9, 371–2.
21. *Ahananuru*, briefly called *Aham*, verses 36, 116, 175, 253, 266 and 238.
22. *Kuruntogai*, 393.
23. *Narrinai*, 358 and 387.
24. *Puram*, 21 and 367; *Aham*, 26 and *Narrinai*, 98.
25. *Puram*,71, 246, 247 and *Aham*, 26.
26. V. Kanakasabhai Pillai: *Tamils Eighteen hundred years ago*, (1904) p. 76. M. Raghava Iyengar: *Cheran Senguttuvan* (Tamil) 2nd edn., 106–7 n. See K.A. Nilakanta Sastri: *The Colas* (1955), p. 58. n. 60 for the criticism of the genealogies attempted so far.
27. *Puram* 65; *Aham* 55, 246.
28. *Aham* 125.
29. *Aham* 141, *Pattinappalai*, 11. 228–82.
30. *Pattinappalai*, 11. 283–4.
31. *Puram* 7, 224; *Porunararruppadai* 11. 141–8. 187–8; *Manimekalai*, Canto. I. i. 39. *Silappadikaram*, Canto V. 11. 90–104: Canto VI, 11. 159–50.
32. K.A. Nilakanta Sastri: *Studies in Chola History and Administration* (1932) pp. 19–38.
33. *Puram*, 74.
34. Incidentally it indicates that *Kalavali* belongs to the Sangam age.
35. K.G. Sesha Aiyar: 'Chera kings of the Sangam Period,' (1937) pp. 125–9.

36. Canto XXVIII 11. 114–22.
37. *Ibid*, Canto XXVI 11. 54–6.
38. See *Puram* 2; *Aham* 65 and 168.
39. K.A.N. Sastri seems to overestimate the value of *Purananuru* when he says: The data furnished by these poems for historical reconstructions will not be the less valuable on account of their being drawn from casual literary pieces rather than from chronicles or other works of a professedly historical nature.' *Studies in Chola History and Administration*. p.1.
40. See V.R.R. Dikshitar: *Studies in Tamil Literature and History* (1936) pp. 229–54.
41. *Puram*, 35. *Padirruppattu*, 13.
42. *Puram*, 26.
43. *Kural*, see for example Nos, 448, 543, 545, 555, 564, 638 and 872.
44. As an example of such unwarranted generalization see V.R.R. Dikshitar's treatment of Indra's festival. *Op. cit.* pp. 305–07.
45. *Puram*, 196; *Perumbanarruppadai*, 405; *Pattinappalai*, 11. 117–20.
46. *Puram*, 160, 390, 398; *Mullaippattu*, 60; *Kuruntogai*, 167, 210.
47. *Puram*, 56, 150; *Malaipadukadam*, 11, 153, 155, 168, 175–8, etc. *Pattinappalai*, 108.
48. *Silappadikaram*, Canto XXX, 1. 189.
49. *Puram*, 279.
50. *Kurinjipattu*, 1. 139.
51. *Puram*, 257; *Perumbanarruppadai*, 69; *Maduraikkanci*, 63.

52. *Puram*, 62; *Silappadikaram*, Canto XVI, 1. 55; *Manimekalai*, Canto XXVIII, lines 240–3 Contra. K.A.N. Sastri: *A History of South India*, p. 130.

53. *Puram*, 230, 289. 368; *Narrinai*, 93; *Pattinappalai*, 11. 5–28; *Porunararrupadai* 11. 245–6. P.T.S. Iyengar gives a diffuse description about the foreign trade in his '*History of the Tamils*,' Ch. XXVIII. The most systematic account is still that of Warmington: 'The Commerce between the Roman Empire and India,' pp. 274 ff.

54. *Maduraikkanci*, 11. 139–44; *Pattinappalai*, 11. 59–117.

55. *Puram*, 183, *Tolkappiyam*, *Poruladhikaram*, 20 and 632.

56. *Puram*, 34, 122, 166, 224.

57. *Silappadikaram*, Canto V, 11, 24–58.

58. *Ibid.* Canto 1. 11. 45–58. See Tolkappiyam 'Karpiyal' sutra 4 and 'Porul' Sutras 104–6 regarding the original two forms of marriage.

59. *Aham*, 7.

60. *Puram*, 246 and 247.

61. *Kural.* See for example, Nos. 51, 55, 56.

62. *Puram*, 85, *Pattinappalai*, 11. 23–6.

63. *Silappadikaram*, Cantos V and VI.

64. *Puram*, 33, mentions in particular the popular dance, *Alliyakkuttu*.

65. Canto VI.

66. The dance which constituted the worship of *Korravai*, the goddess of victory, is vididly described in *Silappadikaram*, Canto XII.

67. *Silappadikaram*, Canto IX, 1. 10.
68. Annual Report of Epigraphy, 1927, II, 24. Some structures in the Chidambaram temple are attributed to Vikrama Chola, too. Apparently, both the kings devoted their attention to the improvement of this temple.
69. The Chola genealogy provided by the 'Vikraman Cholan Ula' and the 'Kalingattupparani' tally in fundamentals with that found in the Kanyakumari inscription of Virarajendra.
70. Contra: T.K. Velu Pillay: The Travancore State Manual. Vol. II. pp. 191–2.
71. Udiyan Cheral is stated to have fed the armies of the Mahabharata battle at Kurukshetra. This is clear instance of mythical fabrication. Some Pandya and Chola kings are also given the same honour in other Sangam poems. However, the attempt made by some to distinguish Udiyan Cheral from Perunchorru Cheral is not convincing.
72. The deduction drawn by K.G. Sesha Aiyar in his 'Chera Kings of the Sangam Period,' by Auvvai Durasami Pillai in his 'Pandai Nalaich Chera Mannargal' (Tamil) and by A. Chidambaranar in his 'Cherar Varalaru' (Tamil) are not free from doubts.
73. P.T.S. Iyengar: History of the Tamils, p. 417. He concludes that the colophons are an inextricable tangle of fact and fiction, of tradition and guess, and therefore, useless for the purpose of constructing genealogical lists of kings." He adds, however, that notes on the life of a few kings can be recovered from these poems.
74. Pulatturai Murriya Kudalur Kilar, the compiler of the Ainkurunuru, was the author of poems 166, 167 and 214 of the Kuruntogai and poem 229 of the Purananuru.

75. Perumbanarruppadai: 306 ff.

76. The suggestion that the Muttaraiyar, who are described as opulent, were probably identical with the Kalabhras, who, defeating the Chera, Chola and Pandyan kings acquired their wealth and position might well be true. If so, the date of Naladi and of several of the Kilkanakku works may be sometime between 4th and 7th century AD.

77. Indra and Indra Vila are mentioned in the Sangam works, but they assumed a greater prominence in the Epics. References to 'Indiran Chirappu' 'Indira Kodanai' and 'Indra Vil' occur only in the Epics but neither in the Sangam works nor in the Devarams.

3

NARRINAI IN ITS HISTORICAL SETTING

It is the view of several scholars that the Tamil classics of old remain to be studied critically from the standpoint of history. Not long ago, Dr. A.L. Basham, formerly Professor of Indian and South Asian histories in the University of London, rightly observed that the Sangam classics in Tamil have not been yet subjected to a critical investigation from the historical point of view.[1] While the world of Tamil scholarship owes an inestimable debt of gratitude to the service rendered by Mahamahopadhyaya Dr. U.V. Swaminatha Aiyar in editing and annotating many of these hidden treasures of literature, it has to be remembered that his was but a pioneer effort in the field. Moreover, in addition to examining the literary characteristics of these works, it is essential that systematic investigations are made into the light that they throw on the life and culture of the people in the past.

There are, however, two kinds of pitfalls which beset adventures of this kind. One is a mis-directed chauvinism which prompts an unwarranted glorification of the past.

Actuated by this motive, legends and fables, fanciful pen-pictures and imaginative descriptions of poets, as well as certain unjustifiable deductions of talented commentators have been frequently pressed into service and made to play the role of history. As a consequence, the dividing line between literature and history has often become narrowed down. A second feature which has recently appeared is an excessive scepticism, resulting in a hypercritical tendency to discard all ideas found in works of literature as valueless for the student of history. Neither of these extreme attitudes is acceptable. While professedly historical works are conspicuous by their absence in south as well as in north India, a considerable amount of historical material can be indirectly gleaned from the vast mass of literary compositions of the past. Even ostensible adulations of kings and chieftains, of victories and endowments, interpreted in their proper light, yield some reliable data. But, by far the most valuable source is provided by the casual and indirect references in the literary works. Particularly in respect of social and cultural history, the light shed by them is of inestimable value. In fact, the more casual the reference in the Sangam classics, the more reliable it becomes as a source of history; its value for the re-construction of history is next in importance only to what has been known as evidence from the hostile camp.

Narrinai forms one of the eight anthologies (Ettuttogai), which constitute a part of what are called the Sangam classics. It has been held by certain writers that the name 'Narrinai,' given to this anthology indicates its superior excellence. The adjective 'Nal' in the name of the work has been interpreted to mean that this collection of poems expounds the ideal features of the Tinais or regions.[2] But it is doubtful whether much can be read into the name nor does the circumstance that in an old verse which catalogues the eight anthologies, Narrinai figures at the outset, by itself, indicate any superiority of this over the other collections of the Ettuttogai.³

The date when the stanzas incorporated in Narrinai were composed cannot be determined definitely. But this work, like certain other classics of the so-called Third Sangam, is assignable to the period ranging from the 1st to the 3rd century AD.⁴ Though doubts have been expressed regarding the date of this Sangam, reliable pieces of evidence support the theory which ascribes it to the early centuries of the Christian era. The discovery in South India of Roman coins, particularly of those belonging to the time of Emperor Augustus, the confirmation of the fact of active commercial contact between Rome and South India provided by the recent finds at Arikamedu and, above all, the striking affinity between the descriptions of this commerce found in the Sangam works and the accounts furnished by the Greek visitors to India during the 1st and 2nd centuries AD make it clear that the Sangam classics belonged to this period. However, the legends connected with the Sangam which call for a belief in the super-natural agency are obviously unhistorical. On the other hand, the contention that the tell-tale word 'Sangam' shows its late origin after Sanskrit had taken root in Tamilaham is beside the point. In the first place Sanskrit had found its way into Tamilaham before the 3rd century AD and secondly the academy appears to have had indigenous names viz., Kudal and Avai, at the outset. This is evident from the Prologue to Tolkappiyam, where it is stated that the work was presented to and accepted by the 'Avai' or the assembly of Nilantaru Tiruvir Pandyan.'

Some scholars think that the Tamil Sangam was organized on the model and in imitation of the 'Dravida Sangha' established by the Jain Vajra Nandi in 470 AD. The natural order of expectation indicates the reverse of this. Vajra Nandi's move might well have been prompted by the desire to create a rival for the Hindu organization already in existence. It is significant to remember in this connection that in later days Jains and Buddhists in South India adopted the phraseology of the Tamil Saiva saints to express their own religious ideas. For instance, in Silappadikaram and Chintamani, the God of the Jains and the conception of salvation are described in terms of the Saivite religion. In these works Aruhan the Jain God is called 'Siva Paramurti,' while the state of ultimate bliss is described as 'Sivagati.'

Moreover, the reference of saint Tirunavukkarasar in the 7th century AD to the Sangam as an established institution of poets shows that it had acquired a standing before his time.[5] Whether there existed from the beginning of the so-called Sangam age a full-fledged academy of poets or a board of censors is a matter open to doubt. The probability is that the wandering bards of the entire Tamil country met at Madurai on certain festive occasions and recited the poems composed by them. Madurai, the Pandyan Capital appears to have been a seat of Tamil learning under royal patronage. The poets attached to the court of the Pandyan king at Madurai might have adjudged the merits of the poems presented by the bards from the different places. This expert body was in all probability the fore-runner of the later Tamil Sangam. However, the difficulty in ascertaining the date and genesis of the institution called the Sangam need not raise any doubt regarding the assignment of the early classics to the opening centuries of the Christian era.

Though the verses embodied in Narrinai were composed before the 3rd century AD it is not known when they were collected and edited. Literary tradition, bequeathed by the early commentators, is that the anthology of Narrinai was prepared under the direction of Pannadu Tanda Maran Valuti. It is difficult to determine the reliability of this piece of tradition. Nor is it possible to determine the exact date of Pannadu Tanda Maran Valuti's reign.

Internal evidence shows that one Bharatan Padiya Perundevanar has affixed invocatory stanzas to five of the eight anthologies, viz., to Narrinai, Ahananuru, Purananuru, Kuruntogai and Ainkurunuru. But controversies regarding the identification of this Perundevanar and his date have not so far led to a definite conclusion. While, therefore, the determination of the identity and date of the scholar who compiled the anthology and of the king who directed the compilation is not easy, the only chronological datum on which we can rely is that the stanzas incorporated in Narrinai were composed some time during the early centuries of the Christian era.

POLITICAL HISTORY

Narrinai refers to several political personages and events. But they are not mentioned with a view to providing an account of the achievements of the rulers or a description of the political events which had occurred. More often than not, the references appear in a casual manner in order to illustrate the situations of love which the poets were describing. It had become almost a convention with the poets of that age to portray the feelings or reaction of lovers by instituting comparisons with prominent political occurrences. For the most part the political events and personalities mentioned by the poets appear to have been contemporaneous with them; but some pertained to men and happenings of an earlier date. The wide popularity which they had attained provided the temptation for the poets to import them into their comparisons so as to make the descriptions impressive and realistic.

However, it is undeniable that the references made were to real personages and events. This conclusion is reinforced by the circumstance that different poets of the same period or of different times refer to the same happenings and personalities. Nevertheless, there are limitations to the historical value of the poetic references which appear in the Sangam classics. Some poets were benefactors at the hands of monarchs and chieftains, and it is too much to expect that in describing events pertaining to their patrons, the poets would not have been influenced by personal bias. A few poets were clearly given to the lavish praise of their patrons. Paranar, for instance, was ostensibly swayed by the temptation to glorify his friends and exaggerate their achievements. A gifted poet, Paranar had the skill to provide a realistic colour to the descriptions. But, reviewing the characteristics of the poets of that age as a class, it would seem that those who yielded to the temptation of providing interested versions were few and far between. Usually the poets of that epoch were remarkably frank and outspoken.

In respect of political history, the most serious, though inevitable, limitation is that no connected account of a ruler or dynasty can be pieced together from the stray references. Nevertheless, it cannot be claimed that even the available data have been fully explored and coordinated. In fact, a systematic study of the Sangam classics from the standpoint of history is a desideratum. A final analysis of the data in conjunction with the determination of the contemporaneity of the poets of particular epochs may yield a basic framework out of a chaotic mass. Even a chronological system may be deduced. A bold attempt was made by the late Sri K.N. Sivaraja Pillai; but, a pioneer in the field, he had to encounter formidable difficulties, as a result of which certain venturesome guesses had to be employed by him in order to fill up unbridgeable gaps. More limited in scope was the attempt made by the late Sri K.G. Sesha Aiyar, for he confined his attention primarily to the Chera dynasty. Thanks to the Padirruppattu, a history of the Chera Kingdom of the Sangam age is in a way possible to be constructed, though there still exist many unsolved problems. More recently, the late Sri S. Vaiyapuri Pillai had made an effort at analysing the facts and fiction contained in early Tamil literature and evolving a chronological scheme. In some respects he has attempted to turn a new leaf in the critical study of Tamil literature. But, while almost all the earlier writers yielded to the temptation of exaggerating the antiquity of Tamil works, Sri Vaiyapuri Pillai seemed to take a subtle delight in proceeding to the other extreme. His attempt to fix the date of Silappadikaram about the 11th century, for instance, seems to make a parody of the scientific method. Nor is consistency one of the merits of Sri Vaiyapuri Pillai's conclusions. In respect of certain works of Tamil literature he has advanced different dates at different times. But it is easier to criticize than to construct. The important need is, as stated earlier, the undertaking of intensive studies of each of the classics from the historical point of view. A systematic attempt at examining the contemporaneity of kings on the one hand and of the poets on the other, and at correlating the events mentioned in the various classics, is bound to help the re-construction of early Tamil history.

The reference found in Narrinai to the three great sovereigns of Tamilaham and their vassals may first be pieced together. It will be followed by an examination of the references to the independent chieftains who ruled in different parts in Tamilnad.

(A) Chera (1) *Udiyan Cheral* Udiyan, the Chera king is mentioned in stanza 113 of Narrinai for the purpose of instituting a comparison. When a loving girl in Palai was informed by her lover that he had to set out in quest of wealth, she was alarmed, and because of her agony at the prospect of the separation, she wept bitterly. The shrill wailing of the girl is compared by the poet to the Ambal Pan or tune called Ambal, played on the flute by the musicians of Udiyan on the field of battle. There is little to suggest that the reference to Udiyan Cheral has been imported in order to praise the Chera monarch or his warlike activity. The comparison is introduced just for the purpose of indicating the nature of the wail. The identity of the king metioned here is beyond dispute. It is true that no dinstinctive qualification of the name 'Udiyan' occurs in the stanza. But since we do not so far know of any Udiyan other than Udiyan Cheral, the famous Perunchorrutiyan Cheralatan, the reference is clearly to this monarch. Apparently the belief that he fed the belligerents in the Mahabharata war is little more than a legend, invented perhaps to depict the monarch's generosity.[6] It may be mentioned in passing that there is plausibility in the suggestion that this king was the hero of the first Decade of Padirruppattu.

Another Chera king is Kuttuvan, mentioned in stanza 105 of Narrinai as the owner of Kudavarai (Kudamalai), flowers from which adorned the tuft of a handsome girl. Apparently Kuttuvan, the Chera king, was a contemporary of the author of this stanza, for it would be out of the way to expect an earlier king to have been mentioned as the owner of the hill. The question arises as to which Kuttuvan is meant in this stanza. Though Chenguttuvan was the most famous Chera sovereign, here it was probably

Palyanai Chel-kelu Kuttuvan who has been thought of, for, in importing the name of the Chera king to indicate the ownership of the hill, the poet might have had the object of referring to the monarch who had won it from the other. Palyanai Chel-Kelu Kuttuvan, 'the possessor of battalions of elephants' was himself a warrior of note, and besides, it was his brother Imayavaramban Neduncheralatan who had extended the dominions to the confines of the Ayirai mountains, situated to the north of the southern border of Tulunadu. Kudamalai, too, had come under his sway. It is probable that it was his brother Palyanai Chel-Kelu Kuttuvan who has been referred to in the stanza, for the acquisition of the hill by his predecessor would have been fresh in the mind of the poet. No special significance could be attached to the mention of Kudamalai if Cheran Chenguttuvan was intended to be specified. Moreover, Palyanai Chel-Kelu Kuttuvan himself is stated to have conquered Umbarkadu (literally Forest of Elephants). Umbarkadu is probably the forest near the borderland of the modern Coimbatore District adjoining the Anamalai Hills. Poet Palai Gautamanar who eulogizes this king in Padirruppattu, gives him credit for having subjugated the whole of Kongunadu. Is it possible that he was the conqueror of Kudavarai which lies to the north-west of Kongunadu? In these circumstances it does not seem venturesome to suggest that the reference to Kuttuvan in stanza 105 of Narrinai is to Palyanai Chel-Kelu Kuttuvan commemorating either his or his brother's victorious glory.

The mention of a king Kuttuvan occurs also in stanza 395, in which a comparison is drawn between the sound of the roaring waves of the sea and the noise of the triumphant drums in the battle fought by Kuttuvan. The reference to Kuttuvan in this stanza seems to have been introduced deliberately in order to stress the victorious achievement of the Chera monarch. Here, too, the full name is not given, and his identity has to be made out entirely from the circumstantial evidence furnished by the stanza. It may be argued that the reference to waves in the piece of comparison is more appropriate to Cheran Chenguttuvan, the great hero of naval victories, as a result of which he earned the title of Kadalpirakkottiya Velkelu Kuttuvan. The same stanza also compares the loving girl with Mandai, the flourishing coastal town. Does the mention of Mandai indicate connection with Cheran Chenguttuvan, famous for his naval supremacy?[7] But, as against all these considerations, there stands the specific qualification provided for Kuttuvan in the stanza. He is described as 'Kadambakattu Yanai Nedunter Kuttuvan," in other words, as Kuttuvan, the owner of mighty elephants and lofty chariots. Weighing the evidence, direct and indirect, it would seem that the reference is in all probability to Palyanai Chel-Kelu Kuttuvan because of the clear allusion to the elephant force of the king.[8]

A Chera monarch, believed to have been mentioned in stanza 18 of Narrinai, is Kanaikkal Irumporai of Tondi. The lover is stated to have gone to the land of this Chera king in quest of wealth. In describing the land, the poet refers to the Chera king's victory over the chieftain called Muvan. The Chera ruler defeated him in battle, and plucking his teeth, carried them to his capital and displayed them on the gates of his palace as a trophy of his victory.[9a] The reference to the king is made obviously in order to indicate the glory and natural wealth of the land to which the lover had betaken himself to acquire wealth. It was a land of hills and valleys, interspersed with perennial waterfalls. A waterfall near the camp where the large army of the Chera king rested seemed to lull the soldiers to sleep by means of its melodious sound. It may be observed that the reference to the king's triumphant victory over Muvan is not directly connected with the description of the land. Perhaps the desire on the part of the poet to praise the king's exploit was responsible for the inclusion of that reference in the stanza.

But the crucial question in respect of this reference is the identification of the Chera king. The stanza in Narrinai merely speaks of the 'Tondipporunan Venvel Teralarundanaipporaiyan.' Kanaikkal is not mentioned, and it is the commentator, the late Sri Pinnattur Narayanaswami Aiyar who has identified the Porayan with Kanaikkal Irumporai. The learned commentator's basis for his deduction is apparently certain details found about one Poygaiyar, the author of Kalavali who is taken to be the author of this stanza as well. The colophon at the end of Kalavali speaks of a fight between Cholan Chengannan and Cheraman Kanaikkal Irumporai and adds that when the Chera king was defeated and imprisoned, the poet Poygaiyar composed a poem in praise of the victor and got the Cheraman released. It must be observed that except in this colophon the name of Kanaikkal Irumporai is not mentioned anywhere else. Two questions emerge; sone is the authenticity of the colophon. The colophon is untrustworthy since it is contradicted by the poem, where stanza 39 states that the Chera king was killed in battle. The other question is whether the author of Kalavali is identical with the poet who composed stanza 18 of Narrinai. One Poygaiyar is the author of Puram 48 and 49; but his patron is said to have been one Cheraman Kokkadaimarpan. On the whole, in the present state of our knowledge it is not possible to hold that the Porayan mentioned in stanza 18 of Narrinai is Kanaikkal Irumporai. In fact, several Porayans figure in the Sangam literature, including Narrinai, but the identification of these rulers is by no means easy.

PORAYAN

Stanza 8 and 346 speak of one Porayan. In Stanza 8, the Porayan referred to, is described as the lord of Tondi. A loving girl wishes her suitor the same measure of high reputation which, Porayan, the master of large chariots, had won for himself. Tondi was originally the capital of Kudanadu, and after the capture of Kudanadu by the Cheras, a member of the ruling family reigned at Tondi. When Kudanadu was divided into Porainadu and Kudanadu for administrative purposes Tondi became the capital of Porainadu. It was apparently from the circumstance that the Cheras ruled over Porainadu that Porayan became one of the surnames of the Chera ruler like 'Kuttuvan' and 'Kongan Porayan,' mentioned in stanza 346 of Narrinai, are spoken of as the lord of Kollimalai. Perhaps the Porayans figuring in both the stanza are identical, for Tondi was situated near Kollimalai. In both the stanzas the prosperity of the region is mentioned, but there is hardly any other detail which helps the identification of the ruler. Anduvan Cheral Irumporai, the first, is stated to have been the founder of the Porayan branch of rulers at Tondi and as many as 18 kings of the line are mentioned. Which of these rulers figures in Narrinai it is not possible to determine.

CHOLAS

The only Chola king mentioned by name in Narrinai is Killivalavan, figuring in stanzas 14, 141 and 390. The reference to this monarch in stanza 14 does not redound to his credit, for here, the ill-repute that had befallen him is specified. It is stated that Killivalavan was disliked by the people because he had set fire to the capital of the Cherala after capturing his fort. These facts are mentioned in the stanza in order to show that a girl's lover had, by deserting her, incurred on odium even more serious than what had befallen Killivalavan on account of his unkind treatment of the Cherala. While this stanza is not flattering to the Chola king, stanza 141 indirectly adverts to the prosperity and glory of the monarch. Here the lover's charming tuft is compared to the black soil in Arisilar in Killivalavan's territory. Incidentally, the king's ambition, his mighty elephantry and array of chariots as well as his triumphant victories are mentioned.

In stanza 390, too, the king's military prowess is praised. But the reference is casual, since it is introduced for the purpose of stating that the leaves (Talai) worn as dress by the loving girl were gathered from the fields around Koyil Venni, which belonged to this monarch. In the Sangam literature, a Killivalavan who died at Kulamurram and another of the same name who died at Kurappalli appear. In all probability, as Dr. G.U. Pope has suggested, the two kings are identical.[9b] He was perhaps the son of Nalamkilli and grandson of Karikalan the Great, who was known also as Perum-tiru-Mavalavan or merely as Valavan. Killivalavan's great military achievement was his decisive triumph over the Chera. An enthusiastic patron of poets, he was himself a poet of same merit.

TITTAN

Tittan, known as Virai Velman Veliyam figures in stanza 58 of Narrinai. His father, who was called Veliyan Tittan, was originally the chieftain of Virai. He attacked Uraiyur which was then under Sendan,[10] defeated and drove him out and established himself there. Veliyan Tittan was succeeded by his son Tittan Veliyan, who figures in Narrinai. The poet adverts to his glory in the course of a comparison. One evening Veliyan Tittan's victorious drums were sounded and conches were blown. In order to witness the gay celebrations the womenfolk of the adjoining villages thronged to the capital city. The desire to witness the celebrations is compared to the eagerness of a girl who wished to go and meet her lover in the evening.

The references to the Cholas include a mention in stanza 400 of the assembly at Uraiyur, which is praised for its unswerving adherence to right principles. A girl exhorts her lover to be as steady as the Uraiyur assembly. The high reputation that the assembly of Uraiyur had acquired is evident from this stanza.

CHOLA CHIEFS

Alisi

Certain chiefs who owed allegiance to the Chola power are found mentioned in Narrinai. One of these was Alisi who ruled over Arcot and its neighbourhood. Stanza 87 of Narrinai speaks of Alisi as a member of the Chola family ruling in Arcot. The poet compares the delight of a girl when she imagined that she met and embraced her lover with the joy of a person when he dreamt that he obtained the delicious gooseberries from the forest of Alisi.

Stanza 390, too, describes Alisi as the lord of Arcot, to which place the beauty of the beloved girl is compared. Alisi was the proud possessor of beautiful chariots and of rich paddy fields in and around Arcot. Kuruntogai (Stanza 257) states that Alisi captured Uraiyur and ruled there. Apparently, this was a later achievement, for no evidence of this triumph is found in Narrinai. Stanza 190 of Narrinai shows that Alisi was the father of Sendan, who was also a brave warrior. Sendan, however, is known to have ruled only in Arcot. It appears, therefore, that Alisi's sovereignty over Uraiyur was a short-lived affair. Arcot continued to be a part of the Chola power, as is evident from stanza 227 which states that the Chola banner was flying over the streets of Arcot.

ANNI

A less powerful Chola chief who ruled over a village near Tanjavur was Anni. Later, the village itself came to be called after him as Annikkudi. Stanza 180 states that Anni was engaged in a fierce conflict with one Periyan, perhaps a chieftain of Cholanadu who ruled over Purandai, or Poriayaru,[11] over a laurel tree and it resulted in the death of Periyan. The stanza says that a woman, who was bemoaning her misery caused by her husband's partiality for a harlot, stated that her ill-will towards her lord could terminate only with her death just as the struggle between Anni and Periyan ended only with the death of one of the two in the battle field. The reference to the chieftains is casual occurring only by way of comparison and hence is quite trustworthy.[12]

A reference to the efficient rule of the Cholas over all the villages of the kingdom appears in stanza 265 of Narrinai sung by Paranar. A comparison is made of the beneficent rule of the Cholas with the bountiful generosity of the lady lover. In passing, it may be mentioned that the same stanza compares the tuft of the lady with that of the peacock in the Kollimalai of Ori. Stanza 227 is interesting, for it refers to the glory of the Chola rule and the prosperity which flourished in Arcot. A comparison is made between the hum of bees around pots of toddy in the streets of Arcot and the uproar caused by the courtship of a girl with her lover. The comparison seems rather far-fetched and inappropriate, though it portrays the increasing growth of the public scandal like the rising hum of bees around the pots of toddy.

Stanza 265 speaks of the beneficent rule of the Cholas over Areru. It indicates the military prowess of Minili, the heroic chieftain of the village, called Param, who defended it efficiently against all incursions by effectively employing his skill in archery. A comparison is made between the efficient rule of Minili over Param and the Chola administration of Areru (265). Incidentally the stanza refers to the practice of the Chola kings wearing Attimalai, the garland of Atti flowers.

THE PANDYAS

The Pandyas kings figuring in Narrinai are but a few, Talayalanganattu Cheruvenra Neduncheliyan being the most prominent among them.[13] The glittering sword of this valiant hero was shining when taken out of its sheath. Therefore, when the battle began, this lustre of the sword, coupled with the volley of arrows which fell incessantly, made it impossible for the girl's lover to reach his destination and meet her. This is the explanation offered by the maid to her mistress for the delay of her lover.

The military prowess of Pandyan Maran Valuti is described in stanza 150. His mighty army, which was assisted by a formidable elephantry, attacked and destroyed the fortifications of his enemies. It is added that the subordinate chieftains under his sway prayed for his long life so that they could enjoy his unfailing protection. Here we have one of the few instances of direct description of a king's prowess, though it is introduced in order to indicate the confidence of the girl that her lover would positively arrive, drawn by submissive horses.

A reference to the celebrated capital of the Pandyan king occurs in stanza 39, in which a comparison is made by the poet Marudan Ilanaganar between the flourishing city of Madurai and the broad shoulders of the lady love. Another and a more direct reference to the splendour of Madurai is found in stanza 298 which speaks of a girl's lover proceeding to that city in order to make his fortune. Incidentally, the Pandyan king, the lord of Madurai, is praised as the owner of a golden chariot. Stanza 379 speaks of the lofty peaks of the Podiyil Hills belonging to the Pandya sovereign. This suggests that the Pandyan king had captured these places from the contemporary Ay. It describes the ruddy eyes of the aggrieved girl-lover which seemed to recall the sight of the rain in Kudavayil of the powerful Chola king as well as her red fingers which resembled the flowers on the Podiyil Hills. The beauty of Marungur, the village belonging to the Pandyan monarch, is compared in another stanza with the charming beauty of the girl lover.

INDEPENDENT CHIEFTAINS

Certain chiefs figure who were for the most part independent of external political control. They were frequently engaged in conflicts with each other and with one or the other of the three powerful monarchs of Tamilaham, viz., the Chera, Chola and Pandya. At times the chieftains were defeated by one or the other of the great powers and were consequently reduced to a position of subordination. But at the earliest opportunity the chieftains regained their independence, and entering into alliance with other rulers, succeeded in maintaining their independent position and thereby a balance of power among the rulers of Tamilaham.

AY ANDIRAN

One of the prominent chieftains mentioned in Narrinai as well as in certain other classics of the Sangam age is Ay Andiran.

His bountiful generosity is referred to in stanza 167, where it is stated that the sound arising from the chariots which were bestowed as gifts filled the entire atmosphere with a sense of plenitude and prosperity. The purpose of mentioning this fact is to indicate that the girl's hero was the lord of a harbour of similar prosperity. The abundance of the gifts given by him in charity is described also in stanza 237.[14] How known facts have been skilfully woven with incredible legends can be seen from Chirupanarrupadai (lines 95–99) where it is described how Ay Andiran procured a blue cloak from a serpent and bestowed it on Lord Siva. The agony felt by Ay Andiran's subjects on account of his death is vividly depicted in Purananuru (Stanzas 240 and 241). An interesting question has arisen regarding the genesis of his name, Andiran. Sri M. Raghava Aiyangar is inclined to think that Andiran is derived from 'Andhra' and that he himself hailed from Andhra Desa and also that he was probably a descendant of the Velir who are believed to have been brought down to the south by Agastya. Plausible as this may seem, it is pertinent to observe in this connection that invariably people belonging to the region immediately to the north of Tamilaham have been spoken of in classical Tamil literature as 'Vadugar.' Why a deviation should have occurred in this case it is difficult to explain.

Kari

Kari, or Malayaman Tirumudikkari, as he was called, was another chief, highly reputed for his enthusiastic patronage of poets. His generosity and skill in war are mentioned in certain stanzas of Narrinai. He is known to have possessed remarkable skill in the use of the bow and arrow. (Stanza 100). The tremendous noise produced by the music of the dancers who had come from distant lands seeking Kari's patronage is compared with the heart-rending shock experienced by a man when his harlot threatened to divulge to his wife his lack of fidelity. The comparison, however, does not seem to be appropriate, for the state of feeling on the part of the musicians is entirely at variance with that of the guilty person in question. Perhaps it is too much to expect comparisons to be applicable in respect of every detail. At any rate, in the numberless comparisons occurring in the early Tamil classics, invariably, one feature alone is sought to be compared. In stanza 170, a lady who was mortified to learn about her husband's illicit association with a harlot, wants the people of the village to rise to a man in the same manner as Kari, collecting his entire force marched against the army of the Aryas and encountered them at Mullur. It may be observed in passing that Mullur was the capital of Malayaman Tirumudikkari. When attacked by Kari the Aryappadai was completely scattered.[15]

In stanza 291, too, the reference to Kari is indirect, for it states that, on account of a man's attachment to a concubine his wife's position had been ruined in the same way as the enemy's forces were destroyed at Mullur by Kari's army. Finally, stanza 320 speaks of one harlot complaining of another of having enticed her paramour; she wanted the entire people of the village to jeer the offender with their conjoint laughter which was to be as loud and effective as the uproar of Kari's people when Ori attacked his territory.[16]

Anji

A chieftain called Anji became prominent in the Kongu country. Stanza 381 of Narrinai tells us that Anji who possessed a powerful force of elephants and cavalry used to bestow chariots liberally on poets. The abundant rain which fell and brought delight and prosperity to the people is compared to Anji's lavish grant of gifts. He is known as Adiyan because he belonged to a family of Adiyas in Cheranadu; but his personal name was Anji.[17] His capital was Tagadur, situated on the hill of Kollikkurram. He fought victorious battles against Peruncheral Irumporai.[18] It was believed that Anji's ancestors had come from out-side and established their position at Tagadur and that later he became lord of Kutiramalai.[19] Several other details about the activities of Anji are revealed by the Sangam classics.[20]

ARUMAN

A petty chieftain who had not been brought under the authority of any superior power was Aruman. He is spoken of as the lord of Sirukudi in stanza 367 of Narrinai. Sirukudi, situated to the north of Kaviri, consisted of tiny houses erected on small posts. The place was, however, rich in natural resources. This stanza, which speaks of the girl lover as a native of this village, provides a direct reference to the ruler of the place. The suggestion of Sri Narayanaswami Aiyar that the girl is compared with Sirukudi, seems rather far-fetched; no feature of the village is comparable with the qualities of the girl.

VANAN

Another chieftain of Sirukudi figuring in this anthology 340 : 9 is Vanan. Here the girl's beautiful bangles are compared to the charming village of Sirukudi. In the course of his description of the abundance of the natural wealth of the place, the poet says that the valai fish used to swim from the irrigation canals into the paddy fields and that even when beaten by the ploughmen it rushed to the bund and back, for it could not scale over it and get beyond. It may be observed in passing that the agriculturists of the village are believed to have ploughed the land efficiently, for the ploughmen are described as 'Chenchal Ulavar.'

Periyan

A chieftain, Periyan by name, figures in stanza 131 of Narrinai. He was the ruler of the village called Poraiyaru, near the Kaviri. An enthusiastic warrior, he was the proud possessor of elegant chariots. He delighted in drinking toddy, and his entire village, Poraiyaru, was known for its perpetual smell of toddy. In this stanza the shoulders of the loving girl are compared to the rich Poraiyaru village.

Talumpan

The chief of Unur, is found mentioned in stanza 300 of Narrinai. A comparison is drawn between the elephant which sought alms at the hands of this unfortunate chieftain and the unsuccessful Panan who interceded on behalf of an errant husband in reconciling him with his wife. The husband had fallen a victim to the seductions of a harlot, and the Panan tried in vain to restore amity between him and his wedded wife.

Pulli

A chieftain of the northernmost region of Tamilaham mentioned in stanza 14 of Narrinai, is Pulli, the lord of the Venkata Hill. Here the reference to the chieftain is direct, for a girl's lover is stated to have betaken himself to the forest of this hill owned by Pulli. His forest is described as dense and dangerous. The chieftain is spoken of as "Kalvarkoman," in the commentary of Narrinai stanza 147 meaning the lord of thieves. Apparently he was a turbulent chieftain and a terror in the neighbourhood.

On the whole, it is undeniable that certain pieces of valuable information regarding the political history of the Tamil country during the early centuries of the Christian era can be gleaned from Narrinai. It is by no means claimed that the data provided are either full or consecutive. Stray pieces of information regarding the kings, chieftains and their activities are all that can be had. Though they do not provide the materials for the re-construction of a systematic political history, the data furnished can serve to supplement the information available in the other classics of the age. In respect of several details they serve as a corroboratory source.

That the Chera, Chola and Pandya were the three outstanding powers of Tamilaham during the Sangam age is clear. It is indisputable that the Pallava power had not yet appeared. A plausible suggestion has been made that the references to wars of the Tamil kings with the Aryas relate to the struggle that the Pallava power had with the indigenous rulers. But the origin of the Pallavas is by no means a settled question. One of the latest theories advanced is that the Pallavas, some of whose kings were called Tirayar, were sailors or maritime chieftains, and that they were invaders from the far eastern region viz., South East Asia. Meanwhile, the old theory that the Pallavas were descendants of the Parthians has regained force. However, there is little doubt that the Pallavas were Sanskritists and it is plausible that in the Sangam age all the patrons of Sanskrit were called Aryas. There is ample evidence to show there were occasional incursions from and to the north. The references to the expeditions of Imayavaramban, Karikala and Cheran Chenguttuvan on the one hand and to the Aryan enemies encountered on the Tamil soil on the other, could not have been utterly baseless fabrications. The achievements were apparently exaggerated; but the legends were in all probability built upon a substratum of truth.

Wars with outsiders apart, there occurred frequent struggles among the powers of Tamilnad themselves. The three kings, their vassals and the independent chieftains were often engaged in conflicts. There is no doubt that preoccupation with war was a dominant characteristic of the age. The cause of hostilities was, more often than not, a desire for the display of military prowess. The passion for developing martial valour and heroism frequently promoted aggressive ventures. Among specific causes of war the most important one was the desire to curb powerful neighbours or an eagerness to obtain possession of coveted places. Narrinai reveals how there arose a conflict between Titiyan and Anni over a laurel tree and this is confirmed by Ahananuru. Ahananuru again shows how Kari, the lord of Mullur killed Ori, the famous archer, and transferred to the Cheras the possession of the beautiful margosa and jack trees on the fertile Kolli Hills.

In the wars of those days archery and elephants seem to have played a prominent part. Kings and noblemen rode in chariots during the fight. The others went on foot, and hand-to-hand fight with sword, spear and dagger was as common as the employment of the bow and arrow from a distance. Martial valour was prized high, and turning one's back to the advancing foe was considered an irrevocable disgrace. A valiant death in the field of battle was held to be a proud privilege of royalty. These high ideals of martial etiquette occasionally bred certain evils. Not infrequently, high-handed actions occurred among belligerents both during and after the battle. Stanza 384 of

Narrinai states that the invading soldiers seized all valuable things belonging to the enemy, as a consequence of which there was little left for the people of the place to live upon. Some paddy which had grown up in the deserted tracts was about all that was available to be used by the destitute people of the land. Again the treatment meted out to the women relatives of the chieftain Pindan by Nannan after his victory was doubtless very cruel. Stanza 270 of Narrinai describes how the women were deprived of their tufts of hair in order to make a rope for dragging elephants. It is incredible that human hair could have given the required strength for the rope. Obviously it was intended as a symbolic demonstration of the might as well as the vindictiveness of Nannan. Stanza 18 of Narrinai, as observed earlier, speaks of the Chera king of Tondi having pulled out the teeth of the vanquished chieftain Muvan and fastened them on the doorway of his own palace as a trophy of victory. More or less similar acts of cruelty and vindictiveness are revealed by certain other Sangam classics as well. Kuruntogai (Stanza 292) states that for the simple offence of a woman having taken a fruit floating on a stream in his garden, Nannan killed her mercilessly, totally disregarding the appeal for clemency made by the woman's relatives who offered to pay gold and elephants to atone for the offence. Purananuru (Stanza 15) shows how the streets of the defeated ruler's capital were ploughed with donkeys and seeds of castor, cotton and various cereals were sown there. It must be admitted that there was a streak of ruthlessness in the treatment of enemies.

But it would be unfair and unhistoric to detach these instances from their context and form general conclusions regarding the ethics of warfare or the prevalent standards of oral behaviour. War has had an inexplicably wonderful code of its own in every clime and in every age. Perhaps what Japan experienced at the hands of 'civilized' enemies very recently is not any the more humane than what happened in certain instances in Tamilnad many centuries ago. In the fight to the finish man has always exhibited his worst traits.

On the other hand, as against the exceptional acts of cruelty there did exist normally a code of ethics in respect of warfare. Before the commencement of attack, the weak, the aged, the brahmins and others not directly involved in war were arranged to be removed from the path of danger. Normally, too, pillage and plunder as well as wanton destruction and devastation did not occur. "Total warfare" is a feature of modern civilisation. The few instances noticed earlier seem to have been the exceptions rather than the rule.

The high ideals which monarchs of the Sangam age kept in view in respect of their duties stand out prominently.[21] The king had of course little of the routine administrative functions which are associated in later times with the heads of states. No doubt, he was the fountain of justice, and personal appeals were made to him against gross injustice. For the rest, the village organisation discharged all the administrative and judicial functions. At a time when the line of demarcation between the state and society was not clearly drawn, the village assemblies and social conventions discharged many of the duties now undertaken by the state. The king was more like a protector, guide and philosopher. Always, even at the war camp, he revelled in the company of poets, musicians and dancers. Little wonder that the court was a seat of light and learning.

The Tamil kings were not only generous patrons of poets but some of them were poets themselves. Among monarchs whose poetic compositions have been incorporated in Narrinai, mention may be made of the Pandyan kings, Ukkiraperuvaluti (Stanza 98), Maran Valuti (Stanza 97 and 301),[22] Arivudai Nambi (Stanza 15), and Muda Tirumaran (Stanzas 105 and 228), the Chera king Marudam Padiya Ilankadungo (Stanza 50) and Palai Padiya Perunkadungo (Stanza 391) and the Chola chieftain Tondaiman Ilantirayar who has to his credit stanzas 94, 99 and 106.

Social Life

While data in respect of political history happen to be indirect, meagre and incoherent, which is perhaps inevitable in a work treating of love, the position is different so far as social life is concerned. Though love affairs are most elaborately dealt with, the reference to the daily life of the people and to their social customs, beliefs and traditions as well as religious ideas and institutions are considerable. A picture of the life of the people can well be gleaned from the situations portrayed in the verses.

The natural divisions of land were the dominant factors which regulated the lives of the Tamils of that age. Tolkappiyam, the earliest grammar of the Tamils now extant, has laid down that the five divisions, namely Kurinchi the land of Hills, Mullai the land of forests, Marudam the land of plains, Palai the desert and Neydal the coastal region had each its distinctive features of life. It has been held by certain writers like Sri P.T. Srinivas Aiyangar that these five divisions mark the stages of transition of the early people all the world over that 'as the South Indian spread from region to region, he developed the stages of culture which each region was calculated to produce.'[23] This view is based on the assumption that South India was the original home of the Tamils, which is not indubitably proved. Further, according to this assumption the transition from the less fertile to the more suitable region would mean that at the final stage of development people lived only in Marudam or Neydal. In fact, it is well known that people continued to remain in all the regions, the Palai not excepted. It is presumable that though people high in the social scale moved from the less fertile to the richer and more suitable region, those of the lower ranks remained in their respective habitat. Whether Tolkappiyam which has postulated the distinctive features of the five regions preceded or succeeded the Classics, assigned by tradition to the third Sangam, is a moot question. The commonly accepted view of the anterior date of Tolkappiyam has been recently challenged by a few writers. The picture it provides seems to be that of a slightly later epoch than that of the Sangam classics. There is more of Sanskrit influence in Tolkappiyam than in some of the Sangam works. The caste divisions and the religious beliefs pertain to a later date. But these are sought to be explained by possible interpolations into the original text. However, the Ahaporul works describe Kalaviyal in active operation; Tolkappiyam, on the other hand, while laying down the features of Kalaviyal also records its decline and abandonment. Politically, too, Tolkappiyam (in Seyyul Iyal, Stanza 391) suggests the existence of four principal kingdoms, which as the annotators would have it, comprised the Pandyamandalam, Malaimandalam, Cholamandalam and Tondaimandalam. This is the picture of Tamilaham of a period later than the 3rd century AD when the Pallavas rose to power in Tondaimandalam. Moreover, Tolkappiyam takes Venkatam as the northern limit of Tamilaham. The extension of the northern boundary should have occurred after the conquest of North Aruvanadu by Karikalan. Narrinai speaks of the country around Venkatam as having remained under Pulli, the Kalvarkoman. The extension of the Chola power up to Venkatam by subduing Pulli's successors should have occurred later.

However, Tolkappiyam, treating the poetics of love, lays down the distinctive characteristics of each region. It distinguishes three bases: the Mudal Porul (the primary factors) the Karupporul (the secondary features, namely deity, food, beast, tree, bird, drum, profession and the type of music produced by yal) and the distinctive tendencies, namely, the company of lovers, separation, the state expecting the lover's arrival or the state bemoaning the lover's absence and *utal* or 'love quarrel.' The Mudalporul, Karupporul and Uripporul of each region are enunciated by him. Thus, it is held that for the Mullai, the Kar season (Winter) and Malai, (the first third part of the night) are appropriate; for Kurinchi the Kutir (autumn) and Yaman (second part of the night); for Marudam all seasons and the last part of the night and daybreak, and for Neydal all seasons and Yerpadu or afternoon and for Palai the spring, summer, as well as noon. Narrinai, too, provides many instances of deviation from these prescriptions.[24] It may be observed that these were of general application; Tolkappiyanar held that the Mudalporul and Karupporul may overlap.[25]

Bearing in mind these general prescriptions let us notice the treatment of love as reflected in Narrinai. Narrinai as well as other works on love hold that the pre-marital love was common among the Tamils of the Sangam age or more probably of a slightly earlier period. The handling of Kalaviyal by the poets suggests that they were not portraying the contemporary situations but what had existed earlier and had given rise to certain conventions. However, it has been said that Kalaviyal corresponded to the Gandharva pattern of marriage which was one of the systems in vogue among the Aryans of old. There is little doubt that Kalaviyal was ennobled almost into a fine art in which certain well-recognised conventions were harmonised with a rustic simplicity and forthrightness. The poets of the age enter into the spirit of the situations of love and describe them with striking vividity. It is held that Kalavu, or what may be called courtship, was adopted only by the higher strata of society in all the five regions. The Adiyar or the servile classes who depended on others for their living are not believed to have figured in the picture. This sounds strange, because love is an elemental feature common to all; but, for one thing, according to the conventions of the age, marriage among the dependants had to be approved of by their masters. Moreover, Ilampuranar, commenting on Sutra 23 of Ahattinai Iyal of Poruladhikaram states that the lower classes were devoid of natural reserve and shyness, as a consequance of which they were unsuited for love of the proper type; he adds that they were entitled to what Tolkappiyar calls Peruntinai (Poruntakkamam) i.e., unnatural or perverted love.

In passing it may be mentioned that the gradations of society known to Narrinai and many of the early classics were based exclusively on occupation. The caste divisions of the later age had not taken hold of Tamil society then, and, therefore the independent earning members of Kuravar, the hunter, the Ulavar, the cultivators, the Ayar, the shepherds, the Paradavar, the fishermen, were all entitled to take to the Kalavu pattern of love.

As observed earlier, the poets who picture the romantic situations were not describing contemporary events which they witnessed. In all probability the situations pertain to a slightly earlier epoch which had become conventional. Poets based their imaginary portraits on such conventions, a few of which might have survived down to their times while the bulk of them had survived down to their times while the bulk of them had vanished. That is one reason why we observe that, more often than not, the man who addresses his love to a damsel was a chieftain or prince (Cherpan); the girl in the picture, too, is a member of an affluent family. She is in a position to have with her a *Toli* or companion who plays the role of a faithful comrade a genuine friend and guide. The companion was usually the daughter of her foster mother. But there is little justification to imagine that the *Toli* belonged to a class of dependants; very often she belonged to the same social positions as the mistress and was one of her neighbours. However, the poets picture the companion as an ideal mate for the girl in love. Her sincere attachment to her mistress, her forbearance, sympathy and understanding as well as her worldly wisdom[26] are all exquisitely portrayed by numerous verses of Narrinai and other Sangam works dealing with love.

The girl who falls in love and enters the Kalavu relationship is, according to ancient Tamil tradition, twelve years of age,[27] while the boy lover is about 16. This may seem strange to us now. Several explanations are possible. Perhaps, in the period in question, the age of maturity was earlier; or perhaps emotional attachment and ideal love independent of physical pleasure commenced early in life; or it might be that the poets in their idealisation of Kalavu or courtship thought that the adolescent period of innocence was eminently suited for their portrayal. But it is significant that according to Tolkappiyar the girl in love is a mature girl which characteristic reserve and shyness.[28] If so, the first of these suggestions alone is acceptable.

Theoretically the Kalavu period was expected to last for a couple of months, though one writer thinks that it lasted for barely a fortnight. The commencement of Kalavu, or what may be literally translated as illicit love but more appropriately taken as courtship, is picturesquely portrayed. When the girl is out attending to her outdoor work, by chance she happens to see an youngster. The young man feels attracted by her and love at first sight springs up between the two. Thereafter, they meet often and their mutual attachment increases in intensity. The fact of their love affair is not generally known to others except to the *Toli*, the bosom friend and constant companion of the girl. The loving girl happens to be sent by her parents to attend to such work as watching the cultivated field in order to protect it from destruction by pests and birds. This affords welcome opportunities for the lovers to meet. An ideal mingling of hearts, or what is described as 'Iyarkai Punarchi' occurs at their meetings during this period. This was no doubt an ideal form of association motivated by spontaneous and natural love. Their exchange of love and ever-increasing attachment from the themes of numerous verses in Narrinai as well as in other Sangam classics dealing with Love. But it is an open question whether it was a union of hearts and nothing more. The references to 'Muyakkam,' to the reddish eyes and to a mother's mention of an unusual smell coming from her tuft are all suggestive.

It would appear that during the Sangam Age fidelity to the lover was rarely, if ever, broken. The Kalavu episode was invariably followed by marriage. Where the parents of the girl objected to the marriage, an embarrassing situation appeared. Perhaps the importance attached to the approval of the parents suggests that the transition to the later system was emerging. At any rate either during or immediately after the Sangam age, Kalavu as an institution tended to decline. Tolkappiyam reveals that the ideal love was sometimes abused and this degeneracy led to its discredit and abandonment by society.[29] Since the literary works of the Sangam epoch which deal with love assume that Kalaviyal in its orthodox form remained in force, this revelation by Tolkappiyam is presumably an indication of the date of Tolkappiyam.

Reviewing the nature of courtship as it prevailed in the Sangam Age, certain features are noticeable. There was generally an intensity of love. Separation of the lovers was a matter of agony. Separations occurred due to various causes. During the period of Kalavu, after meeting each other at an unknown place, they had to part. A longer separation occurred when the man, after having loved the girl had to betake himself to a distant place in order to earn an independent fortune. This separation was a period of ordeal for the lovers and there are numerous verses which depict the trials and tribulations of lovers. It is remarkable that though both the parties were equally moved by intensity of love and consequent agony, poets have dwelt more frequently on the theme of the girl's pang of separation than that of the man. Narrinai has numerous verses depicting the feelings and bewailings of the girls under separation. The grief of the loving girl is not infrequently expressed by her companion. There are lamentations on the part of the companion that her mistress's beauty had vanished. Her physical frame enfeebled, her shoulders had become emaciated and her bangles had become too loose for her hands.[30] Stanzas 79, 236 and 239 go to the extent of stating that the girl considered death to be far better than the wretched life of separation from her lover. Stanzas 37 and 296 show how the girl bemoans her misery on account of separation from her lover during the Kar season, when man and woman find happiness in each other's company. Stanza 304 states that the girl felt her life to be dallying between pleasure and misery, that when the lover remained by her side she felt cheerful in spirit and healthy of body while during his absence all her joy and health had vanished. The girl's unbearable state of separation is vividly described in stanza 61, where it is stated that, unable to get even a wink of sleep, she spent the whole time in having deep sighs of agony. When her mother enquired of her the cause of her sleeplessness, she had to admit the real circumstances responsible for her position.

Though the mother sometimes understands and appreciates the situation, she restrains her daughter from indulging in the romantic venture.[31] She tries to check it by compelling her to remain within the confines of the house. The girl in love tries her best to conceal her romantic entanglement from her mother, because she is sure to be restrained.[32] Stanza 143 shows how even though the mother realised that it was natural for her daughter to embark in Kalavu, she felt it incumbent on her to restrain her and she repented for her failure to check her even at the outset.[33]

The mother reprimands the girl and even belabours her in order to compel her to give up her association with her lover. The mother is really worried over the public slur. She heaps curses on the villagers, and at the heart of hearts she has a feeling that the girl should not be restrained. The reaction of a mother towards the man who eloped with her daughter is indicated in stanza 198; feeling that her daughter's action was not totally wrong, she was only worried as to how the tender girl would stand the trials of the arduous journey through the forest. (Stanza 305).

VELAN VERIYADAL

When the daughter was suffering from love sickness, the mother was in certain cases unable to determine the real cause. There are several instances of the mother invoking the aid of Muruga by holding a ceremony called the *Veriyadal*. The priest conducting the ceremony was believed to pass into a trance and divine the cause of the trouble.[34] The description of *Velan Veriyadal* is found in certain verses.[35]

There was a common belief that people possessed of the spirit of Murugan would be in a state of depression and agony. As a prelude to the treatment it had to be ascertained whether the malady was due to the possession by the spirit of *Muruganangu* (முருகணங்கு). This was determined by consulting a gypsy or sooth-sayer. The sooth-sayer, who was usually an elderly woman, was invited to the house of the affected girl. A measure of paddy was placed in a receptacle in front of an image of Muruga and the girl was asked to keep standing in front of it and worship Muruga. After a time the paddy was sorted into groups of four each and the number of the remaining paddy was believed to indicate the true cause of the malady. If the remaining number of paddy was one, two or three, then the belief was that the malady was brought about through the operation of *Muruganangu* i.e. Muruga's anger.[36] If it was four, then it was adjudged to be a different malady altogether. Where it was thought to have been brought about by *Muruganangu*, immediately the Velan or priest who offered worship to Muruga was invited to the sacred spot set apart for this ceremony. Prayers and offerings were made to God Muruga. The elaborate ceremony accompanied by music, included the offering of goat sacrifice to the deity. There was a gathering of womenfolk in particular. The priest got into a trance and, as if inspired, he gave out the cause of the trouble as well as the remedy.

It is surprising that while *Kalavu* was widely known to be prevalent, the people of the village did not take kindly to individual cases when they came to public notice. Scandal mongering became rife. In the parlance of the age *Ambal* was the term applied to the public comment and the expression of disapprobation. The extreme form of public slur was known as *Alar*. A typical case of *Alar* is described in stanza 149, where it is stated that the women-folk of the village, standing in small or big groups used to scandalise the girl in love, showing their contempt. Pointing to the girl in question they seemed to indicate that she had entered into *Kalavu* association with man.

There was instances of mild sensations developing into abominable scandals. Stanza 249 mentions how *Ambal* turned into vociferous *Alar*. Nachchinarkiniyar would state that *Ambal* was a subdued scandal while Alar was a public uproar.

"அம்பல் முகிழ் முகிழ்த்தல்; அலர் பலரறிய சொன்னிகழ்த்தல்."

The uproar raised by the *Alar* spread quickly and became unbearable for the girls concerned.[37] Kalavu was thus considered an illegitimate and unmoral practice. It is interesting to learn that the village where the slightest suspicion provided the basis of public talk was nicknamed Ambalur (அம்பலூர்). It may be mentioned that the people of Kurinchi would even pursue the man who indulged in Kalavu and attack him. For fear of the girl's mother, on the one hand, and of the public slur on the other, the man used to meet his sweet-heart surreptitiously at dead of night.[38]

Both of these types of restraints were felt by the girl as unjust and unnatural.[39] The companion of the girl who was restrained by the mother and at the same time, was frightened by public odium, gave expression to the unfairness of social standards. There was an under-current of feeling among the lovers that Kalavu was natural and legitimate. Stanza 132 indicates here intensity of love and mentions the lamentations of the girl over the restrictions imposed by her mother and adds that if the lover failed to turn up at night that would prove to be her day of death. The girl deplores the rigour of the mother's control as well as the public watchman's vigil.

Several verses refer to the eagerness on the part of the girl lover to have the formal marriage celebrated soon. Stanza 23 is interesting, for the companion of the mistress states that her lover had been unduly postponing the marriage and that he appeared to be lacking fidelity. Any person guilty of wilful desertion was considered as one devoid of a high moral calibre.[40]

MADALERUTAL

At times, however, it happened that though the loving man was anxious to conduct the marriage, the parents of the girl refused to give their consent.[41] A strange custom of the early Tamils was that the loving man under such a condition used to subject himself to a severe indignity and mortification. In order to impress upon the girl's parents his sincere love and to obtain their approval for the marriage he used to come to the home of the girl riding on an artificial horse made of palmyrah stem and leaves. His dress and appearance would suggest that he was in a forlorn and desperate state. It used to be felt that in the event of failure in his desperate mission he would turn mad. It is said that he wore a garland made of flowers which were not considered sweet-smelling or auspicious.[42] There is no doubt that these flowers were worthless and were never used at all by people. The poet's description of them as 'Villappu'[43] (வில்லாப்பு) i.e. 'those unable to be sold' is a clear pointer to this fact. The artifical horse on which the despondent lover was riding was, however, decorated with bells and clothes.[44] His position, on the whole, was pathetic. If the parents of the girl took pity on him, and if by reason of public opinion and the pressure of the girl, her parents finally agreed to give her in marriage to him, then with great relief and pleasure he gave up his fantastic role. If, however, it happened that the object of his mission was not fulfilled, either he deserted the village and went away or committed suicide. In fact, Madalerutal itself was considered an extreme step. Stanza 377 shows that it was thought far better to lose one's life than to have to resort to Madalerutal.

Where the parents were determined to prevent the alliance, sometimes the lover cleverly eloped with his sweetheart and set up a home either in his village or in some other place. In this matter, invariably the girl's companion played an important role. She fixed with the two lovers the time and the day when they should start unnoticed by others. The moment the matter came to the knowledge of the girl's relatives, they set out to pursue them. But when they met the lovers, invariably the girl expressed her firm resolution to become her lover's life-partner and that there was no use in restraining them from their determined path. It is interesting to find that the mother of the girl sometimes considered this natural and justifiable. On the other hand, her grief was that her daughter would have to pass through arduous pathways and dangerous forests.

MARRIAGE

After the lovers had betaken themselves to the man's house, the relatives of the parties concerned, became reconciled and a formal marriage ceremony was held. But in the vast majority of cases there was no need for Madalerutal or Kondutalaikkalital (கொண்டுதலைக்கழிதல்), for the parents of the girl agreed to the marriage of the lovers.

Generally there did not arise any serious difficulty when the two lovers were more or less of the same social level. Where there was conspicuous disparity in social status, then, as now, obstruction for such alliances appeared from the relatives of the lovers. But even in such cases the determined firmness of the lovers, more often than not, decided the issue and the marriage took place.

A girl of Neydal who was loved by a prince told him that there existed a wide disparity in their social position; he was a wealthy chieftain whereas she was a poor daughter of a fisherman. Her *toli* (தோழி) said that her mistress was engaged in leading the life of a fisher-woman herself and that consequently her body would be emitting the smell of fish which would be detested by him. Therefore, she wanted him to give up the idea of alliance with her.[45]

However, when the parents of the boy and girl were agreeable to the marriage alliance, a preliminary function corresponding to the modern betrothal ceremony was held. A small party of the bridegroom's relatives headed by Brahmins and men of high social status entered the bride's house. Formally they pleaded excuse for delay in fulfilling their pledged word and praise the *toli* the companion of the bride, for her noble efforts in expediting the auspicious function.[46] Prior to the celebration of the marriage the bridegroom had to make a payment of money to the parents of the girl.[47] Having ascertained the price he had to pay for her, and agreeing to pay it, he proceeded to make the preliminary arrangements with Brahmins and noblemen for the conduct of the betrothal ceremony. It would appear that in the Sangam Age the payment of a bride-price was obligatory. There is no reference whatever to a dowry having figured in the settlement of marriages.

Normally the auspicious time for marriage was believed to be the period approaching the harvest season.[48] It was also the season when the Vengai tree flowered, a circumstance probably considered auspicious for the celebration of marriage.[49] For attending the marriage function, the rich bridegroom went in a decorated chariot; those who accompanied the bridegroom went on foot. It is notable that the bridegroom of the Neydal region went to the function with a net and fishing rod.[50] The ceremony conducted was a grand one according to the standards of the times. Instrumental music was played on the occasion.[51] Narrinai does not refer to the use of the sacred symbol *Tali*.[52]

PARATTAYAR

Karpiyal or the wedded life of the married couple invariably followed Kalaviyal. Theoretically the observance of a moral code in conjugal relationship was enjoined on men no less than on women. But there seems to have existed a gulf between theory and practice. Man appears to have often deviated from the lawful path. According to the prescribed tradition of the Tamils, ideal love was of the *Aintinai* type. Both *Kaikkilai* and *Perundinai* were not suited for the higher sections of society. One form of *Perundinai* was man's relationship with Parattayar or public women. Therefore, connections with Parattayar or concubines was looked down upon as unnatural and unbecoming of elegant men. Tolkkappiyanar and Tiruvalluvar condemn this illicit relationship in unmistakable terms. Nevertheless, Narrinai, no less than the other classics of love, reveals, that in actual practice harlotry had become a well established institution; several men fell victims to the paramours of the public women. Therefore, connections with Parattayar or concubines was looked down upon as unnatural and unbecoming of elegant men. Tolkappiyanar and Tiruvalluvar condemn this illicit relationship in unmistakable terms. Nevertheless, Narrinai, no less than the other classics of love, reveals, that in actual practice harlotry had become a well established institution; several men fell victims to the paramours of the public women. It is notable that during the period of pregnancy and confinement of the wife the man was inclined to seek sexual indulgence at the hands of Parattayar.[53] It was but natural that the lawfully wedded wife became furious when she came to know about it. Public opinion, too, condemned such immoral relationship. The Panan and Virali served as mediators between the man and Parattayar. Later, too, when the wedded wife protested and evinced her wrath the Panan tried to intervene and restore cordiality between the husband and wife.[54] Often there sprang up acute rivalry and ill-feeling between the Parattai who had enticed the man and his lawful wife. There is an interesting instance of a Parattai inciting the hatred of the wife against her husband by causing his attachment to herself to be made known to the wife.[55] She sent word that it was he, who, out of infatuation had seized her sweet-smelling tuft of hair. Evidently the Parattai wanted to sow discord between the man and his legitimate partner so that he might permanently come under her own influence. A more or less similar idea is found in stanza 225 in which it is stated that the Parattai openly accused the man within the hearing of the companion of the legal wife. She too, accused the man for having voluntarily sought her association. In one case, on behalf of the mistress her companion burst out furiously against the weak-minded man who had fallen a victim to the amours of a

Parattai, and she scornfully asked him to gratify his physical lust as he liked and never to return to the house of her mistress. Even more arresting is the righteous indignation of a devoted wife who refused to touch her husband on account of his association with a parattai. She reproached him by saying that touching a person who had illicit connection with a Parattai is like touching the discarded pots.[56]

Parattayar seem to have vied with each other in winning the affections of affluent men. Unseemly quarrels and bitter rivalry arose between two Parattayar who competed with each other in capturing the heart of one and the same person. Certain stanzas[57] of Narrinai refer to the piquant situations which arose when a Parattai who had won the heart of a man found to her utter discomfiture that a rival had entered the field.

It is notable that among the Parattayar there are two categories known as *Cheripparattai* and *Kadalparattai*. The *Cheripparattai* appears to have been a public harlot, while the *Kadalparattai* preferred to have relationship with a single individual of her choice. More often than not, she led a virtuous life characterised by fidelity to the chosen person. Little wonder than, of the two classes, the *Kadalparattai* occupied a higher social position than the *Cheripparattai*.

On the whole it is clear that Parattayar constituted a stain on society. Married women sedulously tried to protect their husbands from the seductions of their Parattayar.[58] While recognizing the existence of this foul institution it would be improper to over-emphasise the position it occupied. It is of supreme importance to realize that the Parattayar have received a great attention at the hands of the poets because of the piquant situations which arose in their dealings with men. From the number of stanzas devoted to the handling of themes connected with Parattayar it would be totally improper and unfair to exaggerate the role played by them in the social life of the day. Indeed, it would not be too much to say that it was because of social disapprobation that poets found a special interest in the handling of themes connected with this blot on society. An outspoken characterisation, breathing a bitter condemnation, of this social stain is of a piece with the forthrightness of the poets. It is because society had built up certain standards of conduct that deviations from them received an excessive and almost a disproportionate attention at the hands of the poets of the age. False conventions of depicting the rosier side of life and ignoring the darker one was totally alien to the tendencies of those times.

STANDARDS OF MORAL CONDUCT

Early Tamil society had evolved some conception of true love and norms of moral conduct. The lapses and the protests they provoked reveal the ideals held in view. The virtues of immaculate love and true partnership in life between the husband and wife find their echo in several verses of Narrinai. One of these states that even poison offered by a real lover would not be rejected: (Stanza 355).

"முந்தை இருந்து நட்டோர் கொடுப்பின்

நஞ்சும் உண்பர் நனிநாகரிகர்"

In passing it may be mentioned that these lines bear a tinge of similarity with the precept in Kural 586. Love of a high order which promotes unbounded courage and unselfish sacrifice was known and appreciated. It is this noble feature which the poet Koliyur Kilarmahanar Cheliyanar has in view when he says that a tiger was prepared to attack and kill an elephant for appeasing the hunger of its partner. (Stanza 383).

"கல்லயல் கலித்த கருங்கால் வேங்கை
அலங்கலம் தொடஃ அன்ன குரூஉ
வயப்புனிற்று இரும்பினப் பசித்தென வயப்புலி
புகாமுகஞ் சிதையத் தாக்கிக் களிறட்டு"

It is no doubt poetic imagery that is offered in this excerpt; but it reveals the conception of true love. The idea of depicting it through the illustration of an animal was apparently expected to be significant. It appears to have been realized that ideal love was not physical, much less sexual in character; it was an attachment of spirit. It is this idea which the poet Ammuvanar exemplifies when he says that a loving girl, struck with sorrow that her lover had not turned up as expected, declares that she does not even dread death, but is only anxious that in the life to come, if she is not born as a human being she may forget her lover. She says

"சாதல் அஞ்சேன் அஞ்சுவல் சாவின்
பிறப்புப்பிறி தாகுவது ஆயின்
மறக்குவேன் கொல் லென் காதலன் எனவே"

(Narrinai, 397)

The importance of a nobler love transcending sexual appeal, has been admirably expressed through the appeal of a girl's companion to her lover, calling upon him to be always attached to the girl even long after she loses her physical charm (Stanza 10).

"அண்ணந் தேந்திய வனமுஃ தளரினும்
பொன்னேர் மேனி மணியிற் றுழ்ந்த
நன்னெடுங் கூந்தல் நரையொடு முடிப்பினும்
நீத்த லோம்பு மதி பூக்கே ஊர"

A high standard of moral virtue seems to have been in vogue among family women. Though this was common to all the regions, it was exemplified best in Mullai because it was there that the separation of lovers occurred most and fidelity was on trial, as it were. It is noteworthy that Mullai became a synonymous name for Karpu or chastity. The pang of separation is borne with fortitude controlling the intense feeling of agony; no wonder that numerous verses appear pertaining to this theme. It is considered as an essential virtue of the noble woman to bear the separation with courage.[59] In Stanza 289 the woman having waited long for the arrival of her husband is stated to have cried that just as the fire set on to the felled trees at night by the shepherds get extinguished of their own accord, so, too, her lust would automatically cool itself down.[60] The husband himself knows how longingly his wife would be yearning for his return. Relating how his wife had admirably put up with separation from him on a previous occasion he states that she had remained with her hair unkempt, which showed her immaculate chastity.[61]

The ideal man, too, was expected to lead a moral life. Indulgence with Parattayar was condemned,[62] although as observed earlier, quite a number of men lapsed into immoral ways. (St. 226). In theory the moral code was applicable to man no less than to women. But then, as always, here as all the world over, man made laws and broke them with impunity. Man's ownership of property, his unbounded freedom to go out and his inherent dislike of the humdrum domestic life was perhaps some of the factors responsible for the consequent existence of a class of harlots.

Associated with chastity, certain other virtues were also expected of women. Reverse and restraint, arising from modesty, were considered the most essential of the feminine virtues.

In Stanza 17, Nochi Niyamangilar narrates an incident which illustrates vividly the supreme importance of modesty for women. A girl in love was weeping on account of separation from her lover. Her mother openly consoled her that he would return soon. Then the girl instantaneously realized that she had abandoned her inborn modesty, which was far more precious than life itself. She is stated to have stopped crying and to have resolved upon maintaining her modesty. Again Yeinandaiyar states[63] that during the absence of the husband, modesty is the only impregnable fortification of woman. Narrinai, like the other Sangam works, reveals that the society of that age recognized and upheld certain distinctive feminine virtues. It was idle to expect these virtues among the harlots. Poets of the age deny the existence of these virtues among Parattai and suggest by implication that they constituted the fundamental assets of the well-bred woman of social status.

DIET

Though Narrinai treats largely of love, it throws indirectly considerable light on the habits and customs of the Tamils of the age. The casual nature of the information provided attests its reliability. There was little or no attempt at furnishing a made-up picture. The inevitable limitation of such references is that a full and cogent account of the social life cannot be obtained.

In respect of diet, it is clear that rice formed the staple food. Millet or tinai (திணை) was often a substitute for rice, especially in Kurinchi. Vegetables must have been used for the preparation of accessories, as learnt from other classics. Narrinai, however, mentions 'Karunaikkilangin Porikkari' in Stanza 367. It is notable that the common practice of eating food out of plantain leaves had come into vogue.[64] Fruits were very popular. In Palai even the Vilampalam (wood apple) was used as food. The jackfruit was considered a great delicacy, and there are several references to its wide popularity.[65] It is surprising to learn that Umanar, the salt vendors, ate ripe tamarind fruits to appease their hunger. Gooseberry was popular; in particular, persons journeying through forests or deserts ate them frequently.

Flesh eating was doubtless very common. Goat's meat was most popular, though the flesh of white rats was occasionally used.[66] The Kuravar were very fond of the flesh of the Mulavupanri.[67] It is notable that the elephant's teeth were dried up and kept for use over a considerable time as ivory.[68] Pork, too, was popular with hunters.[69] Meat was thus a principal item of food and usually considerable care was taken to make delicious preparations of meat with the admixture of ghi and condiments.[70] Rice was cooked along with meat and ghi and condiments, and especially on festive occasions, this delicacy figured prominently.

Fish was commonly used not only by the people of Neydal but by others as well. Dried and preserved fish is found mentioned. Mallar ate fried oysters. The Yanar in Palai are stated to have used flesh not only as the part of their diet, but delicacies were prepared out of meat and served on occasions of grand feasts. Though there is no specific reference in Narrinai to the Brahmins having abstained from meat, a verse in Purananuru indicates that they took to an almost exclusively vegetarian diet. It is not known which other classes had begun to abstain from eating flesh. From the circumstance that Tirukkural at a slightly later period preached against the use of animal food. It is probable that even during the Sangam age, perhaps under the influence of the Buddhists and Jains, some sections of the people began to restrict themselves to an exclusively vegetarian diet. Some classes of people observed occasionally fasts connected with certain religious observances (St. 272).

Toddy was as popular as meat and invariably the two went hand in hand. Many are the stanzas which advert to the excessive popularity of this beverage. Toddy was stored in pipes of bamboo as well as in pitchers. The more sour the toddy the greater the relish. There is little doubt that it was a strong and intoxicating drink.[71] Stanza 35 makes it clear that under the influence of toddy a person seemed to become totally transformed.

Toddy was frequently brewed into a hot liquor and taken. In the evening Paratavar invariably enjoyed a drinking bout.[72] That it was shared by relatives and friends on festive occasions is obvious from the references found in Narrinai.[73]

DRESS AND DECORATION

Normally both men and women wore clothes made of cotton. At times girls took to the fanciful dress made of leaves and flowers as a decorative garment.[74] It is seen that the *Talai* (தழை), as this dress formed of leaves and flowers was called, differed in its pattern from place to place. But there is no doubt that in all places it was a special dress worn on extra-ordinary occasions. At times of gay festivals in particular, ladies took to *talai*. Rich ladies used to wear *Kalingam* or fine cloth of cotton. Sheaths of grassy weeds (Korai) were worn[75] principally by people of the hills and forests. It is learnt that Kuravar women adopted the bark of certain trees as their dress.[76]

Attention was paid to personal decoration, particularly by women. The tuft of hair received great care; indeed, there are few verses describing the loving girl which do not advert to the sweet-smelling hair done into a handsome knot. The beautifully made tufts of girls are compared to the outspread feathers of the peacock.[77] That girls often had their hair done into five plaits is learnt from Narrinai as well.[78] Painting eye lashes was another familiar feature of personal decoration on the part of girls.[79]

Both sexes took enthusiastically to garlands. Brahmin ladies adorned themselves with the Mullai flowers.[80] Sweet smelling sandal paste was smeared on the chest.[81] A rather interesting custom was for women to draw decorative designs on their breasts with a fragrant substance, called *Toyyil*, which resembled sandal paste.[82]

Ornaments were immensely popular, and there were several varieties of them. Girls had bracelets and bangles.[83] Bangles were sometimes made of excellent gold and bedecked with precious stones.[84] Anklets were common.[85] Rich girls used to wear, besides these, a heavy chain of gold in eight loops around the waist.[86] It was known as *Kal* (காழ்) or *Kanji* (காஞ்சி). Girls wore also a gold chain known by the name of Ponmanimalai, which was strung with gold coins.[87] Generally, children of the rich had profuse ornaments of gold. Mekalai was an ornament worn around the waist. Girls had the ear-ring, known as *Usal onkulai* (ஊசல் ஒண்குழை). This appears to have been similar to later-day ear-rings called *Simikki* (சிமிக்கி) or *Kudaikkadukhan* (குடைக்கடுக்கன்). Sometimes care was taken to choose ornaments suited to the personal appearance of individuals.[88] This indicates elegance of taste, althought it can hardly be ignored that tastes vary from age to age and from people to people.

Rich people had dishes as well as plates of gold. A girl in one instance is stated to have been accustomed to taking milk out of a golden vessel.[89] Elephants were frequently decorated with gold masks on the forehead and trunk.[90] An artistic sense was displayed in decorating the houses with drawings of decorative designs in front of the entrance.

GAMES AND AMUSEMENTS

It is but natural that the people, young and old, resorted to certain games, pastimes and amusements. Essentially a rural people, living in small villages, with ample leisure and scope for close contact with each other, the Tamils of the Sangam Age appear to have taken enthusiastically to various pastimes. Besides games which were common to the whole of Tamilagam, each Tinai had its distinctive games as well. Youngsters generally took to the game called '*Pandil*' (பாண்டில்)[91] at which gooseberries were moved from one place to another within lines drawn to a pattern on the ground. Those who succeeded in sending the fruit into the assigned places were the winners. Football was a popular game.[92] The football which was made of cotton was sewn over by cotton thread, and hence it was known as Variyanippandu (வரியணிப்பந்து).[93] Girls enjoyed erecting fancy structures like dolls with sand.[94]

Swinging on a pole suspended by ropes was a favourite pastime with girls. The ropes used for the purpose were made out of the fibre of the palm tree.[95]

Kurava girls used to participate in a number of games and frolicsome entertainments on the common space of the village.[96] *Orai* was a popular sport of girls played with dolls.[97] The poet Piran chattanar says that it is unfair and harmful to restrain girls from playing with their mates and participating in outdoor games.[98]

Lovers used to sport in and near brooks. Dance was a favourite entertainment and dances of several kinds were in vogue. On festive occasions, the pattern of dance called Tunangai (துணங்கை) was played.[99] Several other varieties of dance are mentioned in other Sangam classics; Narrinai speaks of one more variety, viz., the Kuravai[100] which was a dance accompanied by the party marking a shrill sound with the tip of the tongue. Occasionally rope dance by experts provided amusement for the people. Music, either to the accompaniment of dance or provided independently, was very much in vogue. Instrumental and vocal music attained a considerable measure of proficiency. Panchery (பாண்சேரி), a part of the village where the professional musicians resided, was a seat of music. The skill of the Panar in the fine arts of music and dance became as proverbial as their distressing poverty. Rich boys used to play on the drum as a piece of entertainment. (Stanza 58).

FESTIVALS

The monotony of life was relieved also by the celebration of festivals from time to time. Some of them were periodic and they took place at specific days of the year, while others were casual, dependent upon the occurrence of happenings, like marriage and birth of a child.

Among the festivals which were celebrated at stated times, the festival of Tai Pongal[101] was an important one. It was a celebration associated with the harvest, ad therefore, it symbolised plenitude and prosperity. Here the reference is to a feast on the first day of the month of Tai by those who had observed fasts on the previous nights. It is not improbable that the Pongal celebration had its genesis in this ceremony.

Another festival common in the Sangam age and ever since then is the bonfire festival on the Krittigai day of the Kartigai month every year.[102] The origin of this festival is traceable to Hindu mythology and astronomy. It was the position of the Krittigai star that determined the day of the festival. Thus it indicates the growing belief in mythology and astronomy. Apart from these specified festivals there were frequent occasions of merry entertainments. Stanza 90 speaks of the village resounding with the festive merriments of the people.

OCCUPATIONS

The people in each Tinai (region) pursued their traditional occupations. Thus the Kuravar in Kurinchi took to hunting and cultivation, the Ulavar in Marudam to agriculture, those in Mullai to the tending of cattle, those in Neydal to fishing and those in Palai to roaming and even to highway robbery. Though these were generally the occupations pursued in the particular regions there were deviations as well. In quite a number of cases people seem to have pursued more then one occupation. Thus some Kuravar took to agriculture alongside with their hunting.[103] In fact, while cultivation was the principal occupation in Mullai, it was adopted as a subsidiary occupation in all other regions, except in Palai. The tilling of the soil was done by buffaloes harnessed to the plough and the process of cultivation was much the same as in later times. (Stanza 60).

Certain features of the occupations, in each of the regions, find casual mention in the poem. Salt manufactured in Neydal was taken in bandies by salt merchants called Umanar to various places in the neighbourhood. This is adverted to in several verses.[104] The salt merchants in Marudam are said to have sold salt in exchange for paddy.¹⁰⁵ Maravar often took to highway robbery. They have been described as 'Koduvil Adavar, Aralaikalvar.' (கொடுவில் ஆடவர் ஆறலைக் கள்வர்). It is learnt that they did not hesitate even to kill people for the sake of robbing them of their belongings.¹⁰⁶

The fishermen of Neydal who were active at night used to dry their nets under the shade of the laurel tree during day time.¹⁰⁷ For the purpose of fishing in the deep wide ocean, fishermen went in their boats, to which mats were fastened. They seem to have acquired considerable skill in using mats in order to take advantage of the wind and sail fast. When they went out fishing at night the fisherman kept burning lights in small dishes (கிளிஞ்சல்). The flames was kept burning with the fish oil.¹⁰⁸

It may be noted that there existed professional washermen. A reference is found to washermen who washed clothes and had them made white and stiff by the use of rice water, viz., water left over from boiling rice. (Stanza 90).

Whatever occupation was pursued, the people in the various regions seem to have applied themselves to their work with earnestness. Women co-operated with them in the occupations wherever possible. In Kurinchi spinning of cotton yarn is known to have been done by women. Widows used to spin a fine variety of cotton.¹⁰⁹ In passing it may be mentioned that cotton was cured by beating it with bow.¹¹⁰ In Mullai milk was curdled and butter taken out of it. The mud pot used for churning the curd was known as *"Tairtali."*¹¹¹ Churning of curd was common not only in the Mullai region but in all other regions, too. It is learnt that early in the morning the sound of churning curd was heard from the houses in Palai and presumably, therefore, from those of other regions as well.¹¹²

Different classes of artisans were at work.[113] There were smiths who took to the making of vessels of brass and copper and jewels of gold.[114] The goldsmith who made jewels pursued his flourishing art and there appears to have existed a great demand for gold ornaments.[115] It is hardly necessary to add that potters were, as in early times, engaged in making vessels, and pots of mud. Potters of the village are said to have been entrusted with the duty of proclaiming to the people the time and date of particular festivals.[116]

The mention of different classes of people like smiths, washermen and potters raises the question regarding the existence of caste in the age of Narrinai of the Sangam age. Sometimes a facile view is advanced that the Tamils of old had no caste distinction and that caste was introduced only by the Aryans. This does not seem to be fully borne out by the known facts. No doubt we hear of Brahmins; but the other divisions are not so clear-cut as in the Aryan system. The Kshatriya is hardly mentioned; on the other hand, people called Maravar, Malavar and others formed the warriors. The duties assigned to the Vaisyas and Sudras, too, were discharged by several classes of people. What appears probable is that there emerged among the Tamils social divisions based upon their occupations which were determined largely by the region in which they lived. Gradually the Kuravar, Ayar, Vellalar, Maravar and Paradavar tended to become endogamous groups. Love and marriage seem to have normally occurred on the basis of these subdivisions. Subdivisions among them also began to appear, e.g. A distinction between Vettuvar and Kuravar had emerged.[117] Moreover, among the Kurinchi people the lower section was known as Kodiyar and Kodichchiyar (கொடியர் and கொடிச்சியர்) while the upper one was Kuravar and Kurattiyar (குறவர் and குறத்தியர்). Subsequently groups pursuing anxiliary occupations appear like the smiths and potters. Though there existed these groups in each of the tinais it was in Marudam that workers of different categories were found indispensable. Perhaps Marudam was the region where the growth of subcastes found a fertile field. While the indigenous divisions proceeded apace, the Aryan caste system in essentials might have mingled with the existing order. In actuality only the rise of the Brahmin caste was the immediate effect of this change. The other subdivisions of the Aryan caste system were later attempted to be yoked into the existing order. By the time of Tolkappiyar, the four-fold system had been recognized and grafted into the indigenous order.[118]

The picture of society we get from Narrinai is on the whole that of a simple business community of people attending to their traditional occupations and leading a simple life. The importance of whole-hearted devotion to work was understood and appreciated. Acquisition of wealth by man was considered essential not only as a pre-requisite of entering wedlock but also for ensuring a happy and prosperous life. There are many references in Narrinai to the lover parting with his sweet-heart for the sake of earning wealth.[119]

Acquisition of wealth did not mean the making of a vast fortune. Need for ensuring the sustenance of the family was the sole aim kept in view. There is little evidence of vulgar worship of mammon. In fact, a lofty conception of wealth and its identification with nobility of character were recognized by the people of this age.

"சான்றோர் செல்வம் என்பது சேர்ந்தோர்
புன்கண் அஞ்சும் பண்பின்
மென்கண் செல்வஞ் செல்வமென்பதுவே"

It was held that fame, happiness and charity are all dependent upon wealth.[120] However, frequently it happened that persons were so intensely attached to their sweet-hearts that they refused to set out to other places in quest of wealth, because they were unwilling to face the ordeal of separation.[121] One infatuated lover said that wealth was not superior to the enjoyment of the company of the girl of his heart.[122] On the other hand, there are several instances of the discerning girl compelling the lover to turn to his duty first and return after a successful acquisition of wealth.

CUSTOMS

Narrinai throws light on certain customs which the Tamils had developed in the Sangam age. Though some customs were specially characteristic of each Tinai, there were certain common ones as well. Hospitality has always been a noted virtue among the Tamils. Its merit was greatly praised by poets of the Sangam age.[123] For guests who turned up even at dead of night the home was expected to provide a hospitable welcome.[124]

The children of the home formed a source of happiness to the family. An errant husband tries to appease his angry wife through the agency of his children.[125] The children endearingly called the father Yendai.[126] The custom of naming the son after his grandfather had come into vogue. Children appear to have been looked after with care. They were trained to walk with the aid of small toys like chariots with three wheels.[127]

In respect of the decoration of the house certain standards of cleanliness prevailed. There were small houses and thatched cottages on the one hand, and big-sized mansions on the other. Even in small houses there was a distinct apartment for the storage of paddy in Marudam, (St. 26) and very probably in other regions as well. After delivery the woman observed pollution for a period, at the end of which, she took an oil bath. For the sake of purification fragrant powders were used. For burning household lamps oil of the laurel was used.[128] Oil extracted from fish was used for burning lamps in boats. There were physicians who treated illness. Pedestrians used to have umbrellas with them.[129] The practice of keeping corpses in pots is adverted to in Stanza 271.

RELIGION

Certain facts concerning the religious beliefs and practices of the early Tamils can be gleaned from Narrinai. There was a widespread belief in spirits.[130] Offerings of food and flowers as well as animal sacrifices were made to spirits.[131] Worship of the spirits was primarily actuated by fear of the evil that might be caused by them. Some spirits were believed to reside in trees,[132] and others in forests and hills. Several references are found in Narrinai to a spirit in the form of a damsel residing in the hill called Kollimalai. This damsel is stated to have been a paragon of beauty.[133] The legendary genesis of this image was that it had been set up by divine agency in order to entice and destroy the *asuras* and *rakshasas* who had been harassing the devotees and saints of the place.

The spirits were supposed to be wandering up and down at the dead of night.[134] Rice offered to the Gods at the Manram or the common place of the villages was believed to be eaten by the spirits.[135]

Apart from the belief in spirits the idea of a personal God[136] had already taken a foot-hold. Muruga appears to have been one of the earliest gods worshipped by the Tamils. Whenever a person was in trouble Muruga was appealed to for protection. How the belief in spirits became merged with the worship of Muruga is seen from the popular faith in 'Muruganangu' or 'becoming possessed by the Muruga'. The belief was that a person who was considered to have been possessed by Muruga became unwell physically and mentally, and that a special offering to the deity accompained by goat sacrifice alone could restore the affected person to the normal state.[137]

The people had such a veneration for Muruga that the parties touched the image of this deity while pledges were taken. Evidently that was considered an assurance of truthful adherence to the pledge.[138]

Muruga, the hill God, was probably worshipped at first in the Kurinchi region. Reference is found in Narrinai to Valli, the Kurava spouse of Muruga.[139] The tradition had gained ground that Muruga was a valiant warrior,[140] though no reference is found here to the accredited Puranic story of his triumph over Surapadma. Nor is there any mention of Siva in this classic. On the other hand, there is a reference to Mayon or Vishnu[141] and to his incarnation as Krsna. Baladeva, too, the elder brother of Krsna is found mentioned. These make it clear that the Aryan legends regarding Vishnu had become assimilated with the religious lore of this time. This is further confirmed by the reference occurring in this work to the divine damsels supposed to be residing in Heaven at the top of the Himalayas. The reference in Stanza 356 to the divine damsels supposed to be residing in Heaven at the top of the Himalayas confirms that the Aryan legendary background had taken deep root in Tamil Nad.

The abstract conception of Divinity, too, had begun to take shape. The idea of God as the Universe is found reflected in the ideas of the times as seen from St. 240. Penance for the purpose realizing god-head was known, and references occur in this anthology to devotees having become immersed in penance on hills.[142] However, it is undeniable that the underlying feature of the religious belief of the time was fear. Gods and spirits were supposed to cause evil when they were offended and periodic offerings were made to appease them.[143] Side by side with this, there had appeared faith in Fate and Karma.[144] Obviously this presupposed a belief in previous life and in the doctrine of transmigration of the soul. Stanza 397 speaks of a loving girl wondering whether she might forget her sweet lover in the next birth should she be born as some creature other than a human being. It is notable that Narrinai does not indicate that any distinctive Jain or Buddhist idea had entered the faith of the people in this age.

SUPERSTITIONS

Not infrequently religious faith merged into superstitious beliefs. The early Tamils had developed their own superstitions, many of which have survived to this day. The chirping of the lizard was considered as a forecast of forthcoming events. The arrival of the lover at the expected time was, for instance, believed to be learnt from the chirping of the lizard.[145] The singing of the cuckoo, too, was another indication of happy things to come.[146] The cry of the crow was believed to foretell the arrival of guests.[147] The consequences of the evil eye were dreaded.[148]

CONCLUSION

Narrinai thus yields certain valuable pieces of information regarding the political and social conditions of the Sangam age.

Unfortunately, the available data are not as full as one would wish. Nevertheless, it is possible to obtain a general picture of the life of the times. On the one hand, a study of the other classics from the historical standpoint may throw more light on the study of Narrinai, and on the other, the attempt at piecing together some of the details found in Narrinai may help the elucidation of similar or comparable data available in the rest of the classics.

ENDNOTES

1. Basham, A.L.: The Wonder that was India (1954),p. 463.
2. See, for example, Sami Chidambaranar; 'Ettuttogaiyum Tamilar Panpadum.' (1957),p. 65, and 'Narrinai Chorpolivugal,' (1942),p. 136
3. "நற்றிணை நல்ல குறுந்தொகை யைங்குறுநூ
   றெருத்த பதிற்றுப்பத் தோங்கு பரிபாடல்
   கற்றறிந்தா ரேத்துங் கலியே யகம் புறமென்
   றித்திறத்த வெட்டுத் தொகை" என்ப.
4. See the author's article on "The Brahmi Inscriptions of South India and the Sangam Age," Tamil Culture, Vol.V. No.2.
5. "நண்பாட்டுப் புலவனுய்ச் சங்கமேறி
   நற்கனகக்கிழி தருமிக்கருளி ஞேன் காண்"

   திருப்பத்தூர் திருத்தாண்டகம்.
   Tirupattur Tiruttandagam. 2. 11. 2.
6. Puram: 2; Aham: 168 and 233. It has been held by some scholars that Udiyam Cheral, the father of Imayavaramban, was different from Perumchorrutiyan since Padirruppattu does

not refer to the latter designation in respect of Udiyam Cheral. But stanzas 168 and 233 of Ahananuru show that the designation applies to the same king. See also 'Silappadikaram, Canto 23:55, and Ibid, Canto 29: Usalvari.

7. Cheran Chenguttuvan is stated to have undertaken a naval expedition against the Kadambas who had been indulging in piracy. In the course of his expedition Chenguttuvan captured the coastal town of Viyalur, which was near Mandai. (Silappadikaram. Canto XXVIIII.11.114–5). But as against this it must be remembered that Mandai had come under the Cheras as early as the time of Imayavaramban Neduncheralatan. (See Aham. 127).

8. Yanaichel probably meant a row of elephants, as may be inferred from the use of the term in Aham, 323.

9a. Narrinai–Stanza 18.

9b. Indian Antiquary, Vol. XXIX, p. 250. Note 2.

10. Kuruntogai, Stanza 258.

11. Sri P. Narayanaswami Aiyar has taken Periyan to stand for Titiyan of Teralundur. Though Titiyan's name is not mentioned in the poem, the reference to the fight over the laurel indicates that Periyan is identical with Titiyan.

12. Anni's conflict with Titiyan is found described in Ahananuru as well. In fact, the allusion to the struggle between the two chiefs would be unintelligible but for the details found in Ahananuru. That a dispute arose between the two, over a laurel tree by Titiyan (Aham St. 45) and that consequent on Anni's cutting down of the tree a fight ensued between the two is evident (Aham St. 126). Anni was killed in the struggle. But Sri Narayana Aiyar has misinterpreted two

other references in Ahananuru. Apparently stanzas 196 and 262 of Ahananuru refer to earlier incidents. Instead of Sri Aiyar's view that Titiyan had plucked out an eye of Anni and that Minili, Anni's son, in revenge killed Titiyan and his heirs, the proper interpretation seems to be that Anni's cows had trespassed into the cultivated fields of the Kosar, who avenged it by plucking Anni's eyes. Mortified by this Anni-Minili, the daughter of Anni adopted a life of renunciation and eventually had the Kosar killed through the aid of Titiyan of Teralundur.

13. Stanza 387. This king, famous for his military valour no less than for his learning and patronage of poets, encountered the combined forces of Yanaikkatchey Mantaram Cheral Irumporai. Cholan Rajasuyam Vetta Perunarkilli, Titiyan, Elini Erumayuran and Irungo Venman (Puram 72, 76, 77 and 79).

14. Numerous references to this chieftain of Podiyilmalai and his munificence are found in Purananuru and Chirupanarruppadai.

15. Ahananuru, 209, 11–17.

16. Kari was one of the seven paragons of charity of the later epoch. He used to present poets with gifts of chariots and was, therefore, called 'Tervanmalayan' (Narrinai 100). During his rule Aryas of the north are stated to have been repulsed by Kari when they attacked his territory. But jealous of his increasing might, Adiyaman Anji of Tagadur besieged and captured Kovalur. The vanquished Kari took refuge under Peruncheral Irumporai who helped him to attack and defeat Ori of Kollimalai. Kari faithfully passed on Ori's territories to the Chera kings. Later Kari induced Irumporai

to attack Tagadur of Anji. This was successfully undertaken by Irumporai, who defeating and killing Anji, passed on Kovalur to Kari.

17. Ahananuru. St. 352. When he was attacked by an enemy, he became frightened and was obliged to take shelter in a forest. He appears to have been called Anji on account of that circumstance. (Ahananuru 115).

18. Padirruppattu, 8th Decad.

19. Purananuru, 99.

20. Once he delayed giving gifts to the poetess Auvvai, who, thereupon became enraged. (Puram, 206). Learning this, he himself approached her and gave her an abundant supply of paddy, clothes and other requirements, upon which she sang in praise of Anji (*Ibid*, 390). When he captured Tirukkovalur, Paranar composed verses in his honour. (Aham, 372). In the battle at Kollikkurram where he fought aginst the combined forces of the Chola and Pandya, he was mortally wounded. (Puram 93).

21. The king was not expected to tax his subjects excessively. Stanza 226.

22. Whether Maran Valuti was identical with Ukkirapperu Valuti or Pannadu Tanda Maran Valuti, it is difficult to determine.

23. History of the Tamils (1929), p. 4.

24. e.g. Stanza 13 is appropriate to Marudam in terms of Uripporul but the Karupporul pertains to Kurinchi.

25. Tol. Ahattinai Iyal, 15. whether Tolkappiyam was or was not anterior to the Ettutogai is still a matter of controversy.

26. Tol. Poruladhikaram–St. 236. A sound mind is necessary for the lady's friend since she has the duty of dispelling the lady's distress.
27. Tol. Poruladhikaram, 96, 206.
28. Tol. Poruladhikaram, *Ibid*.
29. Kalaviyal Sutram, 143.
30. See for e.g. Stanzas 25 and 26.

    Note: St. 46 where the companion of a loving girl says that it would not be proper to abandon pleasure on hand for the sake of wealth which is fleeting.
31. When the girl was unwell, her mother prescribed as a remedy, the cool water from the hill which belonged to the lover of the girl. Stanza 53. That is a subtle indication that the mother knew all about the affair.
32. Stanza 4.
33. Stanza 297 shows how the mother vehemently protested against the association with her lover.
34. e.g. Sts. 34, 173, 244, 268, 274, 282, 288, 322, 373, and 376.
35. Stanzas 173, 258 and 288.
36. Stanza 34 is interesting for, while the mother suspects Anangu, the girl appeals to Muruga in order to clear the doubt.
37. Stanzas 36, 203, 227, 263, 271 and 272.
38. Stanzas 144 and 285.
39. Stanza 63.
40. Stanza 275.

41. e.g. Stanzas 342 and 377.
42. Stanza 152.
43. Stanza 146.
44. Stanza 220.
45. Stanza 45.
46. Stanza 266.
47. Stanza 300.
48. Stanza 22.
49. Stanza 206.
50. Stanza 207.
51. Stanza 93.
52. Nor do we find reference to it in the other Sangam works. But commentators of Tolkappiyam suggest that it had come into vogue at an early age.
53. Stanza 380.
54. Stanza 30.
55. Stanza 100.
56. Stanza 350; Stanzas 260, 340 and 360 also refer to the protests of the wife.
57. Stanza 300 and 320.
58. Stanza 320.
59. Stanza 266.
60. Stanza 289.
61. Stanza 42.
62. Stanza 290.

63. Stanza 43.
64. Stanza 120.
65. Stanza 213, 326 and 353.
66. Stanza 85.
67. Stanza 85, Mallar are known to have burnt snails and eaten them. See also Stanza 280.
68. Stanza 114.
69. Stanza 336.
70. Stanza 41.
71. Stanza 156, 295 and 303.
72. Stanza 239.
73. Stanza 388.
74. e.g. Stanzas 8, 123 and 349.
75. Stanza 60.
76. Stanza 64.
77. Stanzas 264 and 265.
78. Stanzas 96 and 198.
79. e.g. Stanzas 271, 284, 308, 316 and 370.
80. Stanza 321.
81. Stanza 168, 250 and 314.
82. Stanza 225.
83. Stanzas 23 and 239.
84. Stanza 56.
85. Stanza 12. The Chilambu or anklet was worn before the girl attained puberty. A ceremony celebrating the shedding of this ornament was held before she came of age. See Stanza 279.

86. Stanza 66.
87. Stanza 274.
88. Stanza 286.
89. Stanza 297.
90. Stanza 296.
91. Stanza 3.
92. Stanza 324.
93. Stanza 305.
94. Stanza 191
95. Stanzas 90 and 368.
96. Stanza 44.
97. Stanza 68.
98. *Ibid.*
99. Stanza 50.
100. Stanza 276.
101. Stanza 22.
102. Stanza 202.
103. Stanzas 209 and 311.
104. e.g. Stanza 4, 138 and 331.
105. Stanzas 183 and 254.
106. Stanza 352. See also Stanzas 164 and 362.
107. Stanza 258. In the hunt when they came across a whale there was jubilation.
108. Stanzas 175 and 215.
109. Stanza 353.

110. Stanza 353.
111. Stanza 84, (commentary).
112. Stanzas 84 and 12.
113. Stanza 12.
114. Stanza 12.
115. Stanzas 133, 153 and 363.
116. Stanza 200.
117. Stanza 276.
118. Tol. Porul. Stanza 142.
119. e.g. St. 41, 229.
120. Stanza 214.
121. Stanzas 3, 16.
122. Stanza 52.
123. Stanza 120.
124. Stanza 142.
125. Stanza 138.
126. Stanza 221.
127. Stanza 250.
128. Stanza 278.
129. Stanza 374.
130. Stanzas 255 and 398.
131. Stanza 251 and 358.
132. Stanza 343.
133. Stanzas 192 and 201.
134. Stanzas 192, 301 and 319.

135. Stanza 73.
136. Stanza 9.
137. Stanza 251.
138. Stanza 386.
139. Stanza 82.
140. Stanza 34.
141. Stanza 32.
142. Stanzas 141 and 226.
143. Stanza 189.
144. Stanza 185. See Stanzas 88 and 107. It was believed that a person's wealth and ability in this life depended on the beneficence that he had done in his previous life. (Stanza 210.)
145. Stanzas 98, 169 and 333.
146. Stanza 246.
147. Stanza 367.
148. Stanza 155.

4

INSCRIPTIONS OF TAMIL NADU AND THEIR HISTORICAL VALUE

Epigraphy forms the most authentic source of the early and medieval histories of Tamil Nadu. The epigraphic wealth of Tamil Nadu is remarkable; it has been reckoned that Tamil Nadu has well over 40,000 inscriptions, numerically the largest in any State in the whole of India. But many thousands have yet to be copied and published. It is notable that Tamil inscriptions, partially or wholly in Tamil, are found in the neighbouring regions of Malayalam, Telugu and Kannada speaking areas and a few even in Sri Lanka and Malaysia with which Tamil kings had contacts in the past.

The earliest inscriptions are those called the 'Tamil-Brahmi' inscriptions, generally found on the rock-cut beds of natural caverns or on mud pots. They are short, containing barely three or four lines. The total number of these Tamil-Brahmi inscriptions so far discovered is about eighty. The number is likely to increase. Recently Dr. K.V. Raman has discovered an old Brahmi inscription at Arittappatti near Madurai. Most of them were associated with

Jain devotees. They have been found in villages such as Anamalai, Alagarmalai, Mettuppatti, Tiruvadavur, Sittannavasal and Kunrakkudi in the present Madurai and Tirunelveli Districts. They have been reckoned to belong to the 2nd and 1st centuries BC. It is said that a Tamil-Brahmi inscription of about the 1st century BC refers to certain musical instruments. In all probability this is the earliest epigraph in the Tamil country, pertaining to Music. It is interesting to find in some of these inscriptions certain names figuring in the Sangam classics. For example, we find Kadalan Valudi[1], Neduncheliyan and Kadunko[2]. These names are probably those occurring in early Pandyan and Chera history.

Similar to the Tamil-Brahmi inscriptions we find the earlier Asokan Brahmi inscriptions. Professors Haimendorf and Sankalia think the Asokan edicts at Maski, Brahmagiri and Kapbal, for instance, were addressed only to people who could read and write the Asokan-Brahmi. Their language, however, as found in the Tamil country is Tamil. In fact, the difference between Asokan-Brahmi and Tamil-Brahmi inscriptions of the Tamil country is that certain peculiar Tamil letters appear in the latter. These distinctive letters are la (ழ), la (ள), ra (ற) and na (ன).

It is notable that the Tamil-Brahmi script was identical with what is known as the Dravidi script. Evidently the northerners employed this term. A Jaina manuscript, assignable to the 1st century BC, calls it 'Damili.' This Tamil-Brahmi or 'Dravidi' or 'Damili' script is the pattern found in Arikamedu during the 1st and 2nd centuries AD. It is from the Dravidi or Tamil-Brahmi script that there emerged the *Vatteluttu* script about the 3rd century AD; it assumed its full form in the 5th century AD. The Vatteluttu script continued to be in vogue in the Pandyan kingdom down to the 13th century AD and in rare cases even till the 18th century AD.

The Tamil script proper also emerged from the Dravidi or Damili script the 5th century AD, and developing very gradually, assumed its present form only in the 17th century AD.

While considering the question of the evolution of the Tamil script and particularly the early Tamil-Brahmi script it is not irrelevant to speak of its connection, if any, with the pictographic script of the Indus Valley civilization, which continues to be a riddle. Recently, apart from the Finnish and Russian experts Iravadam Mahadevan has devoted much attention to the study of the script of the early Tamil inscriptions. In his "Corpus of Tamil-Brahmi Inscriptions" he examines the palaeography of the Tamil-Brahmi script, its origin and its orthography. He goes on to deal with the grammar of Tamil-Brahmi, phonology, morphology and lexical analysis. The determination of the historical data contained in these Tamil-Brahmi inscriptions is attempted by him. But by far the most fundamental question to which he addressed himself is the connection of the Tamil-Brahmi script with the pictographic Harappan script. He concludes that the former is derived from the Harappan script. Bold and striking as his view is, it still remains to be conclusively proved. In fact the real identification of the Indus script and its relation with a known language can be determined only if we get a bilingual inscription in the Indus script and another script which has been already identified.

Hero-Stones: (Nadukal)

Subsequent to the Tamil-Brahmi inscriptions in the caverns and pottery, there appeared inscriptions engraved on hero-stones. Tolkappiyam speaks of

"காட்சி கால் கோள் நீர்ப்படை நடுகல்" (புறத். 5)

that the hero-stones often contained the name of the hero is seen from a reference in Purananuru:

"அணி மயிற் பீலிசூட்டிப் பெயர் பொறித்து இனி
நட்டனரே கல்லும்." (Puram. 60)

Generally on the hero-stones, either at the top or bottom, details like the name of the hero, the name of the king of the place, his regnal year, when and how the hero met with his death were engraved. Tolkappiyam speaks of six stages in the ritual ceremonies associated with the erection of hero-stones. They were (1) Katchi (காட்சி) i.e. discovery, (2) Kal Kol (கால் கோள்) i.e. invitation, (3) Nirpatai (நீர்ப் படை) i.e. bathing of the stone, (4) Nadutal (நடுதல்) i.e. erection, (5) Perumpadai (பெரும் படை) offering of food and (6) Valttu (வாழ்த்து) blessing. Obviously, considerable importance was attached to the ceremonies of ancestor worship associated with the erection of hero-stones which incidentally throw some light on the social and political history of the early times. In this context mention may be made of the book on the Chengam hero-stones in North Arcot, published by Dr. Nagaswamy. The hero-stones of Chengam are datable from the 5th century AD to 16th century AD. Though he has also referred to some other hero-stones of Tamilaham and Kerala, doubtless there are many others still to be discovered and deciphered. Mailai Seeni Venkataswamy rightly thinks that all the hero-stones belonging to the Sangam age have not been unearthed.[3]

However, the hero-stones of Chengam themselves raise certain intricate problems of chronology. Most of the Chengam hero-stones belong to the age of the Great Pallavas, specifically to the time of the Pallava kings, Simhavishnu, Mahendravarman I, Narasimhavarman I, Nandivarman II and Kampavarman. Excepting those of the time of Kampavarman, the others are all in Vatteluttu script. Startling facts are found in these inscriptions. For instance, Simhavishnu is found to have reigned for more than thirty years while Mahendravarman I ruled for no less than sixty years. Is there some mistake somewhere? Are the earlier sources unreliable? It is not too easy to give a definite answer. It needs further scrutiny and examination. However, the age of the Great Pallavas witnessed the appearance of several long epigraphs in stone and metal. The copper plates are more important and descriptive than the stone inscriptions. The Pallavas were great patrons of learning and they bestowed liberal grants to learned Brahmins as well as to Jaina savants. The court language of the Great Pallavas was Sanskrit. Till the 4th century AD the Pallava inscriptions were in Prakrit and thereafter they were in Sanskrit. From the 7th century they were bilingual, partly in Sanskrit and partly in Tamil in Grantha script. This practice of adopting bilingualism in epigraphy continued for several centuries. The Sanskrit portion contained general exhortations, blessings, names and the achievements of the donors, while the Tamil portion invariably dealt with the boundaries and other details of the lands and other properties gifted. As examples the Pallankovil copper plates and the Kuram Plates may be mentioned. One of the copper plates recently discovered near Velanjeri near Tiruttani is dated in the 9th regnal year of the reign of Pallava Aparajita of the 9th century AD. The Tamil portion states that Aparajita ordered 1000 Kadi of paddy to be provided for offerings to God Subrahmanya enshrined on the top of the Tiruttani hill. It shows incidentally that the famous Tiruttani temple was not constructed by Krishnadeva Raya but only renovated by him.

It may be noted that the Unnaguruvayampalayam plates and the Udayendiram Ceppedugal I were completely in Sanskrit. There was no Tamil portion in them.

The Takua-pa (Siam), or modern Thailand, fragmentary inscription in Tamil is in the 9th century characters. It shows that the Pallava kingdom during the period of Nandivarman III's reign had active commercial relationship with the South East Asian countries. It records the construction of a tank called Sri Avaninaranam by the chief of Nangur and the placing of it under the protection of manikkiramattar.

THE INSCRIPTIONS OF THE PANDYAS

Apart from the legends and the Sangam classics which deal with the early Pandyas, there are several valuable epigraphs of the post-Sangam age. These are the important plates like the Velvikkudi grant of Parantaka Nedunjadayan, the smaller Sinnamanur Plates, the larger Sinnamanur Plates of Rajasimha and the Madras Museum Plates of Jatilavarman. Besides, there are numerous stone inscriptions of this period which are of supreme value in fixing the chronology of certain Pandyan kings. The Anamalai stone inscription of Parantaka is dated in the year 3871 of the Kaliyuga era and calculated on the basis of that it is clear that the inscription of Varaguna is dated in Saka 792, which corresponds to AD 870 and since the inscription is stated to have belonged to the eighth regnal year of the king, the date of the commencement of his reign is determinable. In spite of several doubts and posers about the so-called First Pandyan Empire, the data indicated above are of decisive help to the student of Pandyan history.

In determining the dates, the eras mentioned in inscriptions are of crucial value. In respect of Pandyan history the Kaliyuga era and the Saka era are the most important. The Kaliyuga era is taken to have appeared in 3102 BC, when the

Mahabharata war is said to have commenced. The Saka era corresponds to AD 78 and it is believed by some to have been founded by a Saka king who occupied Ujjaini 137 years after Vikramaditya. Others think that Kanishka was the founder of this era while still others hold that Vema Kadphises was the author of the era. Of these various views suggested it is likely that the theory that Kanishka was the founder of the era is the correct one because of his military prowess and religious eminence. The Saka era was known in South India as the Salivahana Sakabda.

There are several other eras which appear in Indian history like the Vikrama era, the Gupta era, the Saptarshi era and so on. But in respect of South India the Kollam era which commenced in 824–25 AD is important. The absence of a common era in respect of ancient Indian history is a serious obstacle to the reconstruction of the early history of the country.

A peculiar feature of the early Pandyan inscriptions is that they speak of the regnal years of the monarchs in double dates, X years opposite Y years. The exact meaning of this is not clear. Various epigraphists like Burgess, Hultzch, T.A. Gopinatha Rao and Venkayya have furnished different explanations, none of which is convincing. In actuality the procedure adopted is to add up the two figures and reckon the actual year as equivalent to X + Y years.

But though no convincing explanation has been offered so far, this appears to be correct as is inferred from the instance provided by the Larger Sinnamanur Plates where the regnal year 'இரண்டாவதின் எதிர் பதிஞன்காவது' is rendered in the Sanskrit part of the grant as 'Sodase Rajyavarse.'

Again, some inscriptions give the regnal year and the number of days since the commencement of the current regnal year. The lack of uniformity in this matter causes difficulties. Further, the astronomical data provided by some inscriptions create posers because they yield strange and divergent dates. As Prof. K.A. Nilakanta Sastri has pointed out, Inscription No. 422 of 1917 is referred to as belonging to AD 1357 on page 112 and to AD 1445 on page 113 of A.R.E. 1917–8. Again, on page 89 A.R.E., 1923–4, we find Nos. 327 and 334 of 1923 with calculated dates as AD 1278 and AD 1417 respectively ascribed to the same king. In all probability the data furnished in respect of the same king might have caused the variation. It has been claimed very recently by N. Sethuraman in his book on "The Cholas-Mathematics reconstructs the Cholas" that astronomical data can never go wrong. This is perhaps too optimistic a view. How then do we explain the discrepancies in the calculations of Dr. E. Hultzch, J.F. Fleet, L.D. Swamikkannu Pillai and others? Moreover, the calculations of some chronologists are not accepted by historians and linguistic chauvinists. For instance, the conclusions of L.D. Swamikkannu Pillai in respect of Paripadal and Silappadikaram had been questioned by several writers some of whom held that the calculations have been made on inadequate data. True, he had to depend more on Adiyarkkunallar's commentary of Silappadikaram. But in recent years some scholars like Prof. K.A. Nilakanta Sastri who had questioned the 8th century date assigned by Swamikkannu Pillai, have reverted to the chronologist's date. Paripadal, too, is now considered like Kalittogai and Tirumurugarruppadai a later work among the Sangam classics. In this context it is significant to remember that the Sangam Tamils themselves had astronomical knowledge as is evident from the Purananuru and Paripadal. They designated the stars and the planets as Kol.

In respect of Chola chronology though Sethuraman himself is unable to solve certain riddles, his approach is commendable, and he can turn his attention to the history of the Pandyas where the problems to be tackled are more acute.

At the outset, besides stone inscriptions four Copper Plate records of the early Pandyas had been discovered. These are the Copper Plates of Velvikkudi, Srivaramangalam and Sinnamanur (two sets). Now, apart from these four records which throw light on the history of the First Pandyan Empire, ranging from about the 7th to the 10th century AD, two more were newly discovered in 1958. These two are the Dalavaipuram and Sivakasi Plates. These throw fresh light on this period of Pandyan history. Let us consider the details furnished by them.

THE DALAVAIPURAM PLATES OF VIRANARAYANA

They were discovered near the Dalavaipuram village in the Tirunelveli District. Parantaka Viranarayana was the donor of this grant; he was the grandson of Parantaka Nedunjadayan (accn. AD 768), the donor of the Velvikkudi grant. Varaguna Pandya, the brother of Viranarayana who ascended the throne about AD 862, was of a religious disposition and from the present inscription it is learnt that Viranarayana was ruling jointly with his brother for at least 45 years (Prof. Sastri had assigned him only 20 years) and that he gave the gift while camping at Karavandapuram. Maran, apparently identical with Sri Mara Srivallabha, was the father of Varaguna and Parantaka Viranarayana.

In this Copper Plate, however, Viranarayana is said to have defeated his elder brother at Sennilam. It is not known whether this brother was Varaguna, or some other person about whom we do not know anything else, because as far as our knowledge goes, the relationship between Varaguna and Viranarayana was cordial.

Viranarayana acquired Vilinam, conquered the territory of the Kongu to Tenur, captured Vira Tungan and established numerous Brahmadeyas and Devasthanas. In his 45th regnal year while he was camping in the villge of Kalakkudi, a Brahmin (Sri Narayana Kesavan) represented to him that Kadungon who had vanquished the Kalappalar (note the word (களப்பாழரை) in the inscription gifted the villages Tirumangalam and Somajikkurichchi to twelve pious brahmins. Now Sri Narayana Kesavan requested the king to combine the two villages and restore them to him who was entitled to enjoy the two villages.

The Sanskrit portion of the Plates, consisting of 39 verses describe the Prasasti of the donor and his ancestors. Parantaka Viranarayana's mother was Akkalanimmadi of the Pottappi family. He defeated his elder brother at Sennilandai. Was he Varaguna, and if so, was Varaguna born of a different mother?

However, three facts are notable; one is that the duration of the rule given to Viranarayana by the Dalavaipuram Plates is different from that provided by the Larger Sinnamanur Plates; the second is that the practice of incorporating Prasastis in inscriptions had appeared prior to the time of Raja Raja I the Chola, who was believed by early historians to have initiated the practice, and thirdly certain details about the Padyan genealogy and the Kalabhras which were doubted by some scholars are clearly settled.

The Dalavaipuram Plates which Dr. B.G.L. Swamy dismisses as containing routine details, bring out the important facts regarding the Pandyan genealogy and the attack of Tamil Nadu by the Kalabhras, give the lie direct to his contentions. He holds the following ideas:

1. The first is regarding Palyagasalai mudu kudumi Peruvaludi. Dr. Swamy says: "Scholars who attempted to reconstruct the genealogies of the presumed kings of the 'Cankam age' could not accommodate Mudukudmi". Does he discard the colophons to the Puram Verses 7, 9, 12, 15 and 64 of Purananuru? If Kanakasabhai and Pandarathar left him out of Pandyan genealogy that is no reason why Dr. Swamy should follow them. If Sivaraja Pillai thought that 'yaga' could not have been performed so early, reference can be made to verses 122, 166, 224, 361, 397 and 400 to disprove his contention. Any inconvenient fact cannot be dismissed as an interpolation. Prof. K.A.N. Sastri first excluded him and then later said that he was a "more life-like figure than Nediyon." All these run counter to Dr. Swami's stand. His contention that Palyagasalai was only Ter Maran or Rajasimha is not convincing. Ter can be taken in the usual sense. Ter is used also in the sense of 'learned' in the Dalavaipuram Plates.

2. 'Alavariya adhirajas' has been translated by Krishna Sastri as 'driving away numberless great kings.' The exaggeration, if any is pardonable. We have many instances of such exaggerations in inscriptions.

3. Nor can 'Kali Arasan' mean anything but cruel or wicked. As Dr. Swamy himself admits, Srinivasa Aiyangar and several other writers understood the words

in this sense. One cannot discard the meaning just to suit one's own preconceived notions.

4. Dr. Swamy contends that the Kalabhras do not figure in the history of Tamil Nadu. He ignores the reference to 'Kalabhra' in the Velvikkudi Plates and to 'Kalappalar' in the Dalavaipuram Plates. The coins discovered by Ramayya containing the word Kalabhra are thrown into the sea by Dr. Swamy, perhaps because some of them were obtained from a fisherman at Kaverippumpattinam. It is incomprehensible that the name Kalabhra and what is worse 'Kalabhra interregnum' are anathema to him. The obvious reason is that scholars. Tamilologists in particular, associate the decline of the Sangam and the advent of a dark age with the Kalabhras. But the grounds for his contention are not sound. Incidentally it must be urged that the 'Changam' was not held in the Presidency College, or University buildings or in a Seminar Hall. It was often in the court of a cultured king or chieftain or in the company of some learned persons or at times in solitude or in the company of a lover that many of their outpourings emanated.[4] Therefore, the existence of a 'Chankam' or its collapse need not at all depend on the historicity of the Kalabhras. It is also worthwhile remembering that some of the 'Changam Maruviya Nulkal' including several of the Padinenkilkanakku poems appeared in the so-called dark age.

5. However, his aversion to the Sangam led him on, I presume, to lionize the Western Gangas and dismantle the Kalabhras. The burden of his song is that Palyagasalai Mudukudumi Peruvaludi was none other

than Ter Maran or Rajasimha I, that the duration of the so-called Kalabhra rule was confined to about two years and that even this foreign rule was that of the Western Gangas. It must be remembered that while the Kalabhras are mentioned in both the Plates as invaders, the Gangas figure in the Velvikkudi Plates only in two contexts, once as the Anatti of the restoration of Velvikkudi to its heir as Marangari, the gem of the Vaidyaka family and secondly when the daughter of the Ganga king was given in marriage to the Kongu king in which context he defeated a Pallava and other kings. There is no reference to the Western Ganga king having established his rule in Madurai or the Pandyan kingdom. Kongarkon is not a Pandya king; it is used to denote the king of Kongunadu; it is also a term denoting the Cheras.

6. The basic weakness of the contention of Dr. Swamy (and Prof. K.A.N. Sastri) is that they state that Narkorran should have lived through all these generations from Mudukudumi to Nedunjadayan. Here it must be noted that the first was Narkorran (line 35 misprinted as line 31) and the second who prayed for the return of the piece of land was Narchingan (really line 117 and not 103). This cuts the ground from underneath the feet of these scholars.

In fact what I feel is that the time is gone by when chauvinism and regionalism as well as pseudo-scientific attitude vitiated the entire approach. The field of research is neither a Sultanate nor a Tzardom; it is a republic—not under any under any emergency—where the humblest labourer has a right to be heard and even opposed if necessary.

THE SIVAKASI PLATES OF VIRA PANDYA

These form the second set of Plates unearthed recently. The father of Vira Pandya, the donor of the Sivakasi Plates, was Manabharana, while Vira Pandya's brother was Sundra Pandya. From certain Chola inscriptions it is seen that all these three Pandyas (living at the same time) were defeated by Rajadhirajan. Therefore, Prof. K.A. Nilakanta Sastri held that these Plates were issued by Vira Pandya early in the 11th century.

But T.N. Subramanian who had made a more intensive study of the Tamil inscriptions than the professional archaeologists, held that this Vira Pandya belonged to the 10th century AD (accn. AD 946) and that contemporaneous with him there was Manabharanan and Sundara Pandya. This Vira Pandya was identified by him with 'Cholan Talai Konda Vira Pandyan.' But there was more than one 'Cholan talaikonda Vira Pandya.' Moreover, Subramanian's primary basis for his view is palaeography, which cannot obviously be a conclusive source of deduction, particularly in differentiating epigraphs of two succeeding centuries. While Prof. Sastri's view seems to be acceptable, it is surprising that he does not make the position clear in his Colas (1975) on page 222 where he merely states: "One version of Rajadhiraja's prasasti mentions as an introduction to the war with the three Pandyas mentions a conflict with and subjugation of a certain Vikramanarayana." One wishes that the identification of the three Pandyas was clearly made. However, his reference to the three Pandyan opponents and Rajadhiraja in his Pandyan Kingdom (1929) on page 122 is more specific and clears the doubt on the accuracy of the concerned Chola inscription.

Dr. Swamy complains about Prof. Sastri's frequent changes of his interpretations. There is no harm in this if it is inevitable and if it is clearly indicated.

THE KUDUMIYAMALAI INSCRIPTION

One of the famous inscriptions of early South India is the musical inscription of Kudumiyamalai in the old Pudukkottai State. Excepting the music inscription at Tirumayam, a little south of Pudukkottai town, the celebrated Kudumiyamalai inscription is the unique one of its kind in the whole of India. It has been generally assigned to Mahendravarman I. Latterly some scholars have suggested that since Kudumiyamalai and Tirumayam were far away from Mahendravarman's capital and that they were near the Pandyan kingdom, these inscriptions must have appeared under the patronage of the Pandyan kings, and that they must have belonged to a date few centuries later than Mahendravarman's time. But the characters of the Kudumiyamalai and Tirumayam inscriptions are similar to the Pallava script of the 7th century AD. As Dr. Minakshi has pointed out years ago, the formation of the letters is comparable to that of Mahendra's inscriptions at Tiruchchirappalli and South Arcot. Moreover, one of the birudas of Mahendravarman I was 'Sankirna Jati' which means according to Prof. Sambamurti that the king was an expert in the exposition of Sankirna ragas or mixed ragas. Apparently he was very proficient in music.

The Kudumiyamalai inscription is in Sanskrit; but it is interesting to note that just below the colophon, an important note in Tamil characters is found. This was supposed to read as "Ettirkkum Yelirkum ivai uriyavai." It means that the musical notes indicated in the inscriptions are intended for the eight and seven. A label inscribed on the top of the northern side as "*Parvadini*" has been identified as "Parvadini" which meant the *Vina*. The Tamil note in the colophon is therefore taken to mean that the musical notes found in the inscription can be played on the seven stringed and eight-stringed vina. This appears to be the acceptable view. K.R. Srinivasan takes it as "பாட்டிற்கும் யாழ்ற்கும் இவை உரியவை". But obviously the former interpretation is meaningful and correct, particularly in view of the word "Parvadini" found on the northern side of the rock.

A part of the musical inscription at Tirumayam was erased by a later Pandyan king for recording a gift of his to a temple.

CHOLA INSCRIPTIONS

If the epoch of the Imperial Cholas (850–1200) was the golden age of Tamil culture particularly of Tamil literature, it was equally famous in the sphere of Tamil epigraphy. The Chola inscriptions discovered so far are nearly 9000 in number. But the inscriptions useful for the study of the administration of the Chola kingdom are unfortunately below 10% of the total number.

In respect of chronology, apart from the later Chola inscriptions, the accession of Parantaka I is reckoned by counting the number of days that had elapsed since the commencement of the Kaliyuga on the basis of the details found in an epigraph. This datum provides a dependable chronological foothold on the basis of which Kielhorn fixed the date of Parantaka's accession between 15th January and 25th July 907. This constitutes the sheet anchor of Chola chronology of this period.

Recently the State Department of Archaeology has brought to light a copper plate which is the earliest copper plate charter of the Chola dynasty so far known. The plate gives some interesting details about the genealogy of the Cholas. The Plate states that Vijayalaya was the grandson of one Kochchenganan and son of Otriyuran. We do not have confirmation of these facts. It is not possible to have confirmation of these facts. It is not possible to determine whether this Kochchenganan is identical with the ruler of the same name figuring in the Sangam age. Perhaps he was a different ruler.

The Chola Prasastis provide in a grandiloquent manner the achievements of the donor and of his predecessors. They were worded in an ornate and poetic style, often containing gross exaggerations. In fact some of the Meykkirtigal seem to sound like Poykkirtigal. At time the prasastis of some kings were confused with those of others. Nevertheless, several of them are of value in determining the chronology and history of the reigns of the Chola monarchs.

Inscriptions have been found mostly on stone and some on copper plates and other materials. Writings on stone were on rocks, pillars, slabs, pedestals or on the back of images, rims and lids of vases, caskets etc., the walls of temples, the pavement of pillars of colonnades, caves etc. As mentioned earlier, South India is much richer in its epigraphy than North India. Within South India itself Tamil Nadu has the highest record.

Among metals, copper was commonly employed for engraving inscriptions. They were called Cheppedugal in Tamil, Tamrapata, Tamrasasana, Sasanapatra etc., in Sanskrit. The use of copper for writing purposes was not very common up to the 6th century AD and it became popular in the succeeding six or seven centuries. Copper plates were apt to be fabricated in order to establish false titles to property or other claims.

Inscriptions on brass, bronze, silver and gold vessels or images are found; but they are rare.

The contents of the inscriptions in Tamil Nadu, whether they are of the Pallavas, Pandyas, Cholas or feudatory dynasties like the Muttaraiyar or of individuals like Kopperunjinga can be grouped under the following heads, namely, dedicatory, donative, commemorative, administrative, religious and didactic, and occasionally commercial.

By far the largest number of inscriptions were donatory and commemorative. Gifts made to temples, mathas, particular deities, groups of brahmins and individuals figured prominently. The victories of kings were recorded in several inscriptions. Some recorded sales, mortgages and other forms of transfers of property. Further, decisions of disputes between different classes of people or political agreements between different feudatories or chieftains were also engraved. A remarkably valuable inscription is found in Tiruvidaivayil in Tanjavur District which preserves a Devaram of Tirujnana Sambandar, not known otherwise.

Nagaswamy has shown how some inscriptions of the Chola period throw light on the protests of the people on the levy of heavy taxes. For example, Parantaka I imposed a tax of 3000 kalanju in AD 945, when he was involved in a war with the Pandyan kingdom; in AD 1065 Virarajendra leived a surcharge of one Kalanju when he fought with the Vengi kingdom; and even Raja Raja I levied an additional tax of 100 Kasus for the embellishment of the Talaichengadu temple. Protests made by the people were disregarded by him. Raja Raja I ordered the confiscation of lands of those who refused to pay the additional tax. The Tiruvidaimarudur inscription of AD 1000 states that they were made to lie in water or stand in the blazing sun for several hours; their lands also were confiscated. That even articles belonging to them were destroyed is seen from the 13th century inscription at Namakkal. Consequently no-tax campaigns and crude patterns of non-cooperation with the Government were adopted by the people. At times the Government had to reduce the heavy levies. These and similar inscriptions of the Cholas are of immense interest to the student of social history.

Historically accurate inscriptions are not many. One inscription at Tiruvendipuram is an exception. It describes accurately the troubles and difficulties encountered by Raja Raja II and the help he received from his Hoysala contemporary. This is almost an exceptionally authentic and unvarnished record.

Actually in the utilisation of the inscriptions great care has to be bestowed. False claims of victories are sometimes recorded. Some inscriptions contain accounts of legendary kings as found in the Kanyakumari stone inscription. Determination of chronology is a formidable problem. Though several epigraphists like Kielhorn, Fleet, Burgess and Venkayya have worked on the inscriptions, certain wrong calculations have appeared. As Sethuraman points out in his recent book 'The Cholas' the accession date of Rajendra I has been definitely fixed only now as 19th June, while divergent dates were given earlier. Again, it is now settled on the basis of astronomical data that Rajadhiraja I ascended the throne on 8th June AD 1018. Earlier, Kielhorn could only arrive at an approximate date, viz. 23rd May AD 1018. Another instance is that of the date of accession of Vikrama Chola. This was surmised as 29th June 1118 but now Sethuraman has revised it as 13th July AD 1118. Whether the new calculations are all correct remain to be settled.

Certain earlier conclusions regarding the identification of monarchs have now to be revised. Prof. K.A. Nilakanta Sastri has stated on p. 292 of his 'Colas' (1975) thus: "After the death of Virarajendra, Kulottunga marched into the Chola country in good time to get himself accepted as king." But this hypothesis seems to be impossible as shown by Sethuraman, in view of the position of Adhi Rajendra and his inscriptions.

Then the titles Rajakesari and his Parakesari, used alternatively by the Chola kings sometimes cause confusion. For example, Rajamahendra was a Rajakesari who ruled from 1059 to 1063. His younger brother who succeeded him must have been a Parakesari. But really he is known as Rajakesari.

Perhaps the most serious difficulty arises from spurious inscriptions which have appeared. Several fake documents have been unearthed. The inscriptions of Tiruppattur, Kalayarkoil, Iraniyur, Perichchikkovil and Ilayankudi are some of them. These inscriptions have to be carefully studied. Sethuraman shows how some spurious inscriptions were discovered and the persons responsible for them were punished. For example, Inscriptions No. 126 and 127 of 1908 of Tiruppattur, all dated AD 1387, are very remarkable in this respect. An accountant of the village wanted to inherit certain rights for which he was not entitled. He conspired with a goldsmith and an engraver. The engraver engraved a false document on the stone wall of the temple as if the privileges and rights were given by the village assembly to the accountant. Somehow the matter leaked out. The village accountant disappeared. The goldsmith and the engraver were caught and were entrusted with the Kammalar who killed them for intentional forgery and fraud.

Another example is found in an apparently forged copper plate in which certain people known as Yogi paradesis of Akkarai, the adjoining village of Sucindram, put forward claims to certain privileges in the temple at Sucindram.[6]

Perichchikkovil and Iraniyur contain fake records. Prof. K.A.N. Sastri had originally suspected the authenticity of these two records and had stated so in his 'Pandyan kingdom'. But in his 'Colas' he has given a different conclusion. In fact Sethuraman after visiting the two places says that they are fake and spurious.

Again, it must be remembered even in respect of bonafide inscriptions, that all that is found engraved on stone cannot be taken as gospel truth. It must be remembered that the actual wording of the inscriptions might not have been completely framed by the donors themselves.

The details of the inscription were, more often than not, left to the ingenuity of the silpi who executed the engraving. Naturally, the conventional style of framing the epigraphs would have determined in a large measure their form and even their details. This feature accounts for certain otherwise inexplicable anachronisms and incongruous statements appearing in several inscriptions.

Moreover, errors in the actual engraving are occasionally responsible for creating difficulties to the student of history. Slovenliness or inefficiency on the part of the silpi might have been responsible for some mistakes. Several words occurring in the inscriptions of Sucindram, for instance, have not been made out.[7]

Some of the inscriptions have been partly or wholly erased. A few have been damaged. In respect of some new constructions have been erected over places where inscriptions had been engraved. Dr. Hultzch deplored how the renovation of the Ekambaranathar temple at Kanchipuram would destroy certain inscriptions. Actually the apprehended destruction did take place. He wrote with feeling: "What the Mussalmans did not destroy is being demolished by pious Hindus!"

Besides, some of the inscriptions about which we hear from other inscriptions are not now traceable. Some of these inscriptions are those of Tirumanaikkaval, Jambukesvaram, Tiruvidaimarudur, Nidur, Tirukkaravasal, Mayuram, Sivapuram, Alangudi and other places have not been discovered.

It is a lamentable feature that even the available epigraphic matter has not been appropriately used. For instance, Prof. Sastri's monumental book on the Cholas was first written on the basis of the findings discovered up to 1953. The book was re-edited in 1955 and reprinted in 1975. But the epigraphic findings secured between 1935 and 1975 were not made use of in the later publications. Thus the available inscriptions must be traced and copied, remembering that some of the temples are not in good preservation and some are in ruins. Those epigraphs which are traced must be published and in their turn they must be promptly and appropriately utilized. Then alone the history of Tamil Nadu will be properly re-written. In this study some of the prominent inscriptions alone are indicated.

Finally there is a supreme need for coordination between various institutions and individuals working in this field. There must be cooperation between the Archaeological Survey,

Epigraphic Society, State Departments of Archaeology, Universities, learned private bodies interested in History and Archaeology and also the Trustees of Temples. Then alone inscriptions can be discovered, copied, interpreted and edited and utilized for the reconstruction of history.

ENDNOTES

1. 'Valudi' is a Pandyan title as may be seen, for example in Ahananuru: 93 : 3, 130 : 11, 204 : 2, Narrinai : 150 : 4, 358 : 10; Kuruntogai : 345.
2. Kadungo perhaps, as Thiru Arunachalam thinks, refers to Palaipadiya Perunkadungo of the Chera family. He was a poet and prince.
3. Araichchi-Vol. I, No. 2, p. 190. See also the paper on Hero stones and Folk Beliefs by M. Vanamamalai (Journal of Tamil Studies, December 1972, pp. 38–43).
4. To the best of our knowledge, the word 'Sangam' occurs in Appar's Devaram (Tiruppattur Tiruttandaham. 3). But even earlier, in Kalittogai Verses 35 and 68 references are found to the assemblage of talented poets.
5. This account is found in Sethuraman's book on Cholas, p. 166 quoted from South Indian Temple Inscription, vol. III, Pt. II, p. 221.
6. See the author's Sucindram Temple, pp. 201–2.
7. *Ibid*, p. 447.

5

THE BRAHMI INSCRIPTIONS OF SOUTH INDIA AND THE SANGAM AGE

The Brahmi inscriptions which were discovered in the Madurai and Tirunelveli districts early in the century[1] have continued to baffle students of Indian history. Mean while, in 1945, the excavations at Arikamedu have revealed, amidst other interesting material, twenty pot-shreds bearing graffiti which present short inscriptions. In respect of script and language the graffiti show a marked resemblance to the fifty epigraphs of the Madurai and Tirunelveli districts mentioned above.[2] Several attempts have been made to determine the script and language as well as the contents and significance of these inscriptions.

It is indisputable that the characters employed in all those epigraphs are Brahmi, paleographically assigned to about the 3rd century BC. The script resembles in a large measure that of the Bhattiprolu casket inscriptions, the celebrated Asokan epigraphs and the early inscriptions of Sri Lanka. Nevertheless, there appear certain notable differences, too. For instance, the symbol taken to represent da is peculiar to the South Indian Brahmi inscriptions. The symbol for la, which occurs several times here, is totally absent in the Northern Brahmi epigraphs. The formation of 'ma' in the southern records, as a loop with a cross bar, is markedly different from that found in the Asokan and Bhattiprolu inscriptions. The differences have led certain archaeologists to suggest that the script of the Arikamedu graffiti as well as that of the inscriptions lower down in the south belonged to the Dravidi or Damili pattern, as distinct from the North Indian Brahmi of the Asokan type.[3] In the Dravidi or Damili distinctive Tamil letters like la (ழ), la (ள), ra (ற) and na (ன) appear.

It has also been suggested that the Dravidi form of Brahmi is the immediate ancestor of Vatteluttu, which preceded the modern Tamil scripts. This view, propounded by Dr. Buhler, was opposed by Dr. Haraprasada Sastri who thought that Vatteluttu developed from Kharoshti.[4] But it must be observed that Kharoshti, unlike Brahmi, has almost similar symbols for several letters, has fewer loops and is written from right to left. Vatteluttu has decidedly more features in common with Brahmi than with Kharoshti and this seems to confirm the view that it was an adaptation of Brahmi.[5] Vatteluttu was common in South India till about AD 1000 after which, too, for several centuries, it was continued in the Malayalam country.

On the question of the language of the South Indian Brahmi inscription the views of experts vary. Mr. H. Krishna Sastri struggled hard at the identification of the language of these records, and while indicating the numerous derivations from Tamil on the one hand and the several words which were entirely unidentifiable on the other, suggested the view that the language was Early Tamil with an admixture of Prakrit words.[6]

Less circumspect was Mr. K.V. Subrahmania Aiyar who categorically pronounced the language of the inscriptions as Old Tamil. Frequently he was obliged to resort to wild conjectures for the purpose of reading Tamil words into the available material.[7]

The variations in their respective readings too, are striking. For example, what is accepted as 'je' in the Anamalai inscription by Mr. Sastri is taken as 'ku' by Mr. Aiyar. What Mr.Sastri reads as 'jam' in the Tirupparamkunram epigraph is read by Mr. Aiyar as 'la' and so on. Certain words, too, have been translated differently by these two writers. Some translations are palpably wrong, while certain others do not convey any sense whatever.[8]

Dr. C. Narayana Rao, rejecting for the most part the readings of the two above-mentioned epigraphists provides his own, and concludes that the language of the records is the Paisaci form of Prakrit.[9] Arguing that all the contemporary Brahmi inscriptions are in Prakrit, he attempts to furnish a Prakrit derivation to the entire body of epigraphs. For instance the words 'Kotupitavan,' 'kotupiton' 'kutupita,' 'kotupitan; and kutupitvan; occurring in the Kongarpulitangulam, Arittapatti, Murugaltalai, Undankal and Alagarmalai inscriptions respectively, are all construed by him to have emanated from the Pali root 'Kotteti,' while the other writers derive it from the Tamil word 'Kotu,' or 'Kutu' meaning 'to cut.' A Tamil inscription of Narasimhavarman Pallavamalla has employed the term in this sense,[10] and it seems that the Tamil origin is correct. Nor is Dr. Rao's attempt to trace 'Nadu' to a Sanskrit origin from the root 'Nat,' meaning to 'wander' 'convincing. Again, such words as 'Udaiyu,' probably akin to 'udaiyan,' 'eri' meaning a tank, 'tantai' meaning father, 'Makan' meaning son, 'ura,' meaning village, are apparently Tamil words. While Mr. Subrahmania Aiyar's venture to connect 'Ven' with

Venad is far-fetched, we may well accept that the word 'Ven' occurring in some of the inscriptions and derived from 'Vel,' signified a local chief.[11] On the whole, Dr. Rao's position is as untenable as that taken by Mr. Aiyar. Assuredly, Dr. Rao's approval of the view that the prevailing language in the Pandya country of the 3rd and 2nd centuries BC was Paisaci is as startling as it is unsound.[12]

The legitimate inference seems to be that these votive inscriptions are in a hybrid language containing Tamil as well as Prakrit words. If certain words mentioned earlier are Tamil, others like 'pali,' 'upacha' 'cheiya' and 'lena' are Prakrit. The explanation for this strange feature is not far to seek. Buddhist devotees, soaked in Prakrit, the classical language of Buddhism, attempted to have (Prakrit) epigraphs inscribed in a manner that could be understood by the people of the region. That accounts for the strange jumble of words belonging to two different languages. The verbal forms, wherever they can be made out, seem to be in archaic Tamil, but it must be remembered that, for the most part, the inscriptions are content with recording the names of those who had the caverns excavated. It is of supreme importance, therefore, to remember that these epigraphs are not of great value to the study of linguistic development. Arikamedu graffiti have a more pronounced leaning towards Tamil, though they too are not Tamil inscriptions, pure and simple; there are several Prakrit words there too.

It is an indubitable fact that the South Indian Brahmi epigraphs are all associated with the Buddhists. The mountain caverns called Panchapandavarmalai which present the Brahmi inscriptions are located in almost inaccessible heights of mountain slopes, while others are found in out-of-the-way places and still others in the interior of woods. Panchapandavarmalai probably acquired its name from Pandavapabbata, associated with the Buddha's name. Again Kalugumalai, where some of these caverns are found, is the Tamil equivalent for Gridharkuta, or the 'Vulture Peak,' intimately connected with the Buddha's career. Circumstantial evidences show that they were the abodes of Buddhist monks; in particular, the caverns which provide beds with raised elevations for resting the head, resemble the numerous Buddhist monuments of Sri Lanka, containing similar inscriptions.[13] Little wonder, therefore, that the inscriptions are dominated by the Prakrit element, though the authors of these records seem to have struggled hard at making themselves understood by the people of the locality.[14] In these circumstances it is extremely problematic to hold that the languages of these inscriptions are truly representative of the standard of the Tamil language of that time.

Obviously the inferences attempted to be drawn by certain scholars regarding the history of the Tamil language on the basis of such doubtful hypotheses are venturesome, to say the least of it. For instance, depending exclusively on the questionable deductions derived from the above-mentioned Brahmi inscriptions, Dr. N.P. Chakravarti has rushed to the conclusion that the language of the Sangam literature cannot be dated earlier than 500 AD, for, he contends that several centuries should have intervened before the 'crude Tamil of the Brahmi inscriptions' attained the pattern of Sangam classics.[15]

Such a deduction hardly fits in with the known chronology of the literary development of Tamil. In the first place, it is not proved that Tirunanasambandar lived about the middle of the 7th century AD and that Tirunavukkarasar was contemporaneous with him. A considerable span of time must have doubtless intervened between the Sangam Tamil and Devaram Tamil. The syntax and vocabulary of the language of these two epochs appear markedly different. The Devaram hymns are nothing, if not simple, direct and popular invocations, while the Sangam classics are conspicuously archaic and terse.

Nor do the religious and social conditions revealed by the literature of these two epochs show similarity. The Gods mentioned, as well as the rituals and ceremonies adopted, show a pronouncedly different set up. For example, Mayon of the Sangam age became Krishna or Vishnu, and Seyon coalesced with Subrahmania, while Varuna and Indra practically disappeared from the pantheon. The acrimonious rivalry between Hinduism, Jainism and Buddhism which is a dominant feature of the Devaram period has no parallel in the Sangam epoch. Meat and liquor, so popular in the Sangam age, are despised in the era of the hymns.

Assuredly none can think of assigning the Sangam literature posterior to the Devaram hymns.[16] For one thing there is positive reference in Devaram to the Sangam.[17] Besides, Tirunavukkarasar speaks of Pari of old as the paragon of generosity who is none other than the celebrated Pari immortalized in the Sangam literature by Kapilar. The same hymnist refers in a song to Lord Siva's helping a destitute poet, Tarumi, to gain a purse of gold in the 'Sangam.'[18]

Moreover, those who are inclined to assign the Sangam works to a period later than the 2nd or 3rd century AD fail to explain the significant absence of reference to the Pallavas in those classics. Frequently the Muvendar are specified as the great monarchs of Tamilakam and several minor chiefs are mentioned as well; no plausible reason exists for the omission of the Pallavas if they flourished about that time within the traditional limits of Tamilakam. The poets and panar of the Sangam age, who were always in quest of royal patrons could be reasonably expected to have made direct or indirect reference to the Pallavas, if they reigned at Kanchi in the same epoch. On the other hand, the Perumbanarruppadai speaks of Tondaiman Ilantiraiyan who ruled at Kanchipuram in the pre-Pallava period. (The suggested contemporaniety of Trilochana Pallava of the Dekkan, Vijayaditya Chalukya and Karikala Chola is entirely based upon legends which have been incorporated in the late inscriptions of the 11th and 12th centuries AD). Nor could the Sangam poems on the royal patrons have appeared during the period of chaos caused by the Kalabhra invasions of the Tamil Nadu about the 5th century AD. The recent attempts to question the historical validity of the Kalabhra invasions are hardly convincing.

Above all, the data provided by the early Greek geographers confirm in a remarkable measure the details found in the Tamil classics and thereby help the determination of their date. There are several references to 'Yavanas' in the Sangam works, and doubtless, the term denoted Greeks in the first instance.[19] Later, the Romans, Arabs, and all foreigners were called by the same name.

The Greeks, and following them, the Romans had come to South India as traders, and there arose several commercial settlements of Yavanas in the country.[20] A poem describes the prosperous port of Musiri, whither the fine large ships of the Yavanas came bearing gold, making the water white with foam, and returned laden with pepper, along with the rare products of the sea and mountains given by the Chera king.[21] Pepper became the 'Yavanapriya' or the spice dear to the Romans, and it is said that pepper formed more than half the cargo of many a west-bound Roman ship.[22] Pepper, as well as ginger, is mentioned in Graeco-Roman medicine even in the early half of the 1st century AD.

The Yavanas are known to have been employed by South Indian monarchs for rendering certain kinds of service for which they were eminently qualified. There is a reference to Yavana guards, at the palace of the Pandyan king Aryappadaikadanda Nedunceliyan[23] while Roman soldiers are known to have been enlisted in the fighting forces of several Pandyan kings. The Padirruppattu mentions a conflict between the Yavanas and the Chera king, Imayavaramban Nedunjeralatan[24] as a result of which the Yavanas were vanquished and imprisoned, though the cause of the rupture remains a mystery. A song in Mullaippattu depicts the personal appearance of the Yavanas, their distinctive habits as well as their amazing skill in certain arts and crafts. It adds that their spoken language having been unintelligible to the Tamils, the Yavanas were obliged to employ gestures in order to make themselves understood.[25] The astounding skill displayed by the Yavanas in making artistic lamps of brass is adverted to more than once.[26] The Purananuru speaks of the importation of delicious wine which was eagerly sought for by kings and courtiers.[27]

The significance of this literary evidence lies in that it tallies remarkably with the date furnished by the Greek writers of the early centuries of the Christian Era, thereby yielding testimony to the chronology of the Sangam. Pliny describes India of the time of Augustus.[28] The author of the Periplus, who wrote in the latter half of the first century AD describes the conditions of that period, while Ptolemy, the last of the great geographers, who lived about 150 AD speaks of India of the 2nd century AD. Thus it is not extravagant to suppose that it was the Greek description of the commerce of the 1st two centuries AD which was reflected in the Sangam Classics.

Moreover, the hoards of Roman coins unearthed in South India indicate the period when the Roman commerce reached its height.[29] By far the largest number of the coins belongs to Augustus and Tiberius.[30] The references in Roman sources to the two embassies received by Augustus from the Pandyan king[31] and to a temple of Augustus at Muziris[32] tend to confirm the evidence of coins.

In this context the chronological datum furnished by the Arikamedu inscriptions is illuminating. The excavations have revealed that Arikamedu was not only an ancient town and port, evidently identifiable with the 'Poduke' of Ptolemy but also a centre of trade with the Graeco-Roman world. The unique value of the discoveries lies in that they enable us to date the culture of the region almost precisely. On the basis of internal and external evidence, Dr. Mortimer Wheeler concludes that the pottery and the Arretine ware and amphorae, imported from Italy, can be dated to 20–50 AD. He states: "From a convergence of evidence it is here inferred that the sites were first occupied at the end of the 1st century BC, or beginning of the 1st century AD with an inclination towards the later date."[33] Sometime in the 2nd century AD the warehouse in Arikamedu appears to have been deserted, and therefore, the glorious epoch of Arikamedu's industrial and commercial activity ranged about the 1st two centuries of the Christian era. Thus the testimony provided by Arikamedu accords well with the evidence furnished by the Greek writers on the one hand, and by the Sangam Classics on the other. Thereby it reinforces the case for ascribing the Sangam works to about the early centuries of the Christian era, postulated on the basis of the Gajabahu Senguttuvan synchronism.

Consequently the inference is inescapable that the Brahmi inscriptions of South India of c. 3rd century BC to 1st century AD cannot be taken to represent the contemporary language, and that it is clearly unhistoric to post-date the Classics on the basis of these strange records.

The attempt to the reputed linguist to distinguish three stages in the evolution of Tamil, viz., the Primitive Dravidian. Ancient Tamil and Sentamil and to equate Ancient Tamil with the language of the early Brahmi inscriptions of South India seems a misdirected one.[34] His suggestion that originals of the Sangam Classics were composed in the Ancient Tamil of the early Christian era and that the language changed later into Sentamil in which they were written in the 7th century AD is at once interesting and ingenious. But until it is proved that the inscriptions truly represent the then prevalent Tamil language, the line of approach adopted by the learned writer seems unwarranted.

ENDNOTES

1. Annual Report on South Indian Epigraphy for 1912, Plate facing p.57. Idem for 1915—Pl. facing p. 96 and idem for 1918, Pl. facing p. 7.
2. Ancient India, No. 2. p. 109.

    Now about 80 Brahmi inscriptions have been discovered on the whole.
3. Dr. Buhler postulated the view that sometime prior to the 5th century BC the Dravidi script branched itself off from the main stock of Brahmi which was Semitic in origin, and

developed certain peculiarities. (Buhler: Indian Paleography, Appendix 8). But Edward Thomas, Cunningham and Dowson held that the Brahmi script itself was of Dravidian origin and that the northern type is the offshoot of the original. Cunningham in particular believed that Brahmi was derived from a lost pictographic source. Prof. Langden detected the influence of the Mohenjodaro and Harappa script on Brahmi, and this view has been strengthened by the findings of Dr. G.R. Hunter. (See G.R. Hunter: "The Script of Harappa and Mohenjodaro and its connection with other Scripts," pp. 17, 22 and 49.) If the Dravidians were connected with the Indus Valley culture, as appears to have been the case, the Dravidian origin of Brahmi is plausible. See also 'Ancient India' No. 9 (1953) p. 215.

4. Bihar Orissa Research Society Journal, Vol. p. 58.
5. Buhler: Indian Palaeography, p. 73 Contra: *Elements of South Indian Palaeography,* p. 49. Dr. Burnell imagines on grounds, which are uncertain, that the Tamils adopted Vatteluttu from the Phoenician script. T.A.G. Rao demonstrates the affinity of Vatteluttu to Brahmi. See TAS. Vol. I, p. 284.
6. Proceedings of the First All India Oriental Conference, pp. 327–48.
7. Proceedings of the Third All India Oriental Conference, pp. 275–300.
8. For e.g. 'Potatan' in the Kongarpuliyangulam inscriptions is taken to mean 'one belonging to.' Again 'Kaviy' in the Muttuppatti inscription is conjectured to be either a proper name or a cave.
9. *The New Indian Antiquary.* Vol. I, pp. 362–76.

10. *Epigraphia Indica.* Vol. IV, p. 137.
11. The Undankal inscriptions clearly suggest this.
12. An attempt to trace the roots of certain Dravidian words to Paisaci made by K. Amrita Rao seems to be more ingenious than convincing. See "The Dravidian Affinities of the Paisaca Languages of North-Western Asia" in Sir Asutosh Mookherjee Silver Jubilee Volume III. Orientalia, Part 2, pp. 427–32. Prof. K.A. N. Sastri's suggestion that the language of the Arikamedu inscription is 'Monumental Prakrit.'similar to the pattern mentioned in 'Monuments of Sanchi'. Vol I. p. 280, does not explain the presence of Tamil words. See Madras University Journal, Vol. XIV, pp. 3–4.
13. Arikamedu itself appears to have been a Buddhist centre. Not far removed from the Roman warehouse at Arikamedu lies the Kakkayan tope, where a stone image of the Buddha has been discovered.
14. That the Buddhists tried to have their inscriptions engraved in a manner suited to the locality may be seen from the following examples: (a) an epigraph at Maunggun in Burma, comprising quotations from Pali Buddhist scriptures written in characters which resemble the class of South Indian alphabets (*Epigraphia Indica.* Vol. V, pp. 101–2); (b) another on a stupa at Khin-bha-gon in Burma in *Pyu* and *Pali* engraved in the early Telugu-Canarese script of South India (Archaeological Survey of India, Annual Report, 1926–7, pp. 171 ff) and (c) another at Kyundawzu in old Prome containing the formula of Vinaya and Sutta Pitaka engraved in the same early South Indian script (Idem, 1928–9, p. 109). Apparently this script was in vogue there among the South Indian colonists.

15. Presidential address delivered at the All India Historical Congress held at Ahmedabad in December 1954.
16. Not even Mr. S. Vaiyapuri Pillai, who has ascribed the Silappadikaram to the 8th or 9th century AD on grounds which are unconvincing, has assigned the Sangam classis to the post-Devaram period.
17. Tiruttevur Devaram, ii, 10.
18. Tiruputtur Tiruttandagam, ii, line 2. Tirumangai Alvar, who lived in the 8th century, if not earlier, has spoken of 'Sangamukattamil' or the high strandard or Tamil brought into vogue by the Sangam (Periya Tirumoli iii 4—10).
19. In North India, too, they were known as Yavanas. Patanjali refers to the Greeks as Yavanas in his Mahabhashyam.
20. Silappadikaram, V. 9–10.
21. Ahananuru, 149: Purananuru, 343. Compare these data with the accounts of Greek geographers.
22. E.H. Warmington: 'The Commerce between the Roman Empire and India,' p. 182.
23. Silappadikaram, XIV. 62–7.
24. Padirruppattu: 2nd Decad.
25. Mullaippattu, 59–66.
26. Perumbanarrupadai, 316; Nedunalvadai, 101–3.
27. Purananuru, 56.
28. Pliny, *Natural History*, VI, 142–62.
29. See map showing the distribution of Roman coins, fig. 48, *Ancient India*, No. 2, p. 117.

30. R. Sewell: 'Roman coins found in India,' JRAS., 1904, pp. 200 ff. H.G. Rawlinson: 'Intercourse between India and the Western World,' pp. 120–1. E.H. Warmington: 'The Commerce between the Roman Empire and India,' pp. 286–95. The author, in his critical review, agrees with Chwostow who explains the scarcity of Roman coins in Tamil Nadu subsequent to the time of Tiberius by the circumstance that, learning of the popularity of the earlier pattern in South India, the later emperors reissued coins of Augustus and Tiberius, but adds that after the 2nd century AD Romans traded more with the north-west districts of India than with the Tamil States.

31. Starbo: Geography XV, 4 and 73.

32. The Peutingerian Tables.

33. *Ancient India*, op. cit. p. 24.

34. See Dr. Suniti Kumar Chatterji's article on 'Old Tamil, Ancient Tamil and Primitive Dravidian' reproduced in *Tamil Culture*, Vol. V, 1956.

6

ARYAN INFLUENCE IN TAMILAHAM DURING THE SANGAM EPOCH

There is a considerable measure of uncertainty regarding the date of the Aryan advent into Tamilaham. None of the Sangam works indicate when the Aryans entered Tamilaham. Certain writers have held that, not long after the Vedic period, there occurred a mass migration of Aryans to the Deccan and South India including Tamil Nadu and still farther eastwards into the different countries of South-East Asia. Another facile generalisation advanced regarding the migration of the Aryans is that round about 1000 BC they moved southwards reaching even the Tamil country. But this is hardly justified by the known data.

There is a tradition recorded in the Aitareya Brahamana that Visvamitra condemned his fifty sons to live in the southern borders of Aryavarta. These sons of Visvamitra are supposed to have been descendants of Dasyus and it is believed that later on they became the ancestors of the Andhras, Pundras, Sabaras and Pulindas.[1] Assuming that the Brahmanas might be dated to about 1000 BC it is to be remembered that there is no mention of the Tamils in this list.

Certain writers like the late P.T. Srinivasa Iyengar were inclined to treat a reference to Cherapadah occurring in Taitriya Aranyaka as a reference to the Chera kings of the South. But Sayana, the commentator of this Aranyaka, has interpreted Chera to mean snake in that context. The known history of the Chera kingdom does not warrant such an early antiquity for it. Nor do the references occurring in the epics of the Mahabharata and the Ramayana to Tamil Nadu constitute reliable indications of very early Aryan contact.

In fact, it has to be observed that Panini who is believed to have lived about the sixth century BC does not mention the kingdoms in the extreme south. He mentions only the Kalingas among the people of South India. Apparently, by his time the Aryans had little knowledge of the other kingdoms farther south. On the other hand, Katyayana, the grammarian of the 4th century BC, specifies the Chola kingdom. This is to the best of our knowledge, the earliest reference to the extreme south.[2] It is not too much to presume that it was only about the 4th century BC, that the Aryan contact with the Tamil country could have begun. It is significant to remember in this connection that the Manu, who gave a real shape to the laws of the Hindus, considered the Vindhyas as marking the southern limit of Aryavarta and the land farther to the south as a condemned region.[3]

The question arises as to who came first to the Tamil country, the Hindus, Jains or Buddhists. The common view held is that the Hindus were the earliest colonists. But a reexamination of the question suggests that the other possibility is equally worthy of consideration. In the first place, Vijaya, the first king according to the Sinhalese Chronicles and the accredited leader of the Aryan immigrants into Sri Lanka, is assignable to the 5th century BC, though tradition makes him a contemporary of the Buddha. It stands to reason that the Buddhists would have come to Sri Lanka not much earlier than the time when they migrated to South India. Whether the Aryans went to Sri Lanka entirely by the sea route or by land to South India first and thence moved on to Sri Lanka, the Buddhists who were imbued by the missionary zeal would not have failed to come into contact with South India at the earliest opportunity. In any case, sometime between the 5th and 4th centuries BC, Buddhists, and in all probability, the Jains, too, came to the Tamil country in South India.

The view is supported by the Brahmi inscriptions of Madurai, Tirunelveli and Sri Lanka. There have appeared differences of views regarding the date of these inscriptions; some epigraphists assign them to the 3rd century BC, and others to the second and first centuries BC. Palaeography is the principal basis of these deductions: and it is well known that it is not far too dependable a source for determining chronology within a narrow range of time. The view of K.V. Subramania Aiyar that some of the inscriptions are assignable to the 3rd century BC seems to be still valid, though some of the recent epigraphists are inclined to date even the oldest among them to the 2nd century BC. However, generally speaking, the Brahmi inscriptions of South India also support the suggestion that from about 4th century BC, the Jains and Buddhists had begun to come and settle down in Southern India, and that in all probability they preceded the Hindu Aryans.

It is important to remember that the Hindu Aryans did not all migrate to South India at one stretch. The epigraphic evidence as well as the name of groups of Brahmins who were settled at different stages in different places prove this. The designations of groups like 'Narpettennayiravar' and 'Elunurruvar' clearly suggest that waves of immigrants came into the Tamil country. Perhaps the village, Ennaiyiram which literally translates the Sanskrit word *ashtasahasram* (eight thousand) may be one of the places where the community had settled. It is found that now the name survives in a large number of villages where smarta Brahmins live in the Tamil country. Some have suggested that Ennaiyiram was the original name and that later it was sanskritised into 'Ashtasahasram'. The probability seems to have been the reverse of this suggestion. The section of brahmins in the Tamil country known as Vadamas obviously consists of those who came from the north; they claim themselves to be pure in descent from the Aryans. Some of the Sangam poets had names like 'Vadamodankilar', 'Vadama Vannakkan Damodaranar' and Vadaman Vannakkam Perisattan'; these indicate that these poets belonged to groups which had hailed from the north.

There is no doubt that a considerable number of Aryans, particularly of the Brahmin caste had come into the Tamil country some centuries prior to the Sangam age, which is believed to have ranged roughly between the 1st and 3rd centuries AD. The question arises as to whether brahmins alone among the Aryans migrated to the South. Though brahmins were the leaders of the immigrants, there is a great probability that others also accompanied them from the north. The Kshatriyas, as warriors, the Vaisyas as traders and businessmen, as well as the Sudras might have joined them. Ahananuru (279) shows that the Aryans were engaged in taming elephants; it is interesting to learn[4] that elephants themselves were taught and trained through the medium of the Aryan language. Moreover, mention is made of the Aryan dancers of the Kalaikkuttam dance accompanied by drums and rope dancers.[5]

All these indicate that there were Aryan Sudras, too, in the Tamil country of the Sangam age.

A more intriguing question is whether all the brahmins of Tamilaham during the Sangam epoch were immigrants from the north. Did the Aryan brahmins keep themselves aloof from the higher section of the indigenous people in south or did they absorb some of them into their fold? We find certain pieces of evidence pertaining to the Sangam epoch and the succeeding ages which suggest that there appeared a gradual process of amalgamation. The designation 'Vadama' applied to a group only among the brahmins shows that there were others, indigenous to the Tamil country, who became transformed into brahmins.

In this connection, it is well worth noticing the occurrence of terms like 'Melor', 'Uyarndor' and 'Arivar' which occur in Tolkappiyam, the celebrated grammar. The term 'Melor' seems to have specified all persons of high character. From Karpiyal 3, Tolkappiyam, it would appear that it included the first three classes under this designation. There is a slight difference in the denotation of the term as interpreted by the commentators of Tolkappiyam. Ilampuranar interpreted 'Melor' as the devas or celestical beings. Nachchinarkkiniyar provides a very wide interpretation to the term. He states that the norms of conduct prescribed for Vanigar or traders in respect of earning wealth is applicable to brahmins (antanar), arasar (kings) and all those comprised under Velalar. According to him, therefore, 'Melor' denoted those members who followed a high standard of conduct. If that were so, it is a notably democratic conception. References in Tolkappiyam (Tol. Karpiyal 3) and Purananuru (183) show that 'Melor' or men of character could be members of the higher castes.

Equally wide was the denotation of the term 'Uyarndor'. Ilampuranar, the commentator of Tolkappiyam, takes in respect of Sutra No. 27, Uyarndor to mean Antanar and Arasar. But, while commenting on the two succeeding sutras he takes Uyarndor to mean brahmins as well as traders. Perasiriyar, another commentator, holds the term Uyarndor to include brahmins as well as other learned persons. Thus 'Uyarndor' seems to have denoted persons of deep learning and high character. Apparently, in a general sense it comprehended saints, kings, heroes, and brahmins. Used in a specific sense, it denoted also worthy individuals in the three higher groups of the social strata.

As regards the 'Arivar' the interpretations suggested are illuminating. Tolkappiyar does not identify Parppar (brahmins) exclusively with Arivar. Perasiriyar states that 'Arivar' are persons gifted with deep foresight and in this respect he likens them to brahmins, but does not speak of them in identical terms. It is only the Divakaram which equates the term with 'Parppar;' but the basis for this interpretation is not clear. Thus Arivar in the original sense, used by Tolkappiyar, applied to learned men among the people. No exclusive reference to caste or community is implied by the term. This suggests that a certain measure of fluidity existed in the caste system in respect of the Arivar. Perhaps some of the learned Tamils of the indigenous stock were absorbed into the fold of brahmins. One instance pertaining to the 4th century AD is known to us, when for the purpose of conducting sacrifices, certain members of the non-brahmin communities were selected for want of the required number of brahmins. In one of the accounts concerning Brahmins, it is stated that during the time of Mayurasarman of the Kadamba dynasty, some Andhra brahmins selected a number of families from the non-brahmin castes, converted them into brahmins and chose exogamous sept name for them. The fact that some brahmins were described as belonging to the 'Vadamas and 'Brihacharanam' shows that others were indigenous. In this connection it is relevant to consider the genesis of the people in Tamil Nadu known variously as 'Adi Saivas' or 'Sivacharyas' or still later as 'Otuvar'. In respect of customs are manners they imitate the brahmins. Some of them wear the sacred thread. They have been the offlciating priests in the Saiva temples, while quite a few of them continue to be priests in the shrines like those of Kali, Amman and Madan, which are all of pre-Aryan origin. It is probable that some non-brahmins had become merged with brahmins. On the other hand, brahmins who continue as priests in Siva temples, are considered as inferior to other Brahmins. Does this imply that the Siva deity was of non-Aryan origin? In any case these trends suggest that there was a certain measure of fusion among the Aryan and non-Aryan priestly classes.

Not only that. In the early periods of the immigration of the Aryans it would seem that the caste system was not very rigid. At any rate, instances of brahmins having married from other communities are mentioned. Ravana, Vali, Sugriva, Maricha, Subahu, Khara and others are stated to have been children of non-Aryan mothers born of Aryan fathers. Whether or not they were all historical personages or whether all the incident associated with them are true or not, the traditions, regarding their origin suggest that such marriages were not uncommon in the early stages.

It was no doubt in the sphere of religion that the Aryan ideas and practices seem to have influenced prominently the new set-up in Tamilaham. The Aryan brahmins must have been imbued by a certain measure of missionary zeal in their migration to the south, and consequently they were eager to introduce their religious ideas and institutions among the people of their new settlements. They appear to have first worked up their way to royal favour; and, even during the Sangam epoch, several ministers and poets belonged to the Brahmin caste. They were held in high esteem by kings and chieftains. Verses in Purananuru and Padirruppattu state that it was incumbent even on kings to bow down to Brahmins in respect. This high position accorded to them paved the way for their ascendancy and widespread influence among the people of Tamil Nadu as in the rest of South India.

Brahmins in the royal courts induced their patrons to perform yagas or holy sacrifices. Pattinappalai, Padirruppattu and Kalittogai, for instance, refer to great yagas which were conducted on a large scale. The names of kings like 'Palyaga Mudukudumi Peruvaluti' and 'Irayasuyam Vetta Perunarkkilli' provide testimony to the enthusiasm of kings in the performances of sacred sacrifices.

Bestowing gifts on brahmins was held to be a meritorious act of beneficence. Tolkappiyar had declared that giving gifts to brahmins was akin to the performance of sacrifices.

The Vedic lore got currency even during the Sangam epoch. The Vedas were described in Tamil as 'Marai', 'Kelvi', 'Vai Moli', 'Mudu Moli', and 'Yeludakkarppu.' 'Andanalar Nanmarai' and 'Arumarai' were other honorific designations of the Vedas. Specific details regarding the sacrifices like the kind of posts to be erected on occasions of the Yagas, the special dress to be worn by the persons engaged in performing the rituals and ceremonies connected with the sacrifices[7] are indicated in the Sangam works. The Paripadal states that Vishnu emerges from the sacrificial fire.

It is significant that the deities figuring prominently in the Vedas find a more or less equal position in the Sangam works as well. Indra, for instance, is the lord of the celestial gods. In the Sangam age, festivals in honour of Indra were held in the affluent towns and villages.[8] The sacred Mount Meru of the North fiends it echo in the Sangam classics.[9] Tolkappiyam and Paripadal accord the primary place to Vishnu. All the other Gods, Asuras, the Sun and the Moon as well as the natural elements and the five Bhutas are all believed to have emerged from Vishnu. The four-faced Brahma who is entrusted with the creation of the world appears from the navel of Vishnu.[10] Kama and Soma are also like Brahma, the sons of Vishnu. Garuda is the vehicle as well as the banner of Lord Vishnu, while Adisesha, the serpent God, serves as his couch.[11] The various incarnations of Vishnu are mentioned in the Sangam classics.

Muruga is the nephew of Vishnu and the son of Siva and Parvati. He is the God of Kurinchi and is held in great veneration, particularly by the Kuravas. Besides undoubtedly the Tirumurugarruppaddi and Paripadal, other classics like Purananuru,[12] Narrinai[13] and Kuruntogai[14] refer to Muruga. Indra is said to appoint Muruga as the general of the Devas in encountering the opposition of the Asuras headed by Suran. Muruga's exploits and ultimate triumph over Sura are described. Among the places sacred to Muruga, Tirupparunkunram and Tiruchchiralaivai find special mention.

Whether Muruga was an indigenous deity of the Tamils or not has been a subject of controversy. Skanda, Subrahmania and and Kartikeya are names of the same deity occurring in the holy books of the Aryas.[15] But there is no place for this deity in the Vedas. Everything considered, there is a great probability that

Muruga was a popular deity of the Dravidian Tamils and was absorbed into the pantheon by the Aryas.[16] There is also justification to hold that Siva, the 'Mukkatchelvan' of Purananuru, also comes under the same category.

Apart from this, there were several deities of the early Tamils who were not eclipsed. They continue to be worshipped alongside with the Aryan deities; frequently they were assimilated into the existing fold. Thus Korravai, mentioned for instance in Ahananuru (345 : 4), as Kan Amar Chelvi and in Kalittogai (89 : 8) as Perunkattukkorri gets identified with Parvati as the consort of Siva. She, too, has three eyes and the trident. The attributes associated with Korravai are distinctly of the indigenous pattern, and like Siva and Murugan she must have been absorbed in the latter Hindu pantheon.

Besides, a huge host of other deities was known to the Tamils long before their contact with the Aryans. In respect of most of these deities there was a common belief that, if they were not worshipped, harm would befall the people. Some deities were supposed to reside in hills and trees as well as in rivers and tanks. Demons and demonesses were particularly believed to live in these places.

The practice of erecting hero-stones and worshipping them was common among the Tamils of old. Images of Gods and Goddesses were erected in the junction of lanes and streets. Further, in the common meeting place, called the Podiyil, they used to erect a piece of wood and worship it;[17] on the walls of Podiyil they maintained painted images of deities. All these are indications that there was a curious blending of the Aryan and non-Aryan practices in religion. But it must be remembered that the fusion did not permeate the entire society in a uniform manner.

The Aryan pattern, with but a few accretions, remained with the brahmins and the higher sections of the non-brahmins, while the people in the lower rungs stuck mainly to the older indigenous ways, absorbing occasionally the new practices. Festivals were celebrated in honour of the Aryan deities as well as for the rest. There were, for instance, the 'Indra Vila', 'Kartikai Vila', 'Ona Vila' and numerous other festivities connected with the smaller village Gods.

In respect of social life, too, a certain measure of absorption of the northern customs and habits was found. It has been frequently discussed how far the Aryan institution of caste based on Varna or colour had penetrated Tamilaham of the Sangam Age. Clearly the distinction dependent on Varna had appeared. The Tolkappiyam and Purananuru speak of the four-fold division. But two considerations differentiate the Tamilian pattern from the corresponding social structure in the north. In the first place, there is little evidence of the Kshatriya caste as such in Tamilaham; the Chera, Chola and Pandya kings, not to speak of the numerous chieftains were really Sudras. Secondly, there existed numerous subdivisions like Panan, Tudiyan, Parayan, Pulayan, Mallan, Kuttan and Kadamban among the Sudras, purely based on occupation. It would seem, therefore, that in respect of the caste system, too, there was fusion of the Aryan and non-Aryan systems. Prior to the advent of the Aryans, there could have emerged a social division based on occupation, which, in its turn, was determined by the topographical divisions like the Kurinchi, Mullai, Marudam, Neydal and Palai.

The brahmins had begun to live as an exclusive group. They lived in separate streets. Kuruntogai[18] and Perumpanarruppadai,[19] for instance, speak of the streets where brahmins alone lived.

Sirupanarruppadai refers to an essentially Brahmin village, Amur, in Oymanadu.[20] They kept their streets and houses clean. They bathed early in the morning and offered worship. But there were some who took to occupations other than religious. References to these 'Velappappar', otherwise spoken of as 'Urpparppar' and to those who earned their living by cutting conch shells are found.[21] From Padirruppattu[22] it is learnt that some brahmins had become skilled artisans, capable of making fine ornaments. The commentator of Padirruppattu points out that the able craftsman mentioned in the verse was also well-versed in the art of conducting the Yajna. This indicates that a certain measure of fluidity in the choice of occupations prevailed.

There is little doubt that the Aryan brahmins commanded high respect and social influence in Tamilaham even in the Sangam age.[23] This was by virtue of their influence in the royal courts, their association with temples and worship and also their lofty ideals of conduct. It was essentially on account of the royal partronage that they were ensured special protection during occasions of political hostilities.

Though they were in several respects a privileged people, the Aryan brahmins and other immigrants borrowed several customs of the Dravidians, among which may be mentioned the institution of tali-tying which symbolized marriage, the boring of the nose and presenting to the bride the new sari called 'Kurai' by the bridegroom's party before marriage. There was, therefore, a certain measure of admixture in the religious and social set up. But it would by no means be easy to determine the exact proportion of the Aryan and non-Aryan elements in the admixture.

The consideration of the Aryan influence in respect of language is interesting. Brahmins took to Tamil, the native language, alongside with Sanskrit. The result was the entry of Sanskrit words into the parlance and vocabulary of the Tamil language. In respect of the earliest Sangam poems the influence of Sanskrit was practically negligible. But there appeared a gradual increase in the compositions known as the Padinenkilkanakku in which the proportion of Sanskrit words became conspicuous. It is, however, remarkable that several brahmins became Tamil poets; some like Paranar and Kapilar were the most outstanding among them. Certain scholars have estimated that the brahmin poets constituted about one-tenth of the total number of Tamil poets of the Sangam epoch. Perhaps, the percentage was higher for, in several cases the caste to which the poet belonged is difficult to be ascertained. However, it is interesting to find that the Brahmin poets of Tamil took to the language with remarkable enthusiasm. How they relished the indigenous language and its beauties is gathered, for instance, from the fact that 'Kurinjippattu' was composed by the brahmin poet, Kapilar, in order to reveal the sweet charm of Tamil to the Aryan king Brihadatta. This shows the antiquity of Tamil in Tamil Nadu.

By way of conclusion it may be stated that the Tamils of the pre-Aryan age had their own pattern of religious and social institutions, language and literature. But to assert that the pre-Aryan Tamils had 'a rather primitive ad poorish culture',[24] is an understatement. Bishop Caldwell, who wrote at a time when all the Sangam classics had not been brought to light, states that 'the Dravidians, properly so called, had acquired at least the elements of civilization, prior to the arrival amongst them of the brahmins'.[25] The Sangam classics have not only strengthened the force of his observation but have shown that the Tamils of the age had developed their own civilization in a remarkable measure. Prof. K.A. Nilakanta Sastri, who was inclined to exaggerate the influence of Aryanisation of early Tamil country and its language, was constrained to admit later that in the farther south including Tamilaham the Aryans 'were not able to incorporate them (the local inhabitants) into their own society and to root out their languages and their peculiar civilization'[26] No one denies that the infiltration of Aryan influence and of the Sanskrit language penetrated Tamilaham gradually, particularly in the post-Sangam age. But to admit that is not to accept the sweeping statements made by that above-mentioned writer who ought to know better about the Sangam epoch.

ENDNOTES

1. Aitareya Brahmana, VII, 18.
2. Katyayana himself is believed to have been a brahmin of South India.
3. The early Aryans are said to have held the Vindhyas as marking the limit of travelling, for the region to the south of the Vindhyas was known as 'Pariyatra'. It is also said that the Aryans came to identify the South with death and called it Yamyadik or Yamadik, i.e. that which points to the abode of death. Probably this was because the early immigrants were fiercely resisted by the original inhabitants.
4. Mullaippattu 31–37: Malaipadukadam 326–27.
5. Kuruntogai, 7: 3–5
6. Thurston: *Castes and Tribes of Southern India*, Introduction, pp. 45–46. It is surprising that Prof. K.A.N. Sastri has said little about the distinction between the Vadamas and other

Brahmins. Though inclined in general to underestimate the importance of the pre-Aryan culture, as will be shown in the sequel, he adopts a slightly different attitude in his 'Colas' (1975)p. 63, where he says that the striking feature of the culture of the Sangam age is its composite quality.

7. Purananuru, 15 and 166.
8. Ainkurunuru, 62 : 1.
9. Perumpanarruppadai, 429, and Paripadal, 9 : 13.
10. Kalittogai, 2 : 1.
11. Perumpanarruppadai, 371–373
12. Purananuru, 55 : 19.
13. Narrinai, 288 : 10.
14. Kuruntogai, 1 : 3.
15. In the Taittiriya Aranyaka, among the Gayatri mantras of many deities, Shanmukha is mentioned. In the Chhandogya Upanishad Sanatkumara, a great teacher of liberation, is identified with Skanda. But these are all later than the date of the Adichchanaallur finds and of the relics in western Asia.
16. K.A.N. Sastri tried to formulate a view that 'Muruga' is derived from the Persian name 'Murgh'. This is unacceptable. Equally so is the view that 'Muruga' is derived from the African deity 'Murungu' 'Dravidans and Africans' by K.P. Aravanan p.48. Another essay in this collection deals with this question.
17. Pattinappalai, 246–49.
18. Kuruntogai, 277.
19. Perumpanarruppadai, 30.

20. Sirupanarruppadai, 187–88.
21. Ahananuru, 24: 1–3.
22. Padirruppattu, 74: 10–14.
23. Padirruppattu, 24: 6–8.
24. K.A. Nilakanta Sastri: 'The Culture and History of the Tamils' 1963, p.7. Clearly unwarranted is his statement ("Hindu" dated 17-4-1960) that "We do not possess a single line of Tamil literature demonstrably antedating the contact between the pre-Aryan Tamil and Aryan Sanskrit culture." What is the implication of this dogmatic and incorrect statement? Later in the book cited above on p. 129, Prof. K.A.N. Sastri himself states that the proportion of Sanskrit words is rather small in their (Sangam poems) vocabulary. Earlier in this paper itself I have stated that in respect of the earliest Sangam poems, the influence of Sanskrit was practically negligible. See Purananuru verse 1 for example which provides an idea of the purity and antiquity of ancient Tamil.
25. Bishop Caldwell: "Dravidian Comparative Grammar" (1956)p. 113.
26. K.A. Nilakanta Sastri: "A History of South India" (1966), p. 74. It is no chauvinism to state that among all the languages of the world none has had such a clear division into 'Iyal', 'Isai' and 'Nadakam'. Prof. Sastri must have been aware of this.

7

ORIGIN OF MURUGA WORSHIP

It is well known that Muruga was the favourite deity of the Tamils for ages. Apart from the numerous references to Murugan, Velan and Korravai Chelvan in the Sangam classics, a far earlier evidence is seen from the urn burials excavated in Adichchanallur. The excavations have brought to light the Kavidi (a wooden frame with either Muruga's image or the lance, his favourite weapon, at the centre), iron banner base and representations of fowls in bronze and the gold mouth-pieces which were used for covering the mouth of the person who carried the Kavidi in order to maintain purity. The mouth-pieces have some geometrical designs carved on them. A few of the mouth-pieces have holes cut at the ends. Archaeologists believe that the Adichchanallur urn burials are not earlier than the 1st millennium BC. It is older than the other megalithic sites found in Chingleput, South Arcot and other places in South India assigned to a period ranging from 700 BC to 400 BC.

Surprisingly certain relics similar to those of the Adichchanallur finds have been discovered outside India. Mouth-pieces and Vel and other relics of Muruga worship have been found at Enkomi in Cyprus in tombs of the late bronze age. Further, two more or less similar sites are found in Palestine; one at Gaza has besides similar relics of Muruga worship, presents gold fillets or hand-bands, and archaeologists have assigned them to about 2000 BC. In the other site at Gerar relics to those similar of Adichchanallur have been found and these are assigned to about 1200 BC.

How did this resemblance between the Adichchanallur relics and those in Cyprus and Palestine appear? Most probably the ideas of Muruga must have been taken by Tamil traders to Western Asia. It is not likely that they were imported from Western Asia to India or Tamil Nadu. Should this suggestion be held valid, Muruga worship must have originally appeared in Tamil Nadu before 2000 BC.

In this connection it is relevant to note the views of the late Professor Nilakanta Sastri. Professor Sastri in his lecture on Murugan at a meeting of the Archaeological Society of South India, on 22-9-1964, said that Muruga may be an Aryan God for the following reasons:

1. Taitireya Aranyaka and the Upanishads and later Sanskrit literature contain references to Subrahmanya who has been identified with Muruga.
2. The name of the cock is Murgh in old Persian and Muruk in Zend. Hence one is tempted to associate the word with the name Muruga who as a child hugs and plays with the cock as the Mahabharata says.

Prof. K.A. Nilakanta Sastri concludes his talk by saying, "Such data and others not mentioned here seem to show that the Skanda Muruga cycle is no exception to the general rule of

Origin of Muruga Worship 191

Aryan religion and deities being Tamilised, of the mingling of the Great Tradition with the Little".

Now let us try to find out how far the statements of the learned Professor stand to test.

I. Sanskrit scholars fix the age of the Taitireya Aranyaka roughly about the 3rd century BC. The age of the Epics may roughly be placed between 300 BC and AD 300.

If Muruga was a God worshipped by the Aryans, his worship must have been mentioned in the Rig Veda itself. "In Vedic times, the worship of Subrahmanya was unknown; on the other hand, the name appears in the Taitireya Aranyaka Prasana 1, Anuvaka 12, v. 58. There Agni and Vayu are spoken of as the servants or attendants of Indra, called by the name Subrahmanya. We do not have any hymns addressed to him. But in the period of the Epics, we have allusions to the birth of Kartikeya or Subrahmanya. He is spoken of as the son of Rudra or Agni. The Southerners were influenced by this apparently widespread movement, and identifying their own old deity Muruga with Subrahmanya, regarded Him as equal to Indra and Varuna."[1]

Tolkappiyam, the ancient Tamil Grammar, precedes the Ettuttogai and the Pattuppattu. It contains no traces of Jainism and Buddhism and hence it might have been composed either in the 4th century BC or prior to it. In Sutra 2 of the Tolkappiyam-Poruladhikaram, Seyon (Red God) is mentioned as the God of the hilly region. Subrahmanya was never a God of the Mountains in the North.

"The undoubted antiquity of the cult of Muruga among the Tamil is attested by the discovery at the historic urnfield at

Adichchanallur of bronze cocks, iron spears and mouth-pieces of gold leaf similar to those employed by modern worshippers of Muruga when they are on a pilgrimage carrying a Kavadi in fulfilment of a vow."[2] Similar cocks, spears and mouth-pieces were found in the archaeological finds in Syria and Palestine. They may be said to belong to about BC 1200.[3]

All these go to prove that the opinion of Prof. K.A. Nilakanta Sastri in tracing the origin of Muruga to the group of Aryan deities on the basis of references contained in the Sanskrit literature which were earlier to the Sangam literature, is not a satisfactory one.

II. Secondly, Prof. Sastri has tried to trace the word Muruga from Murugh in old Persian and Muruk in Zend. In Persian and Urdu the following are the words springing from the word Murugh:[4]

Murugh	Cock
Murghi	Hen (Urdu)
Murghab	Name of a river in Persia
Murghabi	A watery bird
Murghathesh Khwar	Fire-eater bird

Here we do not find that the word Murugh denotes youth, God, beauty, etc. as in Tamil. Moreover, if the word was used to denote God Muruga in the days of Zend Avesta, it must have found a place in the Vedic literature as the Rig Vedic Aryans were their kith and kin. But we do not find the word in the Vedic literature.

If the word Muruga came to the Tamil country from Persia it would have come by either of two routes—one by the land

and the other by the sea. If it came by land it must have come to North India first and then to South India. If this is true, the word Muruga must be found in the Sanskrit language and there must be many temples to Muruga in Northern India. But surprisingly we neither find the word in the Sanskrit language nor are there many temples dedicated to Muruga or Subrahmanya in the North.

If the word might have come by sea through foreign trade then it must have reached the coastal areas of Sindh, Kathiawar, Maharashtra, Karnataka and Malabar and later to the Tamil country. But we do not find the word in the Sindhi, Maharathi, etc.

We find the word Muruga in the Dravidian languages with different meanings as follows:[5]

Muruku (Tamil)	tenderness, tender age, youth, beauty, akanda.
Murukan (Tamil)	youth, youngman, skanda
Murukan (Malayalam)	Subrahmanyan
Muruku (Tulu)	the young of an animal
Murli (Konda)	young man

Thus it is clear that the word Muruga or Murugu is purely Dravidian in origin. It was used in the Sangam Age in different shades of meanings. A few examples here will suffice:–

1. Murugu-Murugan

   "Arungadi Velan Murugodu Valai"

   "அருங்கடி வேலன் முருகொடு வளைஇ"

   Madurai-k-kanchi, 1.611

2. Murugu-Velvi (Sacrifice or yaga)

   "Padaiyorkku Murugayara"

   "படையோர்க்கு முருகயர"

   Madurai-k-kanchi, 1.38

3. Murugu-Good smell

   "Murugamarpu Murankidakkai"

   "முருகமார்பு முரண்கிடக்கை"

   Pattinappalai, 1.37

4. Murugu-Daivam

   "Murugu meippatta pulatti pola"

   "முருகு மெய்ப்பட்ட புலத்திபோல"

   Purananuru, v. 259

5. Murugu-Velan's frenzic dance

   "Murugayar-n-duvanda muduvay Velan"

   "முருகயர்ந் துவந்த முதுவாய் வேலன்"

   Kurunttogai, v. 362

The Tamil Lexicon Divakaram and Pingalantai have been composed between the 6th and 8th centuries AD (550–750).[6] The Divakaram says that the word Murugu has the meanings of youth, enthusiasm, agil (a kind of tree), firewood and festival. The Pingalantai says that the word has the following meanings: beauty, toddy and lime fruit.

Such meanings of the word 'Murugu' given in Divakaram Pingalantai were not in use in the Sangam literature available to-day. This shows that there must have been many literary works wherein the word Murugu might have found a place with different meanings. This also reveals the antiquity of the word.

In the Sulamani (Nattuppadalam, v. 7), work of the 10th century,[7] the word Murugu was used to denote a festival intended for God Muruga.

"Murugayar Paniyam"

"முருகயர் பாணியும்"

In Naidatham, work of the 16th century AD the word Murugu means honey.

"Murugu voymadu-t-tundali musum"

"முருகு வாய்மடுத் துண்டளி மூசும்"

Manampuripadalam, v. 23

There are some words which have sprung up from the basic name Murugu. They are as follows:

1. Murugiyam—a kind of drum used at the frantic dance of Velan in the hilly country–Tolkappiyam, Porul, S. 18 commentary
2. Murugayartal—Worshipping Lord Muruga
3. Murugutval—becoming older
4. Murugu—a kind of ear ornament
5. Murugan—Lord Muruga (Tirumurugarruppadai, 1.56)
   —young man (Divakaram)
   —Velan (Pingalantai)
6. Murugavarutti sura—a kind of shark (sea-fish)
7. Murugai—a kind of stone

8. Murugai-nandu—a kind of crab

Lexicon, vol. 6, p. 3279

After an etymological study of the words denoting Lord Muruga one is inclined to come to the conclusion that the word Murgh of the old Persian or Muruk of the Zend, helps us little or nothing in tracing the history of the Muruga cult of worship. On the other hand Murugan has been derived from the root of Tamil Murugu which means beauty, fragrance, youth, honey and God.

III. "Dravidic-speaking people were predecessors of the Aryans over most of Northern India, and were the only people likely to have been in possession of a culture as advanced as the Indus culture."[8] Dr. Gurov of Leningrad, one of the scholars who have studied the statuettes in Harappa thinks that the seated figure with a spear might be Muruga. "......The Aryan population of Northern India is not, therefore, a pure race, but contained among others, a strong Dravidian element".[9] "......The Dravidian cults and Dravidian language have begun to influence the religion and speech of the Aryans in Northern India. No trace of the doctrine of Transmigration is found in the Rig-Veda, and yet no other doctrine is peculiarly Indian".

"The most important linguistic family in India outside Indo-Aryan is the Dravidian family......It has become clear that quite a considerable portion of the Sanskrit vocabulary is of Dravidian origin and that this influence has operated over a long period in the history of the language. ... It is evident from this survey that the main influence of Dravidian on Indo-Aryan was concentrated at a particular historical period, mostly between the later Vedic period, and the formation of the classical language.

This is significant from the point of view of the locality where the influence took place. It is not possible that at this period such influence could have been exercised by the Dravidan languages of the South. There was no intensive contacts with South India before the Maurya period by which time the majority of these words had already been adopted by the Indo-Aryan. If the influence took place in North in the Central Gangetic plain and classical Madhyadesa, the assumption that the Pre-Aryan population of this area contained a considerable element of Dravidian speakers would best account for the Dravidian words in Sanskrit. The Dravidian Languages, Kurukh and Malto are preserved even now in Northern India, and may be regarded as islands surviving from a once extensive Dravidian territory. The Dravidian words in the Rig-Veda attest the presence of Dravidian in the North-Western India at that period. Brahui in Baluchistan remains as the modern representative of North Western Dravidian."[11]

The above references of different scholars assert the fact that there were Dravidians in Northern India when the Aryans began to spread both in the Punjab and the Gangetic plain. Hence the Aryans were able to absorb the Dravidian deities into their sphere.

"The ancient, as well as modern worship of Siva and Vishnu and Amba, are forms of fireless worship and they are utterly different from and opposed to the Vedic fire-cult."[12]

"Those Vedic Gods, the etymology of whose names is not patent, and who have no analogies in other Indo-Germanic dialects, must have been originally Dravidian deities. The Aryan God, Varuna, was probably the God of the Dravidian tribes, being on the borders of the sea, to whom the Aryan Rishis, accorded a place in their pantheon. The Aryan Rudra is another God of the Dravidian tribes. He is essentially a mountain deity and could be evolved by the wild mountaineers, say, of the Vindhyan regions and not by dewellers on the plains. His name Rudra meaning the 'Red one' seems to be a translation of the Dravidian name Siva. Korravai, the victorious matron, was the object of worship among the oldest people of the South. The hill-God of the South, the son of Korravai, is Murugan, the fragrant one. The Vedic God, Krishna, corresponds to the God of the Dravidian pastrol tribes. Saivism, i.e., the worship of Siva or Skanda, was prevalent among the mountain tribes long before the advent of the Aryans into the South. According to Dr. Slater, Kali, Siva, and Vishnu are Dravidian deities, though their worship now forms the innermost essence of Indian Culture".[13]

"Indian religion", Sir Charles Elliot, "is commonly regarded as the off-spring of an Aryan religion brought into India by invaders from the North, and modified by contact with the Dravidian civilization. The materials at our disposal hardly permit us to take any other point of view; for the literature of the Vedic Aryans is relatively ancient and full, and we have no information about the old Dravidians comparable with it. But, were our knowledge less one-sided, we might see that it would be more correct to describe the Indian religion as Dravidian religion stimulated and modified by the ideas of foreign invaders. For the greatest deities of Hinduism such as Siva, Krishna, Rama and Durga and some of its most essential doctrines such as metempsychosis and divine incarnations are either totally unknown to the Veda or obscurely adumbrated in it. The chief characteristics of the native Indian religion are not the characteristics of religion in Persia, Greece or other Aryan lands".[14]

Parrinder, E.G. says in his book on African Traditional Religion (1954), that "twenty five tribes in East Africa worship "Murungu" as supreme God and suggests that this God is similar to the Murugan, the Dravidian God and in support of his view he says that the East African 'Murungu' also resides in sacred mountains. But the grounds on which his theory has been advanced seems to be too slender. How does it happen that only twenty five tribes worship 'Murungu'? The mere fact that the temples of the East African 'Murungu' are found in mountains does not provide conclusive evidence of that deity's affiliation with Muruga of the Tamils. The other and distinctive characteristics of Muruga are not found associated with the East African Murungu.

By way of conclusion it may be stated that Murugan was an early Tamilian pre-Aryan God with spear or vel as his weapon and that in course of time he became Aryanised ultimately becoming the Subrahmanya. In fact the literal meaning of Subrahmanya is the one 'dear to the brahmins'.[15] Subsequent to the Aryanisation several legends of the North came to be associated with him. As a consequence Murugan came to be known as Skanda, Somaskanda, Kartikeya and so forth on the basis of various legends. The process of amalgamation is interesting. Muruga of old had married Valli a Veda girl in the typical *Kalavu* love. The Tamils of old before they came under the influence of the Aryans worshipped in the primitive way by strewing paddy and flowers and offering Tinai (the grains of the millet) and honey. Goat was also sacrificed and this early pattern of worship was known as the Velan worship. The Tirumurugarruppadai provides an interesting description of the early rites performed by the Kurava priestess (Kuramakal). She wears two kinds of garments; first she ties round her waist a red thread (cennul) and then she unfurls the cock-banner sacred to the God and applies as paste mustard mixed with ghee, murmuring gently and making obeisance. Garlands, incense, red millet mixed with blood all figure in the process of worship. Finally the blessing of the *pinimukam* appears. This refers either to the peacock or elephant of Muruga. The peacock or snake is distinctively associated with Muruga, the lord of Kurinchi.

Muruga was considered the son of Korravai, the old South Indian Goddess of victorious wars, identified later with Durga-Parvati. Again, it is very significant to note that from early times, Muruga was considered patron of letters and of the Tamil language and culture. (See verses 553 and 563 of Tirumurugarruppadai). It is difficult to decide the genesis of Kantu, as representing Muruga. But was it derived from the Sanskrit Skanda? Or did Kantu represent a post to tie an elephant or a pillar, phallic in origin? It is hazardous to provide a final answer.

The Sanskritised Muruga, or Muruga-Subrahmanya appears to have emerged as seen above, about the time of the Taitrireya Aranyaka, sometime about the 3rd century BC. There is clear evidence of the Sanskritic idea having entered the conception of Subrahmanya, Muruga or Skanda. The Tirumurugarruppadai which provides the idea of the combination of the northern and southern conceptions of Muruga, enumerates the functions performed by the six faces of Muruga. Thus the new name Shanmukha appears. Two of the faces of Subrahmanya are remarkably interesting as pointed out by Kamil V Zelbil. Of these, one represents the tradition according to which Sanatkumara-Skanda taught Narada the esoteric doctrine of the *atman*, 'the Self, and Brahma and Siva the significance of the most sacred syllable *aum* (the first syllable of the Veda) the other interesting face is that which performs the eternal surveillance of the Brahmanic sacrifices.[16]

It is noteworthy that the Aryanised Muruga figures for the first time, to the best of our knowledge, in the temple at Tiruchchendur in the modern Tirunelveli District. The temple is dedicated to Murugan-Subrahmanya and it is believed that it was here that he achieved his great victory over Surapadma.

Various legends sprang up in due course. The Saiva poem Kalladam for instance exalts Tamil and also Sanskrit. It is stated later that Murugan taught not only the Vedas to Agastya, but he taught him Tamil, too.

Perhaps the greatest poet who has sung devotional songs in praise of Muruga-Subrahmanya is the celebrated Arunagirinathar of the 15th century AD. His illustrious Tiruppugal contains the blending of the essence of Saiva Siddhanta philosophy, 'the ancient inheritance of Tamil bardic poetry' and the vast resources of Aryan mythology. The Tamil view of Muruga is a handsome youth of glowing red complexion, dancing in the red morning-sun on top of every hill, his spear adorned with peacock flowers with which he destroys his age-long enemy, the demon of fear (Surapadma).

On the whole, the basic ideas of Muruga are those of the Tamils. They belonged to an earlier age as not only the Adichchanallur excavations have shown, but as the discoveries of an earlier date in Palestine, Syria and Cyprus indicate. The Aryans later adopted Muruga and incorporated him into the composite Hindu fold.

ENDNOTES

1. C.V. Narayana Ayyar: "Origin and Development of Saivism in South India," p. 102. see also.

   T.R. Sesha Ayyangar: "Ancient Dravidians." p. 109

   R. Sathianathaier: "History of India," Vol. I. pp. 170–171. I have discussed this topic with several scholars in Sanskrit and Tamil.

2. K.A.N. Sastri himself says this in his "Development of Religion in South India," pp. 21–22.

3. K.A.N. Sastri: "A History of South India." 1966, p. 57.

4. I am indebted to Janab Muhammad Yusuf Kokan, Reader in Persian and Urdu, University of Madras, for this information.

5. A Dravidian Etymological Dictionary by T. Burrow and M.B. Emeneau p. 336, No. 481.

6. K. Srinivasa Pillai: "Tamil Varalaru." p. 240.

7. *Ibid*: p. 240

8. Mohenjodaro and the Indus Civilisation. Vol. I, p. 42.

9. Grierson: Linguistic Survey of India. Vol. IV, p. 378.

10. K. Ramakrishnaiah: Studies in Dravidian Philology. p. 13.

11. T. Burrow: The Sanskrit Language. pp. 375, 380, 387.

12. P.T. Srinivasa Ayyangar: Stone Age in India. p. 52.

13. T.R. Sesha Ayyangar: Dravidian India. pp. 101–102.

14. Sri Charles Elliot: Hinduism and Buddhism-An Historical Sketch. Book I, p. 15.

15. Tirumurugarruppadai: 552.

16. Kamil V. Zvelebil "A Guide to Murukan" Journal of Tamil Studies, June. 1977, p. 88.

8

THE TEMPLE AS A CULTURE CENTRE

The Hindu temple, like the religion which it represents, has had a long history. Its genesis has been a matter of controversy, some tracing it to the burial site, others to the hero-stones of old, and so on. There is no doubt that in pre-historic times the worship of images in the open, possibly under trees, preceded the erection of temples. Though image worship was common among the people of the Indus valley culture of old, and though they had attained a remarkable measure of progress in the art of building, there is little evidence to show that temples as such had been erected by them. The worship of Mother Goddess, of a male God seated in a yoga-posture, probably the proto-type of the later Siva, as well as the worship of the phallus seem to have been in vogue. But the relics in the sites in which they were discovered do not suggest that they had been enshrined. However, the very fact that they were found among the ruins of destroyed cities does not warrant a definite conclusion as to whether they had been enshrined or not.

Again, during the Vedic period, temples are not known to have existed; there is no reference in the Vedas to worship in temples. Nature worship and adoration of personified elements of Nature, with or without the accompaniment of sacrifices, must have taken place in the open for quite a long time. With the development of settled life and progress in the arts and crafts, temples might have appeared in the age of the Mantras and of the Epics.

By the 4th century BC, the cults of Siva and Vishnu, and particularly of Krishna, had taken distinct shape and worship in enshrined temples to have become popular in and around Mathura. An inscription near Udaipur in Rajputana, belonging to about 150 BC, speaks of a temple of Vasudeva. Erection of temples seems to have received an impetus about the dawn of the Christian era through the Mahayanist influence. The rock-cut chaityas of the 2nd and 1st centuries BC, must have served as models for the Hindus to construct their own shrines. We have specific mention of Hindu temples in the 1st century AD. Temples to Gauri are mentioned in the *Saptasati*, compiled by Hala, the 17th Satavahana king who ruled in the fist quarter of the first century AD.

In the extreme south of India temples are known to have existed in the Sangam age, commonly assigned to the early centuries of the Christian era. The reference to the shrine of 'Mukkatchelvan' is unquestionably to that of Siva, notwithstanding the doubts expressed by some. Senganan who lived towards the close of the Sangam epoch, is reputed to have built 70 temples of Siva. It is notable that the temple and the palace are both indicated in Tamil by one and the same word 'Koil'.

In North and Central India the early structures were either rock-cut temples or those built of wood. In the South, for quite a long time they were constructed only of wood or of bricks and mortar. These early patterns continued till the Western Chalukyas employed stone for the purpose. However, the systematic construction of stone temples began in the South with Mahendravarman I, the Pallava king known as "Vichitrachitta". In fact, he himself has expressed that he took a delight in the construction of temples without the use of brick, timber, metals or mortar.

Temples became very popular from the 7th and 8th centuries onwards with the development of the Bhakti movement. Kings and wealthy men vied with each other in the construction of and endowments to temples. The golden age of temple construction was the period of the Imperial Cholas when the magnificent temple of Tanjore and that of Gangaikondacholapuram appeared along with several others. The tradition of constructing and embellishing temples was continued by the later Pandyas, the Vijayanagar emperors and the Nayak rulers. After the 18th century the construction of huge temples received a set-back in the South with the appearance of the struggle between the Western powers for supremacy and the final establishment of British sovereignty. But the remarkable feature of the history of Hindu temples is that in South India they have not suffered much from the ravages of invaders and iconoclasts, with the result that as compared with the rest of India, the South has fortunately preserved its old temples intact.

It is important to realise that the Hindu pantheon, no less than the style of construction, was a product of the admixture of features developed by various races. There is evidence of the fusion of the Dravidian, Proto-Austroloid and Aryan elements. The controversy over the genesis of Siva worship apart, there is no doubt that Muruga and Korravai became transformed into Subrahmanya and Durga respectively. The practice of having Mithuna sculptures and paintings in temples is probably traceable to Graeco-Roman influence and to Tantric Buddhism. Under the Jain and Buddhistic influence the practice of offering animal sacrifices ended in the Hindu temples as well.

In due course the temple became the pivot of the village. With the popularisation of temple worship by the Nayanmars and Alvars its importance attained a great height. The Bhakti movement laid stress on the idea of a personal God and the emotional appeal made by the movement to devotional prayers had a profound influence in making it popular. Almost every one in the village offered worship at specified times in the temple, while on occasion of special celebrations and festivals, people from far and near used to throng the temples.

The temple became not only a place of worship but the very focus of the entire life of the people of a village. It has been rightly said of Hindu temples that, they were fortresses, treasuries, court-houses, parks, fairs, exhibition sheds, halls of learning and of pleasure, all in one." Several temples have afforded protection for people against marauders and invaders. In various ways temples have proved themselves as agents of poor relief. As landholder, consumer of goods and services and as employer and in short as the focus of social life and development, the temple of medieval times has played a unique role. Above all, the temple as well as the Matha attached to it served as the centre of cultural and educational activity.

What is culture? Perhaps it is one of the over-worked and much-abused words of modern times. In fact, in the name of culture, most uncultured things are done and uncultured ideas are expressed. Though it is not easy to provide a simple and comprehensive definition of culture, its outstanding features may be mentioned. Intellectual attainment thorough knowledge and an intellectual awareness and curiosity are fundamental elements of culture. Besides, culture has intimate relation to social habits and customs, behaviour and morals. In fact, culture has a direct bearing on the way of life as well as on the outlook on life. A person's culture is obviously influenced by one's parentage, social environment and positive scope for self-improvement provided by education and training. It is in respect of these latter facilities that the temple has proved to be a centre of culture.

In the first place, devotees congregating in a temple for worship normally subject themselves to a certain measure of physical and mental discipline. Personal cleanliness, including the taking of baths before going to the temple and the wearing of clean clothes are aids to physical discipline. Fasts on particular days or at specified times of certain sacred days serve as auxiliaries to discipline. More important is the mental cleanliness and the scope for concentration and meditation. True, there is no ostensible test by which these can be measured. They are essentially internal and psychic in character. But by and large, other things being equal, the worshippers have a greater chance for developing these qualities than others.

More positive is the facility for education that the temple provided. During the period when other public agencies like the State had not begun to shoulder the educational responsibility it was primarily the temple and matha which provided the facility for education. Many are the inscriptions of medieval times that speak of the educational facilities provided by temples.

Epigraphs at Tiruvorriyur speak of the recital and teaching of Prabhakara (mimamsa), Rudra, Yamala, Purana, Sivadharma, and Bharata. Besides sacred literature, even subjects like Vyakarana (Grammar) and Astrology were taught. Again the celebrated inscription of Rajendra Chola at Ennayiram registers an endowment for the maintenance of a college for Vedic studies. At Puravasseri near Suchindram there is found an inscription belonging to 1196 AD which registers a gift of land as *kidaivritti* for maintaining two teachers to expound the Rg and Yajur Vedas. The famous epigraph of Vira Rajendra at Tirumukkudal refers to a school maintained in the Jnana Mandapa in the temple for the study of the Vedas, Sastras, Grammar etc. Usually in a spacious Mandapa which could accommodate a large gathering of people, a prominent scholar chanted hymns of the Vedas and expounded them to his ardent listeners. In another Mandapa, the celebrated epic Mahabharata, which has moulded the life and character of the Hindus for ages, was read and explained to the people. The Dharmasastras, embodying the rules of right conduct, the Puranas, Grammar, Rhetoric, Logic, Astronomy, Medicine and other special sciences were taught to those who thronged to learn them.

The Ghatikas and Mathas provided systematic training to pupils in sacred lore. The Ghatikas of Kanchi were perhaps the most outstanding institutions of the kind in South India. Still further south we hear of Salais which were really residential halls of learning. The Salai of Minchirai, the Srivallabhapperumchalai at Kanyakumari and the celebrated Kandalur Salai are known to have served as schools of religious learning. For the Salais provision of a regular income was made from time to time by kings and other wealthy patrons. The identification of Kandalur Salai has been a subject of acute controversy. Most of the South Indian scholars have taken it to mean the harbour at Kandalur and that the mention of it in Chola inscriptions indicates a naval victory off the portstead of Kandalur. But the other interpretation that it referred to a residential hall of learning seems more appropriate. The context in which it occurs and the lines succeeding the reference to Kandalur Salai suggests that it was an institute of learning where free food was provided for scholars. The inscription of Parantaka Pandya, for example, makes it clear:

1. ஸ்வஸ்திஸ்ரீ திருவளரச் செயம் வளர
   தென்னவர் தம்குலம் வளர,
   அருமறை நான்கவை வளர
   வீனத்துலகுந் துயர்நீங்கத்
   தென்மதுரா புரித்தோன்றி
   தேவேந்திர ஜேடினிதிரு

2. ந்து, மன்னர்பிரான் வழுதியர்கோன்
   வடிம்பலம்ப நின்றருளி,
   மால்கடலை எறித்தருளி
   மலையத்துக் கயல்பொறித்துச்
   சேரலீனச் செருவில் வென்று
   திரைகொண்டு வாகை சூடிக் கூப

3. கர் கோன் மகட்குடுப்பக்
   குல விழிருங் கைக்கொண்டு
   கன்னிப்போர் செய்தருளிக்
   காந்தளூர் சாலை கலமறுத்து

மன்னுபுகழ் மறையவர்தம்
மணியம்பலத்திருந்தருளி ஆங்கவர்களற

4. ம் வளர்ப்ப அமைத்த பேராமிரத்தெண்மர்
அவிரோதம் பணிப்பணியால்
மறைபேர்த்துக் கல்நாட்டிப்
பண்டுள்ளபேர் தவிர்த்து
அளப்பனவும் முகப்பனவும்
நிறுப்பனவும் கயலெழுதி அனந்தபுரந் தெம்மாற்கு

It seems that 'Kalamaruttal' does not refer to the destruction of a fleet but the provision for the feeding of a fixed number of persons. Kalam stands for *'unkalam,'* figuratively plates and really the amount of rice for feeding an allotted number of persons—here a specified number of Brahmin scholars. The reference to 'Ayirattenmar' makes it clear that 1008 persons were the permanent members of that institute of learning. Apparently Kandalur Salai was something like an University, similar to those we hear of in Northern India, such as those at Taxila, Nalanda or Vikramasila. This seat of learning was so important that the kings of the three famous dynasties-the Chera, Chola and Pandya vied with each other in securing possession of the celebrated place.

That the Salai at Kanyakumari was another hall of learning or hostel for scholars is evident from several inscriptions. For example, the following epigraphic reference proves this:

"இவ்வூர் ராஜராஜன் சாலைக்கு
சாலாபோகமான ஊர்கள்"

Again: "குமாரி ராஜராஜன் சாலையின் சாலா

போகம் நாஞ்சிநாட்டு மணற்குடி

ஊரோங் கைத்தீட்டு"

The scholars were called Sattar— "ராஜ ராஜேசுவரத்துச் சட்டப்பெருமக்கள் வசம் ஆண்டாண்டு தோறும் இந் நெல்லு அழக்கக் கடவோமாக இசைந்து இக்காசுகொண்ட மணற்குடி ஊரோம்"... and so on.

That 'Kalam' denoted the share of each for the provision of food is clear form several inscriptions. For example, an epigraph of the 14th year of Kulottunga speaks of 'அமுது செய்யக் கற்பித்த கலம்'.

It is true that the education provided in the ghatikas and temples was almost exclusively for Brahmins; but that was in pursuance of the prevalent traditions of the day. It is unfair to condemn age-long practices in the light of modern ideas. Nevertheless, it is true that every society must necessarily change if it is to survive; however, change should not mean a violent break with the past, but a new synthesis of past wisdom and present needs.

It may be observed that it temples and mathas of old, apart from instruction provided for Brahmins, there was also scope for popular education in a limited measure. In many of the South Indian temples recitations and expositions of the Epics and the Puranas took place.

There is inscriptional evidence to show that the practice was in vogue in the temple at Tiruvorriyur, Ennayiram, Tirumukkudal and Tirubhuvani. In the West Coast temples too, it was not unknown. We find at Tirukkadittanam an inscription of Bhaskara

Ravi Varman, assignable to the last decade of the 10th century AD, which mentions the practice of reciting the Mahabharata.

Another institution of popular religious instruction was through the recitation of Tamil hymns before the deities at stated times. The practice of singing the Tiruppadigam, i.e., hymns of the Devaram, Tiruvachakam and Tiruppallandu was in vogue in South India clearly from the 10th century onwards and possibly from a slightly earlier date. The practice of chanting Tiruppadigams must have commenced as early as the reign of the Pallava King Vijay Nandi Vikrama Varman. This is evident from the Tiruvallam inscription, which enumerates the reciters of the Tiruppadigam among the employees of the temple. From the reign of Parantaka Chola I onwards numerous inscriptions speak of endowments made for the recitation of Tiruppadigam and Tiruvaymoli. It appears to have been systematised by Raja Raja I who was a great organizer of the practices and celebrations in the South Indian Temples. An epigraph of Rajendra I mentions a 'Devaranayakan,' apparently a Superintendent of Devaram. This indicates the existence of a department of State which supervised and controlled the performance of this service in various temples.

Discourses and discussions on religious themes seem to have been held in temples or mathas. A piece of very early evidence of religious discourse is found from the Amaravati sculptures where a vast concourse of people is shown listening to what was apparently a disquisition. Even women are found to have attended the discourse. In much later times discourses among the exponents of the different religions of Hinduism, Jainism and Buddhism appear to have been held in temples and Mathas. These were common in the days of the Nayanmars and Alvars. During the medieval period of South Indian history discourses were generally held in the Mathas. These were not confined to brahmins only. Members of the higher sections of the non-brahmin communites also participated in them.

There is another respect in which the moral conduct of the Brahmins as well as of others were influenced by the temple. Vows were taken in front of the temple; the idea was that divine sanctity was attached to such vows. In respect of quite a large number of people who took vows, adherence to the right code of moral conduct would have been a motive force.

Besides sacred literature and devotional songs, music and dance formed a part of the Nityotsavas or the daily services. These appeared prominently during the special celebrations and annual festivals. Almost every big temple maintained its own permanent staff of musicians, vocal and instrumental, Numerous types of musical instruments were in use. Among musical instruments employed in temples, mention is made in inscriptions of Yal or Vinai, Kulai, Udukkai, Kudamula, Kalam as well as Mattalam, Karadigai, Segandi, Kaimani, Parai and Sangu. Here is ample evidence to show that teachers of music and dancing, the Nattuvanars as they are called, were employed by the authorities of the temple to instruct the Devadasis in these arts. Invariably the best musicians, pipers and drummers as well as dancers of the region were enrolled and maintained by the temples. It is no exaggeration to say that these arts owe their development to the temples and royal courts.

Finally, the arts of architecture, sculpture, and painting attained a remarkable progress only in and through the temples. In India, as in ancient Greece, art was the handmaid of religion. The temple was verily the epitome of the architectural and sculptural attainments of the bygone ages. Carving both on metal and wood reached a high degree of progress. Images in bronze, silver and gold were skilfully carved. The Chola Bronzes are world-famous. Painting was developed not only in Buddhist chaityas and viharas but also in Hindu temples.

The temple was an instructive and cultural institution in which people from all walks of life— the architect, the sculptor, the painter, the dancer and the musician, the philosopher and the religious man, the Pauranika, and the poet, each found his place.

The painting on the walls, panelled-ceiling, and gateways of some of the temples show scenic representations of the Ramayana as at Kumbakonam, Kudandai and Tellicherry (Talasseri) or stories from the Mahabharatha as depicted in the wooden ceiling at Vaikom, Cranganore and other temples of Kerala, and in others in Tamil Nadu and Andhra Pradesh. Many temples had spacious halls where the Ramayana, Mahabharata and the Puranas were expounded. For example, the Kuram grant states that a Brahmins scholar was appointed to recite the Mahabharata inside the mandapa of the temple of Vidyavinita Pallavesvara at the village of Paramesvaramangalam.

Most of the temples had also well trained choirs of singers who brought home to the people the best music, literature and religious devotion of the land. Dance performances were also witnessed within the temple precincts, in the spacious Ranga Mandapas in the larger South Indian temples.

Temples are generally treasure-houses of sculpture and iconography. Silpa Sastra emphasises the idea that the worship of images of stone, metal, jewels or clay leads the seeker of liberation form rebirth to his goal.

DECLINE OF THE POSITION AND SERVICE OF THE TEMPLE

Though the formal services provided by the temple are continued to this day it is an unquestionable fact that the temple has suffered in its prestige and appeal so far as the bulk of the people are concerned. There are fewer persons going to the temple and offering worship there than before. There is an atmosphere of apathy, scepticism and even of contempt for the age-long practices and beliefs. The beginnings of these heretical tendencies are traceable to the century when western tradition and western ideas penetrated the land. The age-long veneration and respect for established beliefs and practices witnessed a serious challenge. Many educated people become indifferent to the traditional beliefs while they fail to absorb the really valuable ideas of the West.

One of the important reasons for the growing apathy has been the migration of people from villages to towns and cities. Western education, together with the changed nature of the employment market drew people to urban areas, particularly, the intelligentsia from the villages. The spread of certain new ideas and the contact with the westerners and the realisation of the advances of Science accounted for increasing scepticism. It cannot but be admitted that the activities of the Christian Missionaries openly and otherwise promoted an irreligious attitude among Hindus.

Above all in quite recent times certain political parties have turned against the Hindu religion and its sacred institution, namely the temple. This is, to say the least, most unfortunate. Communal difference may exist especially in the employment field but that need not be prostituted to rouse antipathy to religion as a whole. Hatred of a particular community need not and should not pave the way for atheism. One can understand true atheism arising out of deep study and contemplation; the great Buddha was one of the early atheists. But here the position is different. Lack of initial faith has been worked up to a wholesale condemnation of all that stands on faith. One need not believe in miracles. Which religion in the world is devoid of faith in miracles? But it should be realized that there are different ways of approach to godhood which may vary from individual to individual and from class to class. It is cruel to drive masses of unthinking people into the abyss of apathy, in order to subserve personal or communal ends.

Further, Hinduism stands far above Brahmanism. The mere circumstance that the priesthood is composed of Brahmins or that the sacred lore is Brahmanical in character, does not make Hinduism co-eval with Brahminism. Hinduism is much wider and more comprehensive; it derives its original source from elements outside the Brahmanical fold as well; its genesis is traceable, largely though to Brahmanism, also to Dravidian concepts and practices, proto-Austroloid beliefs and other non-Aryan elements. In this connection it is important to remember that the South Indian temple resembles not only in its structure but also in its organisation the Sumerian temple. The Devadasi system, the annual Tirukkalyanam and other features found in the South Indian Temples have their counterpart in the Sumerian organisation of temples. Even among people connected with the temples directly or otherwise normally 70 per cent of the people were persons other than brahmins as may be seen from numerous inscriptions, for example, from Rajendra Chola I's epigraph at Kolar regarding the various classes of servants employed in a Durga temple. Hence those, out for decrying Aryanism or

Brahmanism, whatever the justification, should keep the South Indian temple from out of their targets of attack.

But the real danger is the passivity and indifference of the average Hindu, the Brahmin included. The external observances are forgotten while the internal or psychic approach to religion is either unknown or is not developed. True, temple-worship may not be needed for those who are spiritually ripe; but in reality, we have more often than not, neither the one nor the other.

In fact we are faced with apathy, scepticism and absorption in materialism. This ought to be arrested if Hinduism is to survive. There is no use of deluding ourselves into the belief that Hinduism is strong enough to overcome these petty onslaughts and minor dangers. In fact we are passing through a critical phase of our history in relation to religion and those who believe in the appearance of avatars to overcome crisis can well feel that such a stage has come very near. A Sankara or Ramanuja, a Ramakrishna Paramahamsa or Vivekananda, a Gandhiji or Aurobindo has to emerge and stem this tide of heresy and apathy.

What is to be done really in order to strengthen the faith in the temple and thereby promote not only piety but also our distinctive culture? A high-power Commission, the Hindu Religious Endowments Commission, is touring the country and collecting evidence concerning the ways and means of rejuvenating the service in temples, the improvement of the training and equipment of the archakas and so on. From the newspapers it is learnt that some witnesses have suggested the creation of institutions for providing archakas with systematic training in agamas and pujas; others have recommended the conducting of religious discourses and preaching by competent persons, while still others have counselled the opening of Colleges giving both secular and religious instruction to pupils. Laudable as these suggestions are, could they be expected to rejuvenate our religion, to infuse enthusiasm among temple-goers and to induce others to develop the age-old habits of worshipping at temples and performing the religious duties enjoined on each of us by custom and tradition? There is no use singing of our past glory; the present deterioration must be faced and the prospects of a bright future ensured. Discourses may attract but a few. Devaram schools also cannot expect to have large numbers of students. Nor would Colleges where religious and secular instruction is provided attract many, even with the bait of scholarships. In an age sunk in gross materialism only that school or college which would provide an opening for employment would be sought. In reality the starting of colleges which can provide a secular and religious instruction should be preceded by an alteration in the curricula of studies. As a preliminary step it may be suggested that *Hindu hostels* can be started, largely with the aid of funds from temples. The residents would have to bear a large part of the expenses themselves; but provision for religious instruction may be made from out of the temple funds. The principal aim should be to offer religious instruction and afford training for a disciplined life. Strikes should be banned and those who indulge in strikes should be totally expelled. But the cynic is sure to scoff at this counsel of perfection.

At the very outset the problem of admission to the hostels would face the authorities. I would straightaway say that membership must be open to all deserving Hindus irrespective of caste. This may be a revolutionary step but it has to be adopted in order to provide for the solidarity of the Hindu fold.

The conditions of admission, the choice of suitable wardens and proctors who must be ideal Hindus in the true sense of the term are all problems bristling with difficulties. But a firm determination to serve the future of the Hindu community and to make it regain its vast glory and culture may, God-willing, help the cause. What temple of old provided has now to be provided by the temple, school, college, and hostel together. Discipline is the supreme need of the hour, discipline at the school, college and in society at large. One of the devices for securing it is by reviving faith in religion and importing it into the various grades of society.

9

THE BHAKTI MOVEMENTS IN TAMIL NADU

In Tamil Nadu leaving aside for the moment other parts of India, Bhaktism in Vaishnavism seems to have had an early start, as stated above. There appeared the Krishna cult and perhaps Madura of the South traced its name to Mathura where the Krishna cult had its great development. It has been suggested, though not proved, that the Southern Madurai became the centre of the Southern Krishna cult. The Yadavas had come to the south and had perhaps developed the worship of Krishna. Even earlier, a section of the Vrsni people seems to have colonized the Pandya country.

However, one thing is certain. The Vaishnava Alvars or devotees had an early origin; the 'Mudal Alvars,' as they are called, are assignable to the 5th century AD and they were followed by a number of Vaishnava devotees till about the 9th century AD. The influence of the Bhagavatas was found among the Alvars. The Alvars were twelve in number. Doubtless the most prominent among them was Nammalvar.

The Alvars worshipped Vishnu, Narayana and Krishna with intense emotion and their outpourings invoke unstinted devotion to this God. It is not necessary to enumerate the names of all the Alvars here. But the most important of them were Tirumangai, Periyalvar and his adopted daughter Andal and above all Nammalvar. Tirumangai was a Marava by caste and, true to the traditions of his caste had taken to highway robbery in his early days. Later he became an ardent devotee of Vaishnavism and sang many moving songs on Vishnu, but some of his songs were primarily directed against Jainism and Buddhism.

Periyalvar of the extreme south had sung touching songs on Lord Krishna, particularly on his birth and early childhood. He also won fame as a successful disputant. Andal is famous for her bondless devotion to God. Considering herself as a *Gopi* she imagined that she was a lover of Sri Ranganatha of Srirangam temple. She sang some enchanting songs on her love for the Lord. Her emotional songs are repeated on occasions of Vashnavite marriages. The next important Alvar was Nammalvar or Satakopa whose *Tiruvoymoli* forms the last and most important part of the *Nalayira Prabandham*. Nammalvar was a deeply learned devotee and his compositions are greatly respected. One of the Alvars, Kulasekhara belonged to the West coast and was a king of Venad in Kerala. His *Mukundamala* quotes a verse from the Bhagavata Purana; this shows that this Purana must have been composed in or before the 9th century AD.

On the whole, the Alvars were early leaders of Tamilian Vaishnavism representing the early Bhagavatism. At their hands there was a marked fusion of Tamil with Sanskrit. Though the Alvars did not actively preach against the caste system, they disregarded caste distinctions; in fact Tiruppan Alvar belonged to the Pana caste. South Indian Vaishnavism has always depended for its strength on the support of the masses. There is a tradition that Tirumangai was a contemporary of the Pallava king Narasimhavarman (AD 630–68) and if this is true, since Tirumangai belonged to the 7th century, it can be concluded that the period of the Alvars ranged from the 5th to the 9th century. The Alvars were followed by Acharyas who developed the philosophical aspect of the religion. The foremost among them was Ramanujachariar, whose influence reached North India.

SAIVISM

About the same time in Tamil Nadu there was the great stir of the Bhakti movement among the Saivites. In respect of India as a whole, some think that Vaishnavism was earlier because Vishnu as such figures in the Rig Veda and some think that Vishnu appeared after Bhagavatism arose. But as noticed earlier Siva as known even in the epoch of the Indus Valley civilization. Some time later there came about a fusion and the Vedic Rudra became identified with the non-Aryan Siva. By the time of the Svetesvatara Upanishad Siva was absorbed in the Vedic pantheon and was given a lofty position as Mahadeva. The earliest specific mention of Siva by a foreigner is traceable to Megasthenes. In the age of the Guptas the worship of Siva assumed a considerable importance; but a Bhakti movement of Saivism is only traceable to South India. Perhaps it commenced in the Kannada country, but it reached a great height in Tamil Nadu. Sixty three Nayanmars or devotees are said to have composed emotional songs employed for the adoration of Siva. They went about the country visiting the Saiva temples and adored Siva with their ecstatic devotion, collected later as the Devarams. It was the great epoch of Saiva bhakti movement which can be said to have ranged from the 7th century AD to 9th century AD. These songs are sung in Saiva temples even to this day and therefore the Bhakti movement initiated by the Nayanmars or Saiva saints had a long influence on the Tamils. The Nayanmars were bitter towards Jainism and Buddhism and that made their activities vigorous and enthralling.

Among the Saiva Nayanmars the most prominent were Jnanasambandhar, Tirunavukkarasar and Sundarar. Sambandar set his songs to music of a high order. Tirujnana Sambandhar's famous Devarams are not only noted for their devotion but also for their contribution to music. Tirunavukkarasar known as Appar, is stated to have been originally a Jain and was converted to Hinduism through the efforts of his sister. Sundarar was the last of the three hymnists. He loved Siva as a friend. He sang the Tiruttondattogai containing an account of 62 saints. He was himself the 63rd saint, according to Nambi Andar Nambi. But there appeared perhaps a little later, the still more famous Manikkavachagar whose outpourings are collected in the Tiruvachagam. They are soul-stirring songs and there is a common saying that he who is not moved by Tiruvachagam will not be moved by any song. His date is the subject of controversy. But in the light of the evidence from the Sinhalese source, Nikaya Sangrahava,[1] and the Pandyan epigraphs of the 9th century AD, Manikkavachagar, a contemporary of Varaguna I, may be assigned to the first half of the 9th century AD.

Saiva Siddhanta of Meykandar, a very popular work on Tamil Saivism, though philosophical, inculcated true devotion to Siva. It came subsequent to the Bhakti movement.

THE "NEW BHAKTI CULT" OF SOUTH INDIA

Later there were undoubtedly many Tamil saints of great devotion and literary skill, like Arunagirinathar, Tayumanavar and Ramalingasvamigal. But though they are famous for their devotional poetry, they appeared at various stages in the history of Tamil Nadu and though they were influenced by the early Nayanmars, they did not belong to the wave of the Bhakti movement of Saivism from the 7th to 9th century AD.

The distinctive features of the Saiva Bhakti movement of the South were that they were imbued by deeply emotional fervour and use of simple language understood by the common people. Unlike the leaders of the Bhakti movement of North India in the medieval period, they did not preach against idolatry and caste, though they disregarded caste distinctions.

THE BHAKTI CULT IN NORTH INDIA

Certain features of the Bhakti movement in North India from about the 12th century AD are different from those in Tamil Nadu both in respect of Vaishnavism and Saivism of the earlier epoch. In the first place, the leading reformers in the North rejected image worship, rituals and other ceremonies and positively opposed the caste system.

Secondly, they had to contend with Islam; but they did not oppose it. They tried to harmonise the two religions, Hinduism and Islam. Various forms of this conciliation and combination could be seen from the teachings of Kabir and Nanak.

Thirdly, it is erroneous to think that the North Indian Bhakti movement owed its origin to South India as has been suggested by some, who hold that, Ramananda a follower of the Visishtadvaita of Ramanuja, was the precursor of North Indian bhakti cult in medieval times. This is not quite accurate. It is admitted that Ramananda was a follower of the creed preached by Ramanuja. But it is wrong to think that Ramananda was a South Indian and that he was born in Mysore. In reality he was a native of Allahabad. But his advocacy of the Visishtadvaita certainly became popular in the North. Moreover, even before Ramananda there were in Maharashtra medieval saints who forestalled him. Nor did the teachings of the Acharyas of the South alone constitute a neo-bhakti cult as K.A.N. Sastri thinks.

Among the medieval saints in Maharashtra prior to Ramananda there were persons of different castes. In fact, they created a mass reolution in their utter disregard of caste. In Maharashtra too there appeared saints belonging to different castes. For instance, there was Namdeva, a tailor (1270–1350) who was a robber-chief in early life. He became an ardent devotee of Vithoba, God of Pandharpur, but later considered Vithoba as no more than a symbol of the supreme soul that pervades the Universe. He was opposed to idol worship and he condemned fasts, pilgrimages, sacrificial ceremonies and all external observances.

Ramananda was a disciple of Ragavananda who belonged to Ramanuja's creed of Visishtadvaita. Ramananda stressed the unity of God and the eradication of the various differences. Though a brahmin, he condemned caste. On his study of the Sastras he proved that the observance of caste discriminations was unnecessary. While the southern leaders of the Bhakti movement merely disregarded caste differences Ramananda and his followers positively condemned caste. In fact, his twelve disciples included a Jat, a barber, cobbler and a Muslim, Kabir. Their devotion to God was devoid of rites and ceremonies. He was thus the harbinger of a rational and coordinated form of religion, though his devotion to Rama was conspicuous, and it appealed to the masses in all parts of Northern India. He was in a sense responsible for the revival of the devotion of the Bhagavatas; only he replaced Krishna and Radha by Rama and Sita.

Kabir of the 15th century was the greatest follower of Ramananda. He tried to harmonise Hinduism with Islam. He thought that Rama was not different from Rahim of the Muslims. His emphasis was pre-eminently on strict moral conduct. Besides condemning the caste system, idol worship, sanctity of baths in sacred rivers and other formalities, he disapproved the orthodox Muslim practices like adherence to Mosques, performance of Sunnat, and the practices like Namaz and Roza. In fact, his creed resembled that of the Sufis, for like them he laid stress on ardent love towards the supreme God. In his propagation of sincere love regardless of formalities and in his stress on religious tolerance, Kabir may be said to have worked towards universal religion. The view that Kabir was influenced by the Upanishadic non-dualism and Islamic monism coloured by Sufi concepts does not seem to be an exaggeration. Even traces of Buddhist thought are traceable in his Kabirpanth. He was not dogmatic at all. He condemned narrow creeds and sectarianism.

There were other saints of North India in the medieval period, like Vallabha (1479–1531) who though born in Andhra

Pradesh went to the north and lived in Benares. A scholar and a devotee, he stressed on the value of detachment from worldly pleasures. He preached devotion to Krishna and urged unconventional love condemning carnal pleasures to appeal to God.

More famous was Chaitanya, a Vaishnava brahmin of Bengal and a contemporary of Vallabha. A social reformer like Ramananda, Kabir Nanak and Tukaram, Chaitanya was strongly opposed to caste distinctions and ceremonies of the Hindus. But he did not condemn idol worship or pilgrimages.

It is significant to note that Jiva Gosvamin, a follower of Chaitanya, wrote a work on the cult of *bhakti* and it is found that the influence of the Bhagavata is unmistakably seen it it.

Nanak (1469–1538), the last of the famous medieval leaders of the Bhakti movement, eventually became the founder of Sikhism which harmonised Hinduism with Islam. The Adi Granth, the Bible of the Sikhs, contains the hymns of Kabir and Nanak. He had no faith in the caste system or in bathing in sacred rivers. Sikhism and Sufism resembled each other closely.

He was a strong advocate of monotheism. According to him God does not belong to any particular people, Muslim or Hindu. Rightly it has been said that Kabir was the spiritual ancestor of Nanak. He urged that the only way of worshipping God is to sing His praises and to meditate on His name.

He laid stress also on practical morality. Nobility of character was emphasised. Sincerity and honesty were given a lofty place. He said: 'Abide pure amidst the impurities of the world; thus shalt thou find the way to religion.'

SUFISM

From the side of Muslims ther were certain leaders besides Kabir who advocated a happy compromise between Hinduism and Islam. Shaik Salim Chishti and Dara Shukoh were the leading members of this school, known as Sufism.

There were some features in common between Vaishnavism and Sufism. In the medieval period both these religions stress the need for self-realisation outside the limitations imposed by rigid dogma. The Islamic concept of equality and brotherhood of man greatly attracted the lower classes of the Hindus who had no access to the temples and the right to read the scriptures. Many of the Muslim mystics, particularly Chishti and his followers, showed a spirit of toleration towards other religions and creeds. They emphasised the essential unity between different religions and that constitutes the kernel of Sufism.

Originally the Sufis were interested in converting Hindus to Islam. But later on many Sufis gave up their evangelistic zeal and instead devoted themselves to a comparative study of the religions and philosophies of India. Abul Fazl and Dara were foremost among them. The intolerant policy of Aurangazeb drove may Sufis to a conspicuous admiration for the Vedanta philosophy and the influence of the Bhakti movement on them was conspicuous. Some Sufis, however even adopted idolatry as another way of worshipping God. Though there were different shades of Sufism, they were all considerably influenced by certain sections of the Bhakti movement. It has been rightly said that "Guru Nanak's thought, in no way differed from that of the Sufis."[2] What would have happened if Sufism had a continuous history of progress?

An important question is whether the Bhakti cult in Northern India is traceable to South India and can be claimed to be a continuation of the neo-bhakti cult of South India by Ramanuja, Nimbaraka and Madhava.[3] This does not appear to be warranted. The differences of the Bhakti movement in North India with those of the teachings of the Acharyas have to be clearly borne in mind though a few ideas may have travelled from here. The generalisation made is not justified.

ENDNOTES

1. 'Nikaya Sangrahava', the Sinhalese Chronicle, p. 18 and C.S. Navaratnam 'Tamils and Ceylon', p.95.

2. N.M. Bhutani: The Cultural Heritage of India, Vol. IV, p.610.

3. See K.A.N. Sastri: History of India II, p.76. A similar sweeping statement is made by S.N. Ganesan: "Due to the influence of Ramanuja, Ramananda, Nimbaraka, Vallabha and Madhava, the whole of North India saw a widespread devotional movement with different ideas about the ways and means of attaining realisation." Bulletin of the Institute of Traditional Cultures, Madras, 1975, Jan. to June, p.76. No one doubts the influence of some ideas of Ramanuja in the north. But this Acharya's ideas were not identical with those of the Alvars of the original Bhakti movement of the South.

10

DATE OF MANIKKAVACHAGAR

One of the disputed questions of South Indian history is the date of Manikkavachagar. For a long time the question centred around the controversy whether Manikkavachagar preceded or succeeded the Devaram Trio. Several scholars held that Manikkavachagar lived long before the Devaram hymnists, probably as early as the Sangam age itself. An equation of greatness with antiquity was largely responsible for the ingenious attempt to push back the date of Manikkavachagar. It was sought to be shown that certain references to Tirunavukkarasar pertain to none other than to Manikkavachagar. But some recent writers have refuted this deduction.[1]

On the other hand, it has been indicated that in his songs Manikkavachagar has referred to Tirujnanasambandar,[2] Tirunavukkarasar[3] and Sundaramurti[4], not by name but by references to their distinctive role as Saiva devotees. These citations seem to show that Manikkavachagar lived subsequent to the Devaram saints.

But even more convincing is the circumstance that Sundarar does not include Manikkavachagar in his Tiruttondattogai. Sundarar had set about the task of recording systematically the names and achievements of Saiva devotees, and it is inexplicable how he could have ignored Manikkavachagar if he had lived before the time of Sundarar[5]. And since Sundarar had not mentioned Manikkavachagar, Sekkilar who faithfully followed the Tiruttondattogai, Sekkilar who faithfully followed the Tiruttondattogai, also omitted the reference to this saint in his Periyapuranam.

The language used by Manikkavachagar is not very different from that of the Devaram hymnists. Even he who runs will find it to be very different from the archaic pattern of the Sangam classics. Moreover, the philosophical views contained in the Tiruvachagam show a development of those found in Devaram.[6]

A specific piece of evidence which shows that Tirunavukkarasar and presumably therefore Tirujnanasambandar had preceded Manikkavachagar is found in his Porrittiru ahaval' in which he adores the Siva enshrined at Sirappalli. The Siva temple at Sirappalli, it is learnt from inscriptions, was originally a Jaina *vihara*. Manikkavachagar has sung in praise of the Siva[7] who was installed by Mahendravarman I in the spot where the Jain *vihara* had flourished earlier. Therefore, he must have been posterior to Mahendravarman I (c. AD 600–630) and Tirunavukkarasar.

Above all, the reference in the present tense to a Pandyan monarch Varaguna in two of his songs,[8] embodied in his Tirukkovai, suggests that Manikkavachagar was a contemporary of a Varaguna the Pandyan king. To the best of our knowledge there was no Varaguna in legend or history anterior to the kings of that name who ruled the First Pandyan Empire.

After the discovery of the larger Sinnamanur plates it is known that in the line of rulers of the First Pandyan Empire there were two Varagunas, the one a grandson of the other. The grandfather has been described as Varaguna Maharaja in the Sinnamanur plates, as Jatila Parantaka Nedujadaiyan in the Velvikkudi grant and as Jatilavarman in the Madras Museum plates. He has been assigned slightly different dates by different scholars but there is little doubt that he was ruling in AD 770, the date of the Anamalai inscription (year 3871 of the Kaliyuga era). From other epigraphic evidence his reign may be taken to have lasted for fifty years—approximately from AD 765 to 815.[9]

The other was his grandson known as Varagunavarman (II), who ruled between AD 862 and 880. Of these two Varagunas, who could have been the contemporary and patron of Manikkavachagar? There is no clear indication on this question in the available sources.[10]

In this connection a clue comes from a Sinhalese source. Nikaya Sangrahava, a Sinhalese chronicle, records that Sena I, the king of Sri Lanka, was converted to the Saiva faith and that his daughter was cured of her dumbness by 'an ascetic clad in the robes of a priest.'[11] It is probable that the ascetic mentioned in this connection was Manikkavachagar, because we have some corroboration of this from the Tamil source.

In the legends connected with the career of Manikkavachagar, described in the Tiruvatavurar Puranam, it is stated that he converted a Buddhist king of Sri Lanka to Saivism and that he cured the king's daughter of dumbness.[12] The story runs that the Sinhalese king had gone with his dumb daughter to Chidambaram to witness the religious controversy between the Buddhist priests of Sri Lanka and Manikkavachagar, and that when the saint performed the miracle of making the dumb princess gain her power of speech, the king and his followers including the Buddhist priests, all embraced Hinduism. One may or may not believe the supernatural element involved in the story. But the coincidence of the story itself in the Tamil Tiruvatavurar Puranam and the Sinhalese Nikaya Sangrahava is striking. It is quite likely that a religious controversy had been held between Manikkavachagar and certain Buddhist priests at Chidambaram in the time of Sena I.

Now the determination of the date of Sena I is not very easy. The traditional date assigned for the reign of Sena I on the basis of the Chulavamsa account is AD 846 to 866. But in the light of the Pandyan epigraphs of the period a correction of 24 years has to be effected in the Chulavamsa chronology. This correction will give the approximate dates AD 822 to 842.[13] Therefore, Manikkavachagar may be assigned to the first half of the 9th century AD. And he must be considered to have been a contemporary of Varaguna I, whose reign ended in AD 815, rather than of Varaguna II, whose reign commenced only in AD 862.

Endnotes

1. See, for example, Sadasiva Pandarattar: "Kalagattin Airattettavatu Veli-ittu Malar" p. 72.
2. Tiruvachagam–Tiruvammanai 8.
3. Thiruvachagam–Tiruchadagam 89.
4. Thiruvachagam–Ennappadigam 6.
5. The contention that the term 'Poyyadimai-illada-pulavar' employed by Sundarar refers to none other than Manikkavachagar is too vague and convincing.
6. The Tamil Plutarch (1946) Note by T.P. Meenakshisundaranar on p. 63.
7. Porrit-tiru-ahaval–line 154 'Sirappalli meviya Sivane porri.
8. Tirukkovai songs Nos. 306 and 327.
9. K.A. Nilakanta Sastri—The Pandyan Kingdom, p. 60.
10. Pandarattar's view favouring Varaguna I on the ground that the Pandyas had lost control over the Cholas by the time of Varaguna II (op. cit p. 75) is not convincing.
11. Nikaya Sangrahava p. 18; See also C.S. Navaratnam: Tamils and Ceylon, p. 95 and C. Rasanayagam: Ancient Jaffna, pp. 253–4.
12. G.U. Pope: The Tiruvachagam–The Legendary History of Manikkavachagar pp. xxx-xxxi (Tiruvatavurar-Puranam, Canto VI.)
13. K.A. Nilakanta Sastri–The Pandyan Kingdom, pp. 70–71.

INDEX

A

Abul Fazl 231
Acharyas 225, 228, 232
Adanur 55
Adhi Rajendra 154
Adichchanallur 6, 189, 190, 192, 201
Adi Granth 230
Adi Saivas 179
Adisesha 181
Adiyaman 127
Adiyan 86
Adiyarkkunallar 21, 57, 142
Agastya 5, 8, 84, 201
Aham 20, 22
Ahananuru 20, 24, 27, 48, 49, 51, 53, 60, 62, 89, 157, 171, 176, 182, 188
Ahatti 95
Aimperungulu 29
Ainkurunuru 47, 48, 65, 71, 187
Aintinai 105
Aitareya Brahamana 173
Aiyar 161
Akkalanimmadi 144
Akkarai 155
Alagarmalai 136, 161
Alagiyapandipuram 59
Alar 101
Alavariya adhirajas 145
Alisi 80
Alliyakkuttu 64
Alvars 54, 55, 56, 57, 208, 214, 223, 224, 225, 232
Amara 214
Ambal 74, 101
Ambalur 101
Amman 179
Ammanai 36, 40, 41
Amur 184
Anamalai 75, 136, 140, 161, 235
Ananda Rangan Pillai 43
Anatti 147
Anbil Plates 25
Andal 224
Andanalar Nanmarai 180
Andhras 173
Andir 84
Anduvan Cheral Irumporai 78
Anji 85
Anni 81, 89, 126, 127, 134
Aparajita 139
Appar 19
Aralaikalvar 118
Arangerrukadai 50
Areru 82
Ariel durant 1, 14, 16
Arikamedu 51, 69, 136, 159, 160, 162, 167, 170
Arittapatti 161
Arivar 177, 178

Arivudai Nambi 92
Aruhan 70
Aruman 86
Arumarai 180
Arumpada Uraiyasiriyar 57
Arunachalam 157
Arunagirinathar 201, 227
Aryans 6, 7, 9, 14, 34, 173, 174, 175, 176, 179, 182, 183, 186, 191, 192, 196, 197, 198, 199, 201
Aryappadaikadanda Nedunjeliyan 24, 166
Aryavarta 173, 174
Ashtasahasram 176
Asokan Brahmi inscriptions 136
Atmanatha Desikar 42
Attimalai 82
Augustus 69, 166, 167, 172
Austroloid 6, 208, 218
Avai 29, 69
Ay 83
Ay Andiran 27, 83, 84
Ayar 95, 119
Ayirai 75

B

Baladeva 52, 123
Balarama 35
Basham, A.L. 67, 125
Bhagavata purana 224
Bhagavatas 223, 229
Bhagavatism 225
Bhutappandiyan 24
Bork 5
Brahmadeyas 144
Brahmagiri 136

Brahmi inscription 19, 125, 135, 136, 159, 160, 161, 162, 163, 168, 175
Brahmi script 9
Brahui language 7
Brihacharanam 179
Brihadatta 185
Brown, G.W. 5
Buhler 160
Burgess 141, 153
Burrow 7

C

Chaitanya 230
Changam Maruviya Nulkal 146
Chakravarti, N.P. 163
Charles Elliot 198
Chenchal Ulavar 87
Chenganan 47
Chenguttuvan 74, 75, 76, 88, 126
Cheppedugal 151
Chera king Atan II 28
Cheraman 77
Cheraman Kokkadaimarpan 77
Cheramanperumal 55
Cheran 76
Cheran Senguttuvan 46, 54
Cheripparattai 107
Chintamani 70
Chirup 84
Chirupanarruppadai 127
Chola inscriptions 211
Cholamandalam 93
Cholamandala Satakam 42
Cholan Talai Konda Vira Pandyan 148
Chulavamsa 236

Coast of Borneo 11
Col. Mackenzie 58
Comal Tank 3

D

Daivam 34
Dalavaipuram 143
Dalavaipuram Plates 143, 144, 145, 146
Damili 136, 137
Damodaranar 176
Dara Shukoh 231
Dasyus 173
Dekkan 165
Dera Ismail Khan 2
Desingarajankadai 41
Dev 218
Deva 214
Devar 34
Devaram 54, 55, 56, 66, 152, 157, 164, 171, 214, 220, 225, 226, 233, 234
Devasthanas 144
Devi 35
Dikshitar 59, 60, 63
Dinnaga 21
Divakaram 178, 194
Dravida Sangha 69
Dubash 43
Dupleix 43

E

Ekambaranathar 37
Ekambaranathar Ula 37
Elam 8, 13
Elamite 5, 14
Elini 5

Elini Erumayuran 127
Elunurruvar 176
Enkomi 190
Ennayiram 210, 213
Enperayam 29
Ettuttogai 20, 22, 49, 51, 52, 60, 68, 69, 191

F

Fleet, J.F. 142
Fr. Heras 3

G

Gajabahu Senguttuvan 19, 21, 26, 51
Gandh 94
Garuda 181
Gopinatha Rao, A. 141
Gupta era 141
Gurov of Leningrad 196

H

Haidar Ali 41
Haimendorf 136
Hala 206
Harappa 2, 6, 137, 169, 196
Harappan inscription 3
Harappan script 3
Haraprasada Sastri 160
Hill 41
Hissar 2
Hultzch, E. 141, 142, 156
Hurrian 5, 6, 14

I

Iberia 15
Ilampuranar 57, 178
Ilayankudi 154

Imaiyar 34
Imayavaramban 45, 75, 88, 125, 126, 166
Imayavaramban Neduncheralatan 27, 166
Indra 21, 33, 35, 49, 60, 61, 63, 66, 164, 181
Indra Vila 66, 183
Indus Valley 205
Iniyavai Narpadu 53
Inna Narpadu 53
Iraiyanar Ahapporul 10, 18, 57
Iraiynar Ahapporulurai 52
Iravadam Mahadevan 3, 137
Iravikkuttippillai 41
Iravikkuttippillaippattu 41
Irayasuyam Vetta Perunarkkilli 180
Irumporais 45
Irunkovel 7

J

Jambukesvaram 156
Jatila Parantaka Nedujadaiyan 235
Jatilavarman 140, 235
Jayankondar 39
Jinji 41
Jnanasambandhar 226

K

Kabir 228, 229, 230, 232
Kabirpanth 229
Kadalan Valudi 136
Kadalparattai 107
Kadalpirakkottiya 76
Kadamba dynasty 178
Kadambakattu Yanai Nedunter Kuttuvan 76
Kadamban 183
Kadiyalur Rudran Kannanar 39
Kadungon 38
Kadunko 136
Kaikkilai 105
Kakkayan tope 170
Kal 212
Kalabhras 66, 144, 145, 146, 147
Kalaikkuttam 176
Kalakkudi 144
Kalambakam 40
Kalanju 152
Kalappalar 144, 146
Kalavali 20, 25, 62, 77
Kalaviyal 93, 94, 95, 98, 105,129
Kalavu 95, 96, 97, 98, 99, 100, 101, 199
Kalayarkoil 154
Kali 179
Kali Arasan 145
Kalinga 113
Kalingattupparani 25, 38, 39
Kalittogai 10, 20, 47, 48, 51, 142, 180, 182
Kaliyuga era 140
Kal Kol 138
Kalladam 201
Kalugumalai 163
Kalumalam 25
Kalvarkoman 87, 93
Kama 33, 181
Kamavel festival 33
Kampavarman 138
Kanaikkal Irumporai 25, 76, 77
Kan Amar Chelvi 182
Kanakasabhai, V. 24

Kanapper 24
Kanchipuram 6, 156
Kanishka 141
Kaniyakulam 41
Kannagi 46
Kanyakumari inscription 25, 153
Kapadapuram 11, 13, 52
Kapbal 136
Kapilar 49, 164, 185
Karavandapuram 143
Kari 84, 85, 89, 127
Karikala 25, 39, 47, 93, 165
Karnataka Savistara Charitam 58
Kartikai Vila 183
Kartikeya 199
Karunakara Tondaiman 38, 39
Karuvur Vanchi 45
Katchi 138
Katyayana 174, 186
Kavadi 192
Kaverippumpattinam 25
Kavidi 189
Kelvi 180
Khan Sahib Sandai 41
Khara 179
Kharoshti 160
Khin-bha-gon 170
Kielhorn 153
Killivalavan 78, 79
Kocar 7, 8
Koccengannan 25
Kochchenganan 151
Kodichchiyar 119
Koduvil Adavar 118
Koilolugu 37, 42
Koliyur Kilarmahanar Cheliyanar 108

Kollam era 141
Kolli Hill 89
Kollikkurram 86
Kollimalai 78, 81, 122, 127
Kongar 27
Kongarkon 147
Kongarpulitangulam 161
Kongan Porayan 78
Kongu Desa Rajakkal 58
Kongunadu 75, 147
Kopperunjinga 152
Korravai 33, 34, 35, 49, 64, 182, 189, 198, 200, 208
Kosar 127
Kotteti 161
Kotupitavan 161
Kovai 36, 38, 39
Kovalur 127, 128
Krishna 224
Krishna cult 223
Kudaikkadukhan 114
Kudal 69
Kudamalai 75
Kudanadu 78
Kudavarai 74, 75
Kudavayil 83
Kudumiyamalai inscription 149
Kulamurram 79
Kulottunga 39, 154
Kulottunga Cholan Ula 38
Kulottunga II 37, 38, 40, 42
Kulottunga III 39
Kulottungan Kovai 39
Kumara Kulottunga 39
Kumarikandam 10
Kunrakkudi 136

Kurai 184
Kural 20, 28, 32
Kuramakal 199
Kuram Plates 139
Kurappalli 79
Kuravai 116
Kurava priestess 199
Kuravar 95, 112, 113, 117, 119
Kuravas 181
Kurinchi 92, 94, 101, 111, 117, 118, 119, 123, 128, 181, 183
Kurinchippattu 49
Kurinjippattu 31, 60, 185
Kurukshetra 65
Kuruntogai 18, 24, 49, 53, 60, 62, 63, 65, 71, 80, 90, 126, 157, 183, 186, 187
Kutir 94
Kutiramalai 86
Kuttan 183
Kuttuvan 75, 78

L

Laksmi 35
Lally 41
Larger Leyden grant 25
Lawan 3
Lawerence 41
Lemuria 11
Lemurian theory 10, 11, 13
Lewan 2, 3
Lothal 4
Lycians 7

M

Madagascar 10
Madan 179
Madras Museum Plates 140, 235
Madurai 10, 11, 70, 82, 83, 175
Maduraikkanci 23, 31
Maduraittalavaralaru 42, 43
Mahabharata 11 18, 74
Mahabhashyam 171
Mahadevan, I 5, 8, 45
Mahamahopadhyaya 67
Mahendravarman 207
Mahendravarman I 138, 149, 234
Mailai Seeni Venkataswamy 138
Malai Nadu 39
Majumdar, R.C. 35
Malaimandalam 93
Malavar 119
Malayaman Tirumudikkari 84, 85
Malepadu Plates 25
Mallan 183
Mallar 112, 131
Manabharana 148
Mandai 76, 126
Mangayarkkarasi 55
Mangudi Marudan 59
Manikkavachagar 55, 226, 233, 235, 236
Manimekalai 20, 21, 25, 53, 60, 61, 62, 64
Manram 29
Manu 174
Marai 180
Marangari 147
Maran Valuti 71, 92, 128
Maravar 118, 119
Maravarman Kulasekhara 39
Maricha 179
Marudam 92, 93, 94, 117, 120, 121, 128, 183

Marungu 83
Maski 136
Maunggun 170
Mayon 52
Mayurasarman 178
Megasthenes 225
Mekalai 114
Melor 177
Meru 181
Mesopotamia 7
Mettuppatti 136
Meykandar 57, 226
Meykkirtigal 151
Minakshi 149
Minili 82, 127
Mohenjodaro 6, 9, 14
Moli 180
Mortimer Wheeler 167
Mudal Alvars 223
Mudaliyar Manuscripts 59
Muda Tirumaran 92
Mudu Moli 180
Muhammad Yusuf Khan 41
Mukkatchelvan 182, 206
Mukundamala 224
Mullai 92, 94, 110, 114, 117, 118, 183
Mullaippattu 60, 63, 166, 171, 186
Mullur 85, 89
Mundi Gak 2
Muruga 34, 49, 52, 100, 122, 123, 129, 181, 182, 187, 189, 190, 192
Murugai 195
Murugai-nandu 196
Murugaltalai 161
Murugan 189, 195
Muruganangu 100, 123
Murugavarutti sura 195
Murugayartal 195
Murugiyam 195
Murugu 194, 195
Murugutval 195
Murungu 199
Musiri 165
Muttaraiyar 53, 152
Muvan 76, 90
Muvendar 44
Muyakkam 97
Muziris 167

N

Nachchinarkiniyar 10, 57
Nadukal 137
Nadutal 138
Nagaswamy 138, 152
Nakkirar 10, 57
Naladi 53
Naladiyar 21
Nalamkilli 79
Nalayira Prabandham 55, 56, 224
Nallanduvanar 47
Namakkal 153
Namaz Gah 2
Nambi Andar Nambi 55, 226
Namdeva 228
Nammalvar 223, 224
Nanak 227, 230, 231
Nanchinad 41, 59
Nanchinad Raja 41
Nandikkalambakam 40
Nandivarman II 138

Nandivarman III 140
Nannan 26, 90
Naraloka Vira 38
Narasimhavarman 225
Narasimhavarman I 138
Narasimhavarman
    Pallavamalla 161
Narayana 224
Narayana Kesavan 144
Narayana Rao, C. 161
Narayanaswami Aiyar 86
Narchingan 147
Narpettennayiravar 176
Narrinai 24, 48, 49, 53, 60, 62, 64, 67, 68, 69, 71, 74, 76, 77, 80, 82, 83, 87, 88, 89, 90, 91, 93, 94, 95, 96, 97, 98, 105, 106, 107, 108, 109, 111, 112, 113, 114, 116, 119, 120, 121, 122, 123, 124, 125, 126, 127, 157, 181, 187
Nathamuni 55
Nayanmars 54
Nediyon 24, 145
Neduncheliyan 44, 82, 136
Neduncheraladan 45, 166
Nedunjeliyan 24
Negroid 12, 13, 14
Nerivayil 27
Neydal 31, 92, 93, 94, 104, 105, 112, 117, 118, 183
Nikaya Sangrahava 226, 235, 236
Nilakanta Sastri, K.A. 61, 64, 142, 145, 147, 148, 154, 155, 185, 186, 188, 190, 192, 228, 232
Nilantaru Tiruvir Pandyan 69
Nimbaraka 232

Nirpatai 138
Nochi Niyamangilar 111
Nyayapravesa 21

O

Ollaiyur 24
Ona Vila 183
Orai 115
Otriyuran 151
Ottakkuttan 37, 40, 42
Otuvar 179
Oymanadu 184

P

Padikkasu Pulavar 42
Padinenkilkanakku 53, 146, 185
Padirruppattu 22, 26, 27, 44, 45, 46, 60, 63, 73, 74, 75, 125, 128, 166, 171, 180, 184, 188
Palai 74, 92, 93, 94, 112, 117, 118, 183
Palai Gautamanar 75
Palai Padiya Perunkadungo 92
Pallankovil copper plates 139
Pallava Aparajita 139
Pallava inscriptions 139
Pallava Narasimhavarman I 19
Pallavan Nandivarman III 40
Palyaga Mudukudumi
    Peruvaluti 145, 180
Palyagasalai Mudukudumi 24
Palyagasalai Mudukudumi Peruvaludi 47, 146
Palyanai 75
Palyanai Chel-kelu Kuttuvan 74, 75
Panan 183
Panar 29, 30, 33, 34, 50, 116

Panchery 116
Pandavapabbata 163
Pandharpur 228
Pandikkovai 38
Pandil 115
Pandy 93
Pannadu Tanda Maran Valuti 71, 128
Paradavar 31, 95, 119
Parakesari 154
Param 82
Parambu 49
Paranar 26, 45, 61, 72, 81, 128, 185
Parani 36, 39, 40
Parantaka I 150, 152
Parantaka Nedunjadayan 140, 143
Parantaka Viranarayana 143, 144
Parattayar 105
Parayan 183
Pari 27, 49, 164
Parimelalagar 57
Paripadal 20, 49, 51, 52, 57, 60, 142, 180, 181, 187
Parppar 178
Parrinder, E.G 199
Parvadini 150
Parvati 35, 181, 182
Patanjali 171
Patinenkilkanakku 20
Pattinappalai 25, 31, 39, 60, 62, 63, 64, 180, 187, 194
Pattuppattu 20, 22, 31, 32, 34, 48, 49, 51, 52, 191
Perichchikkovil 154, 155
Periplus 166
Perisattan 176
Periya Puranam 55, 56

Periyalvar 224
Periyan 81, 87, 126
Periyapuranam 234
Periyatambi Marakkayar 42
Periyavittu Mudaliyar 59
Peru Muttaraiyar 21, 53
Perumbanarruppadai 165
Perumbarrapuliyur Mambi 56
Perumchorrutiyan 125
Perumpadai 138
Perumpanarruppadai 32, 183
Perum-tiru-Mavalavan 79
Perunarkilli 47, 127
Peruncheral Irumporai 86, 127
Perunchorrutiyan Cheralatan 74
Perundalai Sattanar 61
Perundevanar 71
Perundinai 105
Pillaittamil 36, 42
Pindan 90
Pingalantai 194, 195
Pinnattur Narayanaswami Aiyar 77
Piran Chattanar 115
Pliny 18, 166, 171
Podiyil 29, 182
Podiyilmalai 127
Poduke 167
Ponmanimalai 114
Pope, G.U. 79
Porainadu 78
Porayan 78
Poriayaru 81, 87
Porrittiru ahaval 234
Poru 95
Porunar 50

Porunararruppadai 25, 60, 62
Poygai Alvar 25
Poygaiyar 25, 77
Poykkirtigal 151
Poyyamoli Pulavar 39
Prinsep 9
Ptolemy 166, 167
Pugal Chola Nayanar 55
Puhar 61
Pulatturai Murriya Kudalur Kilar 65
Pulayan 183
Pulindas 173
Pulli 87, 93, 94
Pundras 173
Puram 20, 22
Purananuru 20, 21, 22, 23, 24, 25, 27, 31, 34, 44, 45, 46, 47, 48, 49, 51, 53, 60, 62, 63, 65, 71, 84, 90, 112, 127, 128, 138, 142, 145, 166, 171, 177, 180, 181, 182, 183, 187, 188, 194
Purandai 81

R

Radha 229
Ragavananda 228
Raghava Aiyangar, M. 24
Raghava Iyengar, R. 7
Raghunatha Setupati 42
Rajadhiraja I 153
Raja Jai Singh 41
Rajakesari 154
Rajamahendra 37, 154
Raja Raja I 144, 152, 214
Raja Raja II 37, 153
Rajarajacholan Ula 25
Rajasimha 140, 145

Rajasimha plates 140
Rajasuyam Vetta Perunarkilli 127
Rajendra I 37, 153, 214
Rajendra chola I 218
Rama 198, 229
Ramachandran, T.N. 8
Ramalingasvamigal 227
Raman, K.V. 135
Ramananda 228, 229, 230, 232
Ramanuja 219, 228, 232
Ramappayyan Ammanai 40, 41
Ramayana 11, 174, 216
Ranganatha Temple 42
Rangpur 4
Rao, M. 84
Rao, S.R. 3, 4
Ravana 179
Rehman Dheri 2, 3
Rig Veda 7, 191, 225
Rudra 191, 198, 210, 225

S

Sabaras 173
Saiva Nayanmars 54
Saiva Siddhanta 57, 226
Saka era 140
Sambamurti 149
Sambandar 19
Sami Chidambaranar 125
Sanatkumara 187, 200
Sangam age 60, 70, 73, 83, 88, 91, 94, 97, 98, 104, 112, 115, 117, 119, 121, 124, 125, 159, 183, 193
Sangam literature 77, 79
Sangamukattamil 171
Sankalia 6, 136

Sankirna Jati 149
Sankirna ragas 149
Sap 206
Sarasvati 35
Sasanapatra 151
Satakam 36, 42
Satakopa 224
Sekkilar 55, 56, 234
Sena I 236
Senavaraiyar 57
Sendan 79, 80
Sennilam 143
Sennilandai 144
Senghor, L.S. 13
Sesha Aiyar 26, 59, 62, 65, 73
Sethuraman, N. 142, 153
Setupati 41, 42
Seyon 52
Shaik Salim Chishti 231
Silappadikaram 10, 19, 20, 21, 22, 24, 25, 26, 27, 30, 33, 34, 46, 50, 51, 53, 54, 57, 61, 62, 63, 64, 65, 70, 73, 126, 142, 171
Simhavishnu 138
Simikki 114
Sinnamanur Plates 48, 140, 141, 144, 235
Sirukudi 86
Sirupanarruppadai 60, 184
Sirupancamulam 21
Sita 229
Siva 6, 27, 34, 52, 56, 123, 179, 181, 182, 197, 198, 200, 205, 206, 208, 225, 226, 234
Sivacharyas 179
Sivagati 70
Siva Jnana Bodham 57

Sivakasi Plates 143, 148
Siva Paramurti 70
Sivaraja Pillai, K.N. 72
Skanda 199
Snowden, Jr. 16
Soma 181
Somajikkurichchi 144
Somaskanda 199
Sri Mara Srivallabha 143
Srinivasa Iyengar, P.T. 145, 174
Srinivasan, K.R. 150
Srinivasa Pillai, K. 202
Srirangam 37, 42, 224
Sthalamahatmyas 58
Sthalapuranas 57
Subahu 179
Subrahmania Aiyar 161
Subrahmanya 199
Subrahmania Aiyar, K.V. 161, 175
Subramanian, T.N. 148
Sugriva 179
Sulamani 195
Sundaramurti 4, 55, 233
Sundara Pandya 148
Sundarar 5, 226, 234, 237
Suniti Kumar Chatterji 172
Suran 181
Surapadma 123, 201
Swaminatha Aiyar, U.V. 67
Swamikkannu Pillai, L.D. 142
Swamy, B.G.L. 144, 145, 149

T

Tagadur 86, 127, 128
Tairt 118
Taitireya Aranyaka 174, 190, 191

Takkayagapparani 40
Takua-pa (Siam) 140
Talai 79, 113
Talaichengadu temple 152
Talayalanganam 24, 44
Talayalanganattu Cheruvenra Neduncheliyan 82
Talayalankanam battle 48
Tali 105
Tamil-Brahmi inscriptions 135, 136, 137
Tamil-Brahmi script 137
Tamrapata 151
Tamrasasana 151
Tanjai Vanan Kovai 39
Tarumi 164
Tayumanavar 227
Tellarrerinda Nandivarman 40
Ten Madurai 10, 13, 52
Tenur 144
Ter Maran 145, 147
Tervanmalayan 127
Tiberius 167, 172
Tinai 47, 68, 111, 115, 117, 120, 121, 199
Tiruchirappalli 41
Tirujnana Sambandar 55, 152
Tirukadugam 21
Tirukkovai 38, 234
Tirukkural 53, 57, 112
Tirumala Nayak 40, 41
Tirumandiram 55
Tirumangai 224, 225
Tirumangai Alvar 56, 171
Tirumangalam 144
Tirumayam inscriptions 149
Tirumular 55
Tirumurais 55
Tirumurugarruppadai 20, 4, 49, 51, 60, 142, 195, 199, 200, 203
Tirunanasambandar 163
Tirunavukkarasar 70, 163, 164, 226, 233, 234
Tirunelveli 136, 143, 159, 175, 201
Tirupparamkunram 161
Tiruttani 139
Tiruttevar Tevaram 59
Tiruttondar Puranam 55
Tiruttondattogai 226, 234
Tiruvachagam 55, 226, 234, 237
Tiruvadavur 136
Tiruvalangadu Plates 25
Tiruvalluvamalai 60
Tiruvalluvar 105, 106
Tiruvanchaikkalam 45
Tiruvatavurar Puranam 235
Tiruvaymoli 214
Tiruvendipuram 153
Tiruvengadam Pillai 43
Tiruvidaimarudur inscription 152
Tiruvidaivayil 152
Tiruvilaiyadal Puranam 56, 57
Tiruvoymoli 224
Titiyan 89, 126, 127
Tittan 79
Toli 94, 96, 97, 106
Tolkappiyam 11, 34, 48, 52, 53, 57, 64, 69, 92, 93, 94, 97, 98, 128, 130, 137, 138, 177, 178, 181, 183, 191, 195

Tondaiman Ilantiraiyan 165
Tondaimandalam 42
Tondaimandala Satakam 42
Tondi 26, 76, 78, 90
Tondipporunan Venvel 77
Toyyil 114
Trilochana Pallava 165
Tudiyan 183
Tukaram 230
Tulunadu 75
Turai 47
Tyagasamudra 38

U

Udayendiram Ceppedugal I 139
Udiyam Cheral 27
Udiyan 45, 65, 74
Udiyancheral 45
Ujjaini 141
Ukkiraperuvaluti 92
Ula 95
Umbarkadu 75
Undankal inscriptions 170
Unnaguruvayampalayam Plates 139
Upanishads 190
Ur 94
Uraiyasiriyar 57
Uraiyur 6, 55, 79, 80, 81
Urpparppar 184
Usal onkulai 114
Uyarndor 177, 178

V

Vadama 177
Vadaman Vannakkam Perisattan 176
Vadamas 179

Vadamodankilar 176
Vadugar 84
Vai Moli 180
Vais 119
Vaishnava Alvars 54
Vaiyapuri Pillai 73, 171
Vajra Nandi 60, 69, 70
Vakaipparandalai 25
Valavan 79
Vali 179
Vallabha 229, 230
Valttu 138
Vanamamalai 157
Vanan 39, 86
Vanchi 26, 45
Vanigar 177
Varaguna 140, 143, 144, 226, 234, 235, 236, 237
Varaguna II 236
Varagunavarman 235
Variyanippandu 115
Varuna 35, 49, 52, 164, 191, 197
Vatteluttu 136, 139, 160, 169
Vayu 191
Velan 189
Velanjeri 139
Velan Veriyadal 99, 100
Velappappar 184
Velir 7, 26
Veliyan 79
Velvikkudi Grant 18, 140, 143, 235
Velvikkudi Plate 48, 143, 146, 147
Venad 41, 162, 224
Vendan 52
Vengi 152
Venkata Hill 87

Venkayya 141, 153
Venni 25
Vijay 214
Vijayaditya Chalukya 165
Vijayalaya 151
Vaiyapuri Pillai, S. 73
Vikrama Chola 37, 38, 40, 65, 153
Vikramacholan Ula 25
Vikramaditya 141
Vikramaditya VI 40
Vikrama era 141
Villappu 102
Vira Rajen 210
Virali 106
Viraliyar 33, 34, 50
Viranarayana 143, 144
Virarajendra 40, 152, 154
Vira Tungan 144
Vishnu 4, 33, 52, 123, 164, 180, 181, 197, 198, 206, 224, 225
Visishtadvaita 228

Vithoba 228
Viyalur 126

W

Warmington, E.H. 59, 171, 172
Will 1, 14, 16

Y

Yajna 184
Yal 50, 215
Yanaichel 126
Yavanapriya 165
Yavanas 165, 166, 171
Yeludakkarppu 180
Yendai 121
Yerpadu 94
Yertur 7
Yusuf Kokan 202

Z

Zend Avesta 192

www.ingramcontent.com/pod-product-compliance
Lightning Source LLC
Chambersburg PA
CBHW070728160426
43192CB00009B/1363